CHRIS DEVON

C++ for game development

Contents

Introduction to Game Development with C++

Why C++ is Essential in Game Development
Game development is a multifaceted discipline that requires a balance of technical expertise, creative vision, and an understanding of both software engineering and game design principles. Among the numerous programming languages available for game development, C++ stands out as a primary choice for both industry veterans and aspiring developers. This chapter delves into the reasons why C++ is essential in game development, highlighting its advantages, historical significance, and the specific features that make it particularly suited for this domain.

1. Performance and Efficiency

One of the most significant advantages of C++ is its performance. Games often require real-time processing capabilities to deliver smooth graphics, responsive controls, and immersive experiences. C++ allows developers to write low-level code that can directly interact with hardware, optimizing memory usage and processing speed. This is crucial in resource-intensive applications like video games, where every millisecond counts.

C++ offers several features that contribute to its efficiency:

- **Manual Memory Management**: While this can introduce complexity, it also allows developers to optimize memory allocation and deallocation, resulting in lower overhead. This capability is vital for managing

1

resources in large, complex game worlds.

- **Compiled Language**: C++ is a compiled language, meaning that code is translated directly into machine language, resulting in faster execution times compared to interpreted languages. This allows for better performance in computationally heavy tasks such as physics calculations, rendering, and artificial intelligence.

2. Object-Oriented Programming (OOP)

C++ supports object-oriented programming, a paradigm that emphasizes the use of objects and classes. This model is particularly effective for game development because it facilitates the organization of code into manageable components, reflecting real-world entities within the game world.

Key aspects of OOP in C++ that benefit game development include:

- **Encapsulation**: By bundling data and methods that operate on that data within classes, developers can create modular and maintainable code. This makes it easier to manage game entities such as players, enemies, and items.
- **Inheritance**: C++ allows developers to create new classes based on existing ones. This is particularly useful for creating complex game hierarchies, such as different types of characters or objects that share common behaviors or properties. For example, a base class "Character" can be inherited by subclasses like "PlayerCharacter" and "EnemyCharacter," each with specific attributes and methods.
- **Polymorphism**: This feature enables developers to use a single interface to represent different underlying data types. In game development, this allows for flexibility when dealing with various types of game entities that share common functionalities, such as rendering, movement, and interaction.

3. Extensive Libraries and Frameworks

C++ has a rich ecosystem of libraries and frameworks specifically designed for game development. These tools provide developers with pre-built functionalities that can significantly speed up the development process. Some notable libraries and frameworks include:

- **Unreal Engine**: One of the most popular game engines, Unreal Engine is built using C++ and provides a comprehensive suite of tools for 3D game development. Its high-performance rendering capabilities and robust physics engine make it a go-to choice for AAA game developers.
- **SDL (Simple DirectMedia Layer)**: A widely-used library that provides low-level access to audio, keyboard, mouse, joystick, and graphics hardware via OpenGL and Direct3D. SDL is particularly useful for developing cross-platform games.
- **SFML (Simple and Fast Multimedia Library)**: Another multimedia library that simplifies the process of creating 2D games. SFML provides a user-friendly API for graphics, audio, and networking, making it an excellent choice for indie developers.

These libraries and frameworks not only enhance productivity but also ensure that developers can focus on game mechanics and design rather than low-level system details.

4. Cross-Platform Development

C++'s ability to compile on multiple platforms is a significant advantage for game developers who wish to reach a broader audience. With proper planning and architecture, games developed in C++ can be easily ported to various operating systems, including Windows, macOS, Linux, and even consoles like PlayStation and Xbox.

This cross-platform capability is largely due to:

- **Standardized Language Features**: C++ is standardized by the ISO, ensuring that code written in C++ can be compiled on any system that supports the standard. This uniformity reduces compatibility issues and increases the likelihood of success across different platforms.
- **Integration with Cross-Platform Engines**: Many game engines and

frameworks support C++, facilitating the process of developing games that can run on multiple devices. This is particularly advantageous in the current market, where players expect to access games on various platforms, including PCs, consoles, and mobile devices.

5. Community and Industry Support

C++ has a long-standing presence in the game development industry, leading to a vast community of developers and extensive resources available for learning and troubleshooting. This community support is crucial for both new and experienced developers, as they can find answers to technical questions, share experiences, and access a wealth of tutorials, forums, and documentation.

Additionally, many educational institutions offer courses in C++ specifically for game development. This widespread availability of learning resources means that newcomers can easily find the knowledge they need to get started in game programming.

6. Legacy and Historical Significance

C++ has played a pivotal role in the evolution of game development since its inception. Many of the foundational game engines and technologies were built using C++, including id Software's Quake engine and Epic Games' Unreal Engine. As a result, a large portion of the gaming industry's infrastructure relies on C++, establishing it as a cornerstone of modern game development.

The historical significance of C++ in game development cannot be overstated. Many popular franchises, including Call of Duty, Assassin's Creed, and The Legend of Zelda, have roots in C++. This legacy contributes to the language's credibility and ongoing relevance in the industry.

7. Future-Proofing Your Skills

As technology evolves, the demand for skilled game developers continues to grow. C++ remains a relevant and sought-after language in the gaming industry, making it an excellent choice for those looking to build a career in game development.

Learning C++ not only provides a strong foundation in programming principles but also opens doors to various opportunities within the tech industry. As many advanced technologies, including game engines and performance-critical applications, still rely on C++, mastering the language will equip developers with skills that are valuable beyond just game development.

In conclusion, C++ is an essential language in game development due to its performance capabilities, support for object-oriented programming, extensive libraries and frameworks, cross-platform compatibility, and a strong community. Its historical significance and continued relevance make it a top choice for both new and experienced developers looking to create engaging and high-performance games.

Understanding why C++ is vital in this field sets the stage for a deeper exploration of game development principles, techniques, and best practices, which will be covered in subsequent chapters. As you embark on your journey into the world of game development with C++, you will discover not only the power of the language but also the limitless possibilities it offers for creating immersive and memorable gaming experiences.

Overview of Game Engines and Frameworks: Unity, Unreal, SDL, SFML

In the realm of game development, engines and frameworks serve as the backbone for creating, managing, and deploying games across various platforms. These tools provide developers with essential functionalities, enabling them to focus on game design and mechanics rather than low-level technicalities. This section provides an in-depth overview of some of the most popular game engines and frameworks, namely Unity, Unreal Engine, SDL, and SFML, detailing their features, strengths, and ideal use cases.

Unity

Unity is one of the most widely used game engines in the world, favored for its versatility, user-friendly interface, and extensive support for both 2D and 3D game development. Originally launched in 2005, Unity has evolved into a comprehensive ecosystem that caters to a diverse range of developers, from indie creators to large studios.

Key Features:

- **Cross-Platform Development**: Unity supports over 25 platforms, including mobile (iOS, Android), console (PlayStation, Xbox, Nintendo Switch), and desktop (Windows, macOS, Linux). This broad compatibility makes it an attractive choice for developers looking to reach a wider audience.
- **Visual Editor**: The Unity Editor offers a powerful drag-and-drop interface, making it accessible for beginners and allowing rapid prototyping. Developers can manipulate game objects, manage assets, and configure scenes without needing extensive coding experience.
- **Asset Store**: Unity's Asset Store is a vast marketplace where developers can buy and sell assets, tools, and scripts. This resource saves time and enhances productivity by providing pre-built components that can be integrated into projects.
- **Scripting with C#**: Unity utilizes C# as its primary scripting language, allowing developers to write scripts for game logic, UI behavior, and more. This choice is particularly beneficial as C# is easier to learn than C++, making Unity a popular entry point for new developers.
- **Strong Community and Documentation**: Unity boasts a large and active community, with extensive documentation, tutorials, and forums available. This support network is invaluable for both newcomers and experienced developers seeking solutions to specific challenges.

Ideal Use Cases: Unity is suitable for a wide range of game genres, from 2D mobile games to complex 3D environments. Its flexibility and ease of use make it an excellent choice for indie developers, prototyping, and educational purposes.

Unreal Engine

Unreal Engine, developed by Epic Games, is renowned for its stunning graphics capabilities and robust feature set, making it a preferred engine for high-fidelity 3D games. First released in 1998 with the launch of the original Unreal game, it has undergone numerous iterations, with Unreal Engine 5 being the latest version.

Key Features:

- **High-Quality Graphics**: Unreal Engine excels in rendering high-quality visuals, thanks to its powerful rendering engine and advanced features like real-time ray tracing. This capability makes it particularly appealing for AAA game development, cinematic experiences, and virtual reality applications.
- **Blueprint Visual Scripting**: Unreal Engine offers a unique visual scripting system called Blueprints, allowing developers to create game logic without writing traditional code. This feature is especially useful for designers who may not have a programming background.
- **Robust Physics and Animation**: The engine includes advanced physics and animation systems, facilitating realistic movements, environmental interactions, and character behaviors. This attention to detail is critical in creating immersive gameplay experiences.
- **Marketplace**: Like Unity, Unreal Engine has a Marketplace where developers can find assets, plugins, and tools to enhance their projects. The availability of high-quality resources can significantly accelerate development time.
- **C++ Programming**: For developers who prefer deeper control and optimization, Unreal Engine allows for extensive C++ programming. This flexibility makes it possible to fine-tune performance-critical components of a game.

Ideal Use Cases: Unreal Engine is ideal for large-scale projects that demand cutting-edge graphics and complex gameplay mechanics, such as first-person shooters, RPGs, and open-world games. It is also a popular choice in industries beyond gaming, including film and architecture, due to its powerful visualization capabilities.

SDL (Simple DirectMedia Layer)

SDL is a low-level, cross-platform development library designed to provide a simple interface for managing multimedia, graphics, audio, and input. First released in 1998, SDL has become a foundational tool for many game developers, particularly those creating 2D games.

Key Features:

- **Cross-Platform Compatibility**: SDL supports a wide range of platforms, including Windows, macOS, Linux, iOS, and Android. This makes it a versatile choice for developers aiming for broad reach.
- **Low-Level Access**: SDL provides low-level access to graphics and audio systems, giving developers control over rendering and audio playback. This feature is particularly beneficial for developers who want to optimize performance and tailor experiences to their specific needs.
- **Simple API**: The API of SDL is straightforward and easy to use, making it accessible for beginners and enabling rapid prototyping. Developers can quickly set up window management, handle input devices, and play sound effects.
- **Focus on 2D Graphics**: While SDL can be used for 3D graphics, it is primarily optimized for 2D games. Developers can leverage its features to create sprite-based games, platformers, and more.
- **Open Source**: SDL is open-source, which allows developers to modify the codebase to suit their needs. This transparency fosters a collaborative community where developers can contribute improvements and extensions.

Ideal Use Cases: SDL is well-suited for indie developers and hobbyists focused on creating 2D games, educational projects, or smaller-scale titles. Its simplicity and efficiency make it an excellent choice for rapid development cycles.

SFML (Simple and Fast Multimedia Library)

SFML is a multimedia library that provides a higher-level interface compared to SDL while still maintaining a focus on simplicity and performance. It is particularly favored by developers who prefer a C++-oriented approach.

Key Features:

- **C++ Friendly**: SFML is designed with C++ in mind, providing an object-oriented API that feels natural to C++ developers. This makes it easier to integrate into existing C++ projects and leverage the language's features.
- **2D Graphics and Audio Support**: SFML excels in handling 2D graphics, audio, and network operations, making it a comprehensive solution for developing 2D games. Its features include sprite handling, sound playback, and networking capabilities.
- **Simplicity and Learning Curve**: SFML is known for its straightforward API and ease of use, making it an excellent choice for beginners. The library abstracts many complexities involved in game development, allowing developers to focus on game design.
- **Cross-Platform Functionality**: Similar to SDL, SFML supports multiple platforms, including Windows, macOS, and Linux, enabling developers to build games that run on various operating systems.
- **Active Community and Resources**: SFML has a supportive community with a wealth of tutorials, documentation, and sample projects. This accessibility can significantly enhance the learning experience for new developers.

Ideal Use Cases: SFML is ideal for 2D game development, particularly for indie projects, educational purposes, and rapid prototyping. Its focus on simplicity makes it a great choice for developers looking to create games without the complexities of larger engines.

Each of these game engines and frameworks—Unity, Unreal Engine, SDL, and SFML—brings unique strengths and capabilities to the table, catering to different types of developers and project requirements. Unity's versatility and user-friendliness make it a favorite among indie developers, while Unreal Engine's high-quality graphics appeal to those creating AAA titles. SDL and SFML provide low-level access and simplicity, making them excellent choices for developers focused on 2D game development.

As a C++ developer entering the world of game development, understanding these tools will be crucial for selecting the right environment for your projects. In the next chapters, we will explore how to leverage C++ within these engines and frameworks, enabling you to create compelling and immersive gaming experiences.

Core Game Development Concepts: Game Loop, Rendering, Input Handling

Game development involves a multitude of complex systems that must work together seamlessly to create an engaging and interactive experience. Understanding the foundational concepts that underpin these systems is crucial for any game developer, especially when using a versatile language like C++. This section will delve into three core concepts: the game loop, rendering, and input handling, outlining their importance and how they function in the context of game development.

The Game Loop

The game loop is the heartbeat of any video game, responsible for updating the game state, rendering graphics, and processing user input in a continuous cycle. It is what makes games dynamic and interactive, allowing for real-time changes and events.

Structure of the Game Loop

A typical game loop consists of three primary phases:

1. **Processing Input**: This phase captures and processes player inputs from various devices (keyboard, mouse, game controller, etc.). The game needs to interpret these inputs to modify game state accordingly.
2. **Updating Game State**: After processing input, the game loop updates

the game state based on the input received and the rules defined in the game logic. This includes moving characters, handling collisions, updating scores, and managing the game world.

3. **Rendering**: The final phase of the loop involves rendering the game's visuals. This process converts the updated game state into graphics displayed on the screen, allowing players to see the results of their actions and the changes in the game world.

Sample Game Loop Implementation

Here's a simple example of a game loop structure in C++:

```cpp
#include <iostream>
#include <chrono>

class Game {
public:
    void run() {
        bool isRunning = true;

        while (isRunning) {
            // Process Input
            processInput();

            // Update Game State
            update();

            // Render
            render();

            // Sleep for a
fixed time to maintain a steady frame rate
            std::this_thread::sleep_for
(std::chrono::milliseconds(16));
// Approx 60 FPS
        }
    }
```

```
private:
    void processInput() {
        // Handle input events (keyboard, mouse, etc.)
    }

    void update() {
        // Update game objects and state
    }

    void render() {
        // Render the game scene
    }
};
```

Importance of the Game Loop

The game loop is essential for maintaining a smooth and responsive gameplay experience. A well-structured game loop ensures that the game runs at a consistent frame rate, preventing issues like stuttering or lag. Additionally, it allows developers to implement features such as time-based movements and animations, which can enhance the overall gaming experience.

Rendering

Rendering is the process of converting game data (such as geometry, textures, and lighting) into the visual representation displayed on the screen. It plays a crucial role in creating the immersive environments that players interact with.

Types of Rendering

1. **2D Rendering**: In 2D games, rendering involves drawing sprites and textures on the screen. This process can be relatively straightforward, utilizing graphics libraries such as SDL or SFML. Basic operations include drawing images, shapes, and text.
2. **3D Rendering**: 3D rendering is more complex and involves creating three-dimensional representations of objects and environments. This includes managing vertices, meshes, textures, and lighting. Most modern

game engines, like Unity and Unreal, provide powerful rendering engines that handle the intricacies of 3D graphics.

Rendering Pipeline

The rendering pipeline typically follows these stages:

1. **Geometry Stage**: This stage involves transforming 3D models into 2D projections based on the camera's perspective. It includes operations like translation, rotation, and scaling.
2. **Rasterization**: In this stage, the projected shapes are converted into pixels or fragments on the screen. This step is crucial for determining which parts of the geometry are visible and how they should be rendered.
3. **Fragment Processing**: Here, each pixel is processed, applying textures, colors, and lighting calculations. This step is essential for achieving the desired visual effects.
4. **Output Merger**: The final stage combines the processed fragments and outputs the resulting image to the screen.

Performance Considerations

Rendering can be computationally intensive, especially in graphics-heavy games. Developers must optimize rendering processes to ensure smooth performance. Techniques such as culling (removing objects not visible to the camera), level of detail (LOD), and batching (grouping draw calls) can significantly improve rendering efficiency.

Input Handling

Input handling is a critical component of game development that directly impacts gameplay and player experience. It involves capturing and interpreting player inputs from various devices to control characters, navigate menus, and interact with the game world.

Types of Input Devices

1. **Keyboard**: A standard input device for many games, allowing players

to execute actions using key presses. Keyboards are often used for movement, actions, and menu navigation.

2. **Mouse**: Primarily used for pointing, clicking, and navigating 3D environments. The mouse's precision makes it essential for games that require aiming or selection.

3. **Game Controllers**: These devices, including gamepads and joysticks, offer an alternative input method, particularly for console gaming. Controllers provide analog input and multiple buttons, enhancing the gameplay experience.

4. **Touchscreens**: For mobile games, touchscreens are a primary input method. They enable direct interaction with the game through taps, swipes, and multi-touch gestures.

Handling Input Events

Input handling typically follows an event-driven model, where input events (like key presses or mouse movements) are captured and processed by the game loop. Here's a simplified approach to handling keyboard input in C++:

```cpp
#include <iostream>
#include <unordered_map>

class InputManager {
public:
    void update() {
        // Simulate capturing input state
// In a real implementation, this would interface with the OS or
graphics library
        for (const auto& key : keys) {
keys[key.first] = false;
// Reset all keys to not pressed
        }

        // Example of capturing key states
        if (isKeyPressed('W'))
keys['W'] = true; // Move forward
        if (isKeyPressed('S'))
```

```
keys['S'] = true; // Move backward
    }

    bool isKeyPressed(char key) {
        // Placeholder for
 actual key state checking logic
        return false;
// Implement actual input state check
    }

    bool isKeyDown(char key) {
        return keys[key];
    }

private:
    std::unordered_map<char,
bool> keys; // Store the state of each key
};
```

Input Mapping and Actions

To create a user-friendly experience, developers often implement an input mapping system that allows them to define which actions correspond to specific inputs. For example, a player might use the "W" key to move forward, the "A" key to move left, and the mouse to aim. This abstraction allows for easy changes to control schemes, accommodating player preferences and accessibility needs.

Best Practices for Input Handling

1. **Keep It Responsive**: Input handling should be as immediate as possible to ensure that player actions are reflected without noticeable delay.
2. **Implement Input Polling**: Regularly polling input states in the game loop allows for real-time updates and helps maintain responsiveness.
3. **Provide Customization Options**: Allowing players to customize controls enhances user experience. Consider providing an options menu where players can remap keys or adjust sensitivity.
4. **Handle Edge Cases**: Ensure that your input handling accounts for

scenarios like simultaneous key presses or controller disconnections to prevent gameplay issues.

Mastering core game development concepts such as the game loop, rendering, and input handling is essential for creating engaging and interactive games. These concepts serve as the foundation upon which more complex systems are built, enabling developers to craft immersive experiences that captivate players.

Setting Up Your Development Environment: IDEs, Compilers, and Tools

Creating a robust game development environment is crucial for efficient workflow and productivity. A well-configured development environment enables developers to write, test, and debug code effectively. In this section, we will explore essential components of a development environment for C++ game development, including Integrated Development Environments (IDEs), compilers, and various tools that streamline the development process.

Integrated Development Environments (IDEs)

An IDE is a software application that provides comprehensive facilities for software development. It typically includes a source code editor, build automation tools, a debugger, and often integrates with version control systems. Using an IDE can significantly enhance your coding efficiency and streamline the development workflow.

Popular IDEs for C++ Game Development
Visual Studio:

- **Overview**: Visual Studio is one of the most widely used IDEs for C++ development, especially on Windows. It offers powerful features such as IntelliSense (code completion), debugging tools, and an integrated build system.

- **Features**: Visual Studio supports a variety of project types, including game development projects that utilize DirectX and other game libraries. The IDE also integrates well with Microsoft's Azure cloud services and has excellent support for version control systems.
- **Best Use Case**: Ideal for developers working on Windows-based games or those using the Microsoft ecosystem.

CLion:

- **Overview**: Developed by JetBrains, CLion is a cross-platform IDE that specializes in C and C++. It provides advanced code analysis, smart code completion, and support for CMake projects, which is essential for managing complex game development setups.
- **Features**: CLion's built-in debugger and integration with various version control systems make it a powerful tool for collaborative game development. Its refactoring tools and testing support enhance code quality and maintainability.
- **Best Use Case**: Suitable for developers who prefer a modern interface and advanced code management features, especially when working on multi-platform games.

Code::Blocks:

- **Overview**: Code::Blocks is an open-source, cross-platform IDE that is lightweight and highly customizable. It supports multiple compilers and can be adapted to various workflows.
- **Features**: With a straightforward interface, Code::Blocks is easy to use for beginners. It includes a built-in debugger and supports plugins, allowing developers to extend its functionality.
- **Best Use Case**: Ideal for beginners and small projects or for developers who need a simple, lightweight IDE.

Eclipse CDT:

- **Overview**: Eclipse is a versatile IDE known primarily for Java development but also supports C++ through the C/C++ Development Tooling (CDT) plugin.
- **Features**: Eclipse provides a powerful debugging environment and support for various build systems, making it suitable for complex projects. Its extensible architecture allows developers to integrate additional tools and plugins easily.
- **Best Use Case**: Best for developers already familiar with the Eclipse environment or those working on large-scale projects that benefit from extensive plugin support.

Visual Studio Code (VS Code):

- **Overview**: While not a traditional IDE, VS Code is a powerful, open-source code editor that can be extended into a full-fledged development environment through extensions.
- **Features**: With support for debugging, integrated terminal, and numerous plugins for C++ development, VS Code is highly configurable. The C++ extension adds features like IntelliSense, debugging capabilities, and code navigation.
- **Best Use Case**: Suitable for developers looking for a lightweight, customizable environment, especially when working on cross-platform projects.

Compilers

A compiler is essential for converting the source code written in C++ into executable programs. Different compilers offer varying levels of optimization, error checking, and support for C++ standards.

Popular C++ Compilers

GCC (GNU Compiler Collection):

- **Overview**: GCC is a free and open-source compiler suite widely used for C and C++ development across multiple platforms.

- **Features**: Known for its performance and support for the latest C++ standards, GCC is a go-to choice for many developers. It provides robust optimization capabilities and generates efficient binaries.
- **Best Use Case**: Ideal for Linux-based development and for those who require a powerful compiler with extensive features.

Clang:

- **Overview**: Clang is another open-source compiler that is part of the LLVM project. It is known for its fast compilation times and user-friendly error messages.
- **Features**: Clang supports modern C++ features and offers excellent optimization options. It also provides a modular architecture, allowing for easy integration with other tools.
- **Best Use Case**: Well-suited for cross-platform development and when using modern C++ standards, particularly on macOS and Linux.

Microsoft Visual C++ (MSVC):

- **Overview**: MSVC is a proprietary compiler provided with Visual Studio, primarily targeting Windows development.
- **Features**: MSVC offers comprehensive support for the Windows API and DirectX, making it an excellent choice for developing Windows games. It also includes advanced optimization techniques and debugging tools.
- **Best Use Case**: Recommended for developers focused on Windows-based game development.

Intel C++ Compiler:

- **Overview**: The Intel C++ Compiler (ICC) is designed to produce highly optimized code for Intel processors.
- **Features**: It offers advanced optimization techniques specifically tailored for Intel architecture, enhancing performance for CPU-intensive

applications, including games.

- **Best Use Case**: Best for performance-critical applications where optimization for Intel hardware is paramount.

Essential Development Tools

In addition to IDEs and compilers, various tools can enhance your game development process, making it more efficient and organized.

Version Control Systems (VCS):

- **Overview**: Version control is essential for managing changes to your codebase, allowing multiple developers to collaborate effectively and track changes over time.
- **Popular Options**:
- **Git**: The most widely used distributed version control system. Tools like GitHub or GitLab provide platforms for hosting Git repositories and managing collaborative projects.
- **Subversion (SVN)**: A centralized version control system suitable for projects that require strict version control workflows.
- **Best Use Case**: Use Git for most projects, especially when working with teams, due to its flexibility and widespread adoption.

Build Systems:

- **Overview**: Build systems automate the process of compiling and linking code into executable programs, simplifying project management.
- **Popular Options**:
- **CMake**: A cross-platform build system that generates build files for various platforms and compilers. CMake simplifies project setup and makes it easier to manage complex builds.
- **Make**: A widely used tool for managing build processes, especially in Unix-like environments. It allows developers to specify how to compile and link the program.
- **Best Use Case**: Use CMake for cross-platform projects and Make for

simpler, Unix-based projects.

Debugging Tools:

- **Overview**: Debugging tools help identify and fix issues in your code. They allow developers to step through code, inspect variables, and analyze the flow of execution.
- **Popular Options**:
- **GDB (GNU Debugger)**: A powerful command-line debugger that works with GCC and other compilers. It allows you to run your program step-by-step and inspect the state at any point.
- **Visual Studio Debugger**: Integrated within Visual Studio, this debugger provides a user-friendly interface with advanced debugging features.
- **Best Use Case**: Use GDB for command-line debugging in Unix-based systems, and Visual Studio Debugger for Windows-based development.

Profiling Tools:

- **Overview**: Profiling tools analyze the performance of your game, helping identify bottlenecks and optimize code.
- **Popular Options**:
- **Valgrind**: A programming tool for memory debugging, memory leak detection, and profiling. Valgrind can help identify performance issues related to memory usage.
- **Visual Studio Profiler**: Integrated within Visual Studio, it provides insights into performance and helps identify slow code paths.
- **Best Use Case**: Use Valgrind for memory profiling and Visual Studio Profiler for CPU performance analysis.

Graphics and Sound Tools:

- **Overview**: For game development, integrating graphics and audio is crucial to enhance the player experience.

- **Popular Options**:
- **Adobe Photoshop or GIMP**: Used for creating and editing 2D graphics and textures.
- **FMOD or OpenAL**: Libraries for integrating audio into games, enabling sound effects and music playback.
- **Best Use Case**: Use Adobe Photoshop for high-quality graphics and FMOD for sophisticated audio management.

Setting up a well-structured development environment is essential for successful C++ game development. Selecting the right IDE, compiler, and tools tailored to your project's needs can significantly enhance productivity and streamline the development process.

Project Structure and Best Practices for Game Development Projects

Creating a well-organized project structure is vital for the success of any game development project. A clear structure facilitates collaboration, code maintenance, and future scalability. In this section, we will explore best practices for organizing your game development projects, covering the directory structure, naming conventions, coding standards, and the importance of documentation.

Importance of Project Structure

A well-defined project structure helps developers navigate the codebase efficiently, making it easier to locate files and understand the organization of the project. It also enables better collaboration among team members by providing a common framework that everyone can follow. A consistent structure is especially critical in larger projects where multiple developers are working concurrently.

Recommended Directory Structure

The following is a recommended directory structure for a C++ game development project:

```
bash

/MyGameProject │ ├───────

/src              # Source code │ ├───────
    /core         # Core game logic │ ├───────
    /entities     # Game entities (e.g., characters,
    items) │ ├───────
    /components   # Game components (e.g., physics,
    rendering) │ ├───────
    /scenes       # Game scenes (e.g., main menu,
    levels) │ ├───────
    /resources     # Resource management (e.g., textures,
    audio) │ └───────
    main.cpp      # Entry point of the application │ ├───────

/include          # Header files │ ├───────
    /core         # Header files for core logic │ ├───────
    /entities     # Header files for entities │ ├───────
    /components   # Header files for components │ └───────
    /scenes       # Header files for scenes │ ├───────

/resources        # Game assets │ ├───────
    /images       # Image assets (textures, sprites) │ ├───────
    /sounds       # Audio files (music, sound effects) │ └───────
    /fonts        # Font files │ ├───────

/build            # Build files and binaries │ ├───────

/docs             # Documentation │ ├───────

/tests            # Unit tests and test scripts │ ├───────

CMakeLists.txt    # CMake build configuration ├───────
README.md         # Project overview and setup
instructions └───────
```

```
LICENSE            # License information
```

Explanation of Directory Structure

- **/src**: This directory contains all source code files. Organizing code into subdirectories based on functionality helps maintain clarity.
- **/include**: This directory houses header files that define interfaces for the source code in the /src directory. Keeping headers separate from implementation files encourages modular design.
- **/resources**: This folder holds all game assets, such as images, sounds, and fonts. Organizing assets by type makes it easier to manage and update them.
- **/build**: This directory is where build artifacts and binaries are generated. Keeping build files separate from source code avoids clutter.
- **/docs**: Documentation is crucial for long-term maintenance. Use this folder for project documentation, including design decisions, coding standards, and user manuals.
- **/tests**: Having a dedicated folder for unit tests and testing scripts helps ensure that your game remains stable as you add new features.
- **CMakeLists.txt**: This file is essential for configuring the build process if you are using CMake. It defines project settings, source files, and dependencies.
- **README.md**: This markdown file provides an overview of the project, including setup instructions, usage, and any other relevant information for developers or users.
- **LICENSE**: Always include a license file to specify the terms under which your project can be used or modified.

Naming Conventions

Using consistent naming conventions for files, classes, and variables is crucial for enhancing code readability and maintainability. Here are some best practices:

1. **File Names**: Use lowercase letters with underscores to separate words (e.g., game_scene.cpp). This convention helps distinguish source files from header files.
2. **Class Names**: Use CamelCase for class names (e.g., PlayerCharacter, GameEngine). This makes it easy to identify classes in your code.
3. **Function Names**: Use lowercase letters with underscores (e.g., initialize_game, update_player). This style is consistent with many C++ coding standards and helps differentiate functions from classes.
4. **Variable Names**: Use descriptive names that convey the purpose of the variable. Stick to a consistent style, either CamelCase or snake_case, for clarity (e.g., playerScore or player_score).
5. **Constants**: Define constants in uppercase letters with underscores (e.g., MAX_PLAYERS). This convention helps to differentiate constant values from regular variables.

Coding Standards

Following coding standards is essential for maintaining a clean codebase, especially in team environments. Here are some recommended practices:

1. **Commenting**: Write clear and concise comments to explain complex logic or to provide context for specific sections of code. Use docstrings to describe classes and functions, including parameters and return values.
2. **Code Structure**: Maintain a consistent structure within files. Group related functions together, and use whitespace effectively to separate logical blocks of code.
3. **Error Handling**: Implement robust error handling to ensure the game can gracefully handle unexpected situations. Use exceptions for critical errors and validate user input where necessary.
4. **Modularity**: Design code in a modular way, encapsulating related functionalities within classes or modules. This approach promotes code reusability and simplifies testing.
5. **Version Control Commits**: Commit code regularly to your version control system with meaningful commit messages that describe the

changes made. This practice helps maintain a clear history of development.

Documentation Practices

Good documentation is vital for any development project, serving as a guide for both current and future developers. Here are best practices for maintaining effective documentation:

1. **Project Overview**: Provide a comprehensive project overview in the README file, including the project's purpose, features, and any dependencies.
2. **Setup Instructions**: Clearly outline the steps required to set up the development environment and build the project. Include information on required tools, libraries, and installation instructions.
3. **Code Documentation**: Use inline comments and docstrings to describe classes, functions, and key variables. This practice helps other developers understand your code quickly.
4. **Design Documentation**: Maintain documentation that outlines the architecture and design decisions made during development. This can include diagrams, flowcharts, and explanations of key components.
5. **Changelog**: Keep a changelog that records changes made to the project over time, including bug fixes, new features, and improvements.

Establishing a well-structured project organization and adhering to best practices is fundamental to successful C++ game development. A clear directory structure, consistent naming conventions, coding standards, and thorough documentation create a solid foundation for development, making it easier for teams to collaborate effectively and ensuring the longevity and maintainability of the project.

In the next chapter, we will explore essential C++ concepts and techniques that form the backbone of game development, equipping you with the knowledge to create sophisticated and engaging games.

Core C++ Concepts for Game Programming

Core C++ Concepts for Game Programming
Essential C++ Syntax and Concepts: Variables, Functions, Loops
C++ is a powerful programming language that serves as the backbone of many game development projects. Understanding its fundamental syntax and concepts is crucial for creating efficient and effective games. In this chapter, we will delve into the essential elements of C++, focusing on variables, functions, and loops. These building blocks will enable you to write clean and performant code that is foundational for game programming.

Variables

Variables are essential for storing and manipulating data in any programming language, including C++. They act as containers for holding values that can change during program execution. C++ supports several variable types, including primitive types (such as integers and floating-point numbers) and user-defined types (such as classes and structures).

Declaring Variables

In C++, you declare a variable by specifying its type followed by its name. The syntax is as follows:

```
type variableName;
```

For example, to declare an integer variable called score, you would write:

```
int score;
```

You can also initialize a variable at the time of declaration:

```
int score = 0;
```

Types of Variables

C++ has various built-in data types, including:

Integer Types: Used to store whole numbers.

- int: Standard integer type (typically 4 bytes).
- short: Short integer type (usually 2 bytes).
- long: Long integer type (at least 4 bytes).
- long long: Extended long integer type (at least 8 bytes).

Floating-Point Types: Used to store decimal numbers.

- float: Single-precision floating-point (typically 4 bytes).
- double: Double-precision floating-point (typically 8 bytes).
- long double: Extended precision floating-point (size varies).

Character Types: Used to store single characters.

- char: Typically 1 byte, can store single characters or small integers.

Boolean Types: Used to store true/false values.

- bool: Can hold true or false.

User-Defined Types: Includes structures, unions, enums, and classes. These allow for the creation of complex data types tailored to your specific needs.

Variable Scope

Variable scope defines the context within which a variable can be accessed. There are three primary scopes in C++:

Local Scope: Variables declared within a function or block are accessible only within that function or block.

```
void exampleFunction() {
    int localVar = 5; // Accessible only within this function
}
```

Global Scope: Variables declared outside of any function are accessible throughout the entire program.

```
int globalVar = 10; // Accessible in any function

void anotherFunction() {
    // globalVar can be accessed here
}
```

Class Scope: Variables declared within a class are accessible by all member functions of that class.

```
class Game {
private:
    int playerHealth; // Accessible only within Game class

public:
    void setHealth(int health) {
        playerHealth = health;
    }
};
```

Functions

Functions are fundamental building blocks in C++ that allow you to group code into reusable units. They help organize code and improve readability by breaking down complex operations into manageable parts.

Declaring and Defining Functions

The syntax for declaring a function in C++ is as follows:

```
returnType functionName(parameterType parameterName) {
    // Function body
}
```

For example, a simple function that adds two integers could be declared as follows:

```
int add(int a, int b) {
    return a + b;
}
```

To call this function, you would use:

```
int result = add(5, 3); // result now holds the value 8
```

Function Overloading

C++ allows for function overloading, where multiple functions can have the same name but different parameter lists. This feature enhances code readability and usability.

```
int multiply(int a, int b) {
    return a * b;
}

double multiply(double a, double b) {
    return a * b;
}
```

In the example above, both multiply functions can coexist, and the appropriate one will be called based on the argument types passed.

Inline Functions

C++ also supports inline functions, which suggest to the compiler that it should insert the function's code directly into the calling code rather than performing a traditional function call. This can improve performance, especially for small, frequently called functions.

```
inline int square(int x) {
    return x * x;
}
```

Recursive Functions

A recursive function is one that calls itself to solve a smaller instance of the same problem. This technique can be particularly useful in game programming for tasks such as traversing trees or managing game states.

```
int factorial(int n) {
    if (n <= 1) return 1;
    return n * factorial(n - 1);
}
```

Loops

Loops are control structures that allow you to execute a block of code multiple times. They are essential in game programming for tasks like updating game states, handling input, or rendering graphics.

Types of Loops

C++ supports several types of loops:

For Loop: The for loop is used when the number of iterations is known beforehand.

```
for (int i = 0; i < 10; i++) {
    // Code to execute 10 times
}
```

While Loop: The while loop is used when the number of iterations is not known, and execution continues as long as a condition is true.

```
int count = 0;
while (count < 10) {
    // Code to execute until count is 10
    count++;
}
```

Do-While Loop: The do-while loop guarantees that the loop body will execute at least once, as the condition is checked after executing the block of code.

```
int count = 0;
do {
    // Code to execute
    count++;
} while (count < 10);
```

Break and Continue Statements

In loops, you can use the break statement to exit the loop prematurely or the continue statement to skip the current iteration and proceed to the next.

```
for (int i = 0; i < 10; i++) {
    if (i == 5) break; // Exit the loop when i is 5
}

for (int i = 0; i < 10; i++) {
    if (i % 2 == 0) continue; // Skip even numbers
    // Code for odd numbers
}
```

Mastering the essential syntax and concepts of C++—including variables, functions, and loops—is crucial for effective game programming. These fundamental elements empower developers to write efficient, organized, and reusable code, forming the foundation for more complex programming paradigms and game mechanics.

Object-Oriented Programming (OOP) in Game Design

Object-Oriented Programming (OOP) is a programming paradigm that uses "objects" to represent data and methods. This approach is fundamental in game design, as it provides a way to model real-world entities and their interactions in a way that is both intuitive and manageable. By structuring your code with OOP principles, you can create more organized, scalable, and maintainable game applications. In this section, we will explore the core concepts of OOP—encapsulation, inheritance, polymorphism, and abstraction—and how they apply to game development.

Core Concepts of OOP

1. Encapsulation

Encapsulation is the concept of bundling data (attributes) and methods (functions) that operate on that data into a single unit, known as a class. This helps restrict direct access to some of the object's components, which can enhance the integrity of the data and promote modularity.

Example of Encapsulation:

cpp

```cpp
class Player {
private:
    int health;
    int score;

public:
```

```cpp
    Player() : health(100), score(0) {}

    void takeDamage(int damage) {
        health -= damage;
        if (health < 0) health = 0; // Prevent negative health
    }

    int getHealth() const {
        return health;
    }

    void increaseScore(int points) {
        score += points;
    }

    int getScore() const {
        return score;
    }
};
```

In this example, the Player class encapsulates the player's health and score. The health and score attributes are private, meaning they cannot be accessed directly from outside the class. Instead, public methods are provided to modify and retrieve these attributes, ensuring controlled access.

2. Inheritance

Inheritance is a mechanism that allows one class (the derived class) to inherit attributes and methods from another class (the base class). This promotes code reuse and establishes a hierarchical relationship between classes.

Example of Inheritance:

```cpp
cpp

class Character {
protected:
    int health;
```

```cpp
    int attackPower;

public:
    Character(int h, int a) : health(h), attackPower(a) {}

    void attack(Character& target) {
        target.takeDamage(attackPower);
    }

    virtual void takeDamage(int damage) {
        health -= damage;
    }

    int getHealth() const {
        return health;
    }
};

class Enemy : public Character {
public:
    Enemy() : Character(50, 10) {} // Inherit health and attack
    power from Character

    void takeDamage(int damage) override {
        health -= damage / 2; // Enemies take half damage
    }
};

class Player : public Character {
public:
    Player() : Character(100, 20) {} // Inherit health and attack
    power from Character

    void takeDamage(int damage) override {
        health -= damage; // Players take full damage
    }
};
```

In this example, both Player and Enemy classes inherit from the Character base class. This means they share common functionality, such as the attack method, while still being able to implement their specific behaviors for taking damage.

3. Polymorphism

Polymorphism allows methods to do different things based on the object that it is acting upon, enabling you to write more flexible and extensible code. In C++, polymorphism is typically achieved through function overriding and virtual functions.

Example of Polymorphism:

In the previous code example, both Player and Enemy classes override the takeDamage method. This means that when you call takeDamage on a Character reference, the appropriate method for the actual object type will be executed.

```cpp
Character* character = new Player();
character->takeDamage(30); // Calls Player's takeDamage method

character = new Enemy();
character->takeDamage(30); // Calls Enemy's takeDamage method
```

Here, polymorphism enables the same function call to produce different results based on the actual object type, allowing for dynamic behavior in your game design.

4. Abstraction

Abstraction is the concept of hiding the complex implementation details of a system while exposing only the necessary parts. In C++, you can achieve abstraction through abstract classes and interfaces.

Example of Abstraction:

```cpp
class GameObject {
public:
```

```cpp
    virtual void update() = 0; // Pure virtual function
    virtual void render() = 0; // Pure virtual function
};

class Player : public GameObject {
public:
    void update() override {
        // Update player logic
    }

    void render() override {
        // Render player graphics
    }
};

class Enemy : public GameObject {
public:
    void update() override {
        // Update enemy logic
    }

    void render() override {
        // Render enemy graphics
    }
};
```

In this example, GameObject is an abstract class that defines a common interface for all game objects. The update and render methods are pure virtual functions, meaning that any class inheriting from GameObject must provide implementations for these methods. This allows you to treat all game objects uniformly while hiding their internal workings.

Benefits of OOP in Game Development

1. **Modularity**: OOP promotes modular design, making it easier to manage and maintain code. Each class can be developed and tested independently.
2. **Code Reusability**: Inheritance allows for code reuse, reducing redun-

dancy and the likelihood of errors. You can create new classes based on existing ones without rewriting code.

3. **Scalability**: As games grow in complexity, OOP provides a clear structure that makes it easier to scale projects. New features can be added by creating new classes or extending existing ones.

4. **Maintainability**: Encapsulation and abstraction help keep the codebase clean and manageable, making it easier to debug and update.

5. **Dynamic Behavior**: Polymorphism enables dynamic behavior in games, allowing for more flexible and responsive interactions between game objects.

Implementing OOP in Game Design

To effectively implement OOP in your game design, consider the following best practices:

- **Design Class Hierarchies**: Plan your class hierarchy carefully. Identify base classes that share common properties and methods, and design derived classes to handle specific behaviors.
- **Use Interfaces**: Define interfaces for common behaviors to promote flexibility. For example, you might create an interface for all interactive objects in your game.
- **Favor Composition over Inheritance**: While inheritance is a powerful tool, it can lead to tight coupling. Favor composition (using classes as members of other classes) when it makes sense for your design.
- **Document Your Code**: Use comments and documentation to describe the purpose and functionality of classes and methods. This will aid both your future self and other developers working on the project.
- **Test Extensively**: Test your classes and methods to ensure they work as intended. Unit testing can help identify issues early and improve code quality.

Object-Oriented Programming is a vital aspect of game design that allows developers to create structured, modular, and maintainable code. By leveraging encapsulation, inheritance, polymorphism, and abstraction, you can model complex game mechanics and interactions in an intuitive manner. Understanding these OOP principles is essential for any game developer using C++, and it sets the foundation for creating robust and scalable game architectures.

Pointers, References, and Dynamic Memory Management

Understanding pointers, references, and dynamic memory management is crucial for effective game programming in C++. These concepts enable you to manage memory efficiently, create complex data structures, and optimize performance—essential elements in the demanding field of game development. In this section, we will cover each of these topics in detail, providing you with a comprehensive understanding of how to utilize them in your game projects.

Pointers
What are Pointers?
A pointer is a variable that holds the memory address of another variable. In C++, pointers are powerful tools that allow you to manipulate memory directly, making them essential for dynamic data structures, resource management, and performance optimization.

Declaring and Using Pointers
To declare a pointer, you use the * operator, and you can assign it the address of a variable using the address-of operator &.
Example:

```
cpp

int x = 10;
int* ptr = &x; // ptr now holds the address of x

std::cout << "Value of x: " << *ptr << std::endl; // Dereferencing
ptr to access value of x
```

In this example, ptr is a pointer to an integer, and it holds the address of x. By dereferencing the pointer using the * operator, you can access the value of x.

Pointer Arithmetic

Pointers can also be incremented or decremented, allowing for easy manipulation of arrays and other contiguous data structures.

Example:

```
cpp

int arr[] = {1, 2, 3, 4, 5};
int* ptr = arr; // Points to the first element of the array

for (int i = 0; i < 5; ++i) {
    std::cout << *(ptr + i) << " "; // Accessing array elements
    using pointer arithmetic
}
```

In this example, ptr points to the first element of the array arr. By incrementing the pointer, you can traverse the array.

References

What are References?

A reference is an alias for another variable. Unlike pointers, references cannot be null and must be initialized when they are declared. They provide a safer and more convenient way to handle data without the need for explicit dereferencing.

Declaring and Using References

To declare a reference, you use the & operator in the variable declaration.

Example:

```cpp
int y = 20;
int& ref = y; // ref is a reference to y

std::cout << "Value of y: " << ref << std::endl; // Accessing the
value through reference
ref = 30; // Modifying the value of y through the reference

std::cout << "New value of y: " << y << std::endl; // Outputs 30
```

In this example, ref is a reference to y. Any changes made to ref directly affect y.

Differences Between Pointers and References

While both pointers and references can be used to manipulate variables indirectly, they have key differences:

- **Nullability**: Pointers can be null, whereas references cannot.
- **Reassignment**: Pointers can be reassigned to point to different variables, while references remain bound to the variable they were initialized with.
- **Syntax**: References use simpler syntax, eliminating the need for dereferencing.

Dynamic Memory Management

Dynamic memory management allows you to allocate and deallocate memory at runtime using the new and delete operators. This is particularly important in game development, where the memory requirements can vary significantly depending on the game's state.

Allocating Memory Dynamically

To allocate memory for a variable or an array dynamically, you use the new operator.

Example:

```cpp
int* dynamicArray = new int[5]; // Allocate an array of 5 integers

for (int i = 0; i < 5; ++i) {
    dynamicArray[i] = i * 10; // Initialize the array
}

for (int i = 0; i < 5; ++i) {
    std::cout << dynamicArray[i] << " "; // Access array elements
}

// Deallocate the memory when done
delete[] dynamicArray;
```

In this example, we allocate memory for an array of integers dynamically. It's crucial to use delete[] to free the allocated memory, preventing memory leaks.

Deallocating Memory

When using dynamic memory allocation, you must manually manage the memory to avoid memory leaks and dangling pointers. The delete operator is used to deallocate memory previously allocated with new.

Example:

```cpp
int* singleValue = new int(5); // Allocate a single integer
dynamically
std::cout << "Value: " << *singleValue << std::endl;

// Deallocate the memory
delete singleValue;
```

In this example, a single integer is allocated, and it is important to call delete to free the allocated memory.

Smart Pointers

C++11 introduced smart pointers—std::unique_ptr, std::shared_ptr, and std::weak_ptr—which automatically manage memory. They help prevent memory leaks and dangling pointers by automatically deallocating memory when the pointer goes out of scope or is no longer needed.

Example of std::unique_ptr:

cpp

```
#include <memory>

void example() {
    std::unique_ptr<int> smartPtr(new int(10)); // Allocate memory
    using a smart pointer
    std::cout << "Value: " << *smartPtr << std::endl;
} // Memory is automatically deallocated here
```

In this example, std::unique_ptr manages the memory for an integer. When the smart pointer goes out of scope, it automatically deletes the allocated memory.

Best Practices for Memory Management

1. **Always Deallocate Memory**: If you use new to allocate memory, ensure you pair it with delete or delete[] to avoid memory leaks.
2. **Use Smart Pointers**: Leverage smart pointers for automatic memory management and to prevent common memory management errors.
3. **Initialize Pointers**: Always initialize pointers to avoid undefined behavior. If a pointer may not point to valid memory, consider using nullptr.
4. **Avoid Memory Leaks**: Regularly test your game for memory leaks using tools like Valgrind or built-in profiling tools in IDEs.
5. **Limit Pointer Usage**: Use references when possible instead of pointers, as they are safer and less prone to errors.

Mastering pointers, references, and dynamic memory management is essential for efficient game development in C++. These concepts not only enhance your ability to manage resources effectively but also contribute to the overall performance and stability of your games. By utilizing pointers and references correctly, and implementing robust memory management strategies, you can ensure that your game runs smoothly and efficiently.

In the next chapter, we will explore advanced C++ features and techniques that further enhance our ability to create high-performance games, including templates, operator overloading, and the Standard Template Library (STL).

Using Smart Pointers for Safe Memory Handling in Games

As game development becomes increasingly complex, effective memory management is critical to creating high-performance applications. C++ offers powerful tools for managing memory dynamically, but traditional techniques can lead to issues such as memory leaks, dangling pointers, and excessive resource usage. Smart pointers were introduced in C++11 as a robust solution to these challenges, enabling developers to handle memory more safely and efficiently. In this section, we will explore the various types of smart pointers, their use cases, and best practices for utilizing them in game development.

What are Smart Pointers?

Smart pointers are wrapper classes that manage the memory of dynamically allocated objects. They automatically handle memory deallocation when the object is no longer needed, significantly reducing the risk of memory leaks. The three main types of smart pointers in C++ are std::unique_ptr, std::shared_ptr, and std::weak_ptr.

Types of Smart Pointers
1. std::unique_ptr
std::unique_ptr represents sole ownership of an object. This means that only one unique_ptr can point to a particular object at any time, ensuring

that the object is automatically deallocated when the unique_ptr goes out of scope or is explicitly reset.

Key Features:

- **Non-Copyable**: std::unique_ptr cannot be copied. It can only be moved, ensuring unique ownership.
- **Automatic Cleanup**: Memory is automatically released when the unique_ptr is destroyed.

Example:

```cpp
cpp

#include <iostream>
#include <memory>

class GameObject {
public:
    GameObject() { std::cout << "GameObject created\n"; }
    ~GameObject() { std::cout << "GameObject destroyed\n"; }
};

void createGameObject() {
    std::unique_ptr<GameObject> obj(new GameObject());
    // obj will automatically clean up when it goes out of scope
}

int main() {
    createGameObject(); // Output: GameObject created, GameObject
    destroyed
    return 0;
}
```

In this example, the GameObject is automatically destroyed when the unique_ptr goes out of scope, demonstrating effective resource management.

2. std::shared_ptr

std::shared_ptr allows multiple pointers to share ownership of the same object. It maintains a reference count, which keeps track of how many shared_ptr instances point to the same object. The object is only destroyed when the last shared_ptr pointing to it is destroyed or reset.

Key Features:

- **Shared Ownership**: Multiple shared_ptr instances can point to the same object.
- **Reference Counting**: Automatically manages the reference count to clean up memory when it's no longer in use.

Example:

```cpp
cpp

#include <iostream>
#include <memory>

class Enemy {
public:
    Enemy() { std::cout << "Enemy created\n"; }
    ~Enemy() { std::cout << "Enemy destroyed\n"; }
};

void spawnEnemy(std::shared_ptr<Enemy> enemy) {
    std::cout << "Enemy spawned\n";
}

int main() {
    std::shared_ptr<Enemy> enemy1(new Enemy());
    spawnEnemy(enemy1); // Output: Enemy created, Enemy spawned

    {
        std::shared_ptr<Enemy> enemy2 = enemy1; // Share ownership
        std::cout << "Shared ownership established\n"; // Output:
        Shared ownership established
    } // enemy2 goes out of scope, but enemy1 still exists
```

```
    // Output: Enemy destroyed after enemy1 goes out of scope
    return 0;
}
```

In this example, enemy1 and enemy2 share ownership of the same Enemy instance. The destructor is only called once all shared_ptr instances pointing to the object are out of scope.

3. std::weak_ptr

std::weak_ptr is used in conjunction with std::shared_ptr to break reference cycles that could lead to memory leaks. A weak_ptr does not affect the reference count of the shared_ptr. This is particularly useful in scenarios where you want to observe an object managed by shared_ptr without extending its lifetime.

Key Features:

- **No Ownership**: It does not own the object, thus preventing cyclic references.
- **Observation**: Allows access to the managed object if it still exists.

Example:

```cpp
#include <iostream>
#include <memory>

class Player {
public:
    Player() { std::cout << "Player created\n"; }
    ~Player() { std::cout << "Player destroyed\n"; }
};

class Game {
public:
```

```cpp
    void setPlayer(std::shared_ptr<Player> p) {
        player = p; // Store shared_ptr
    }

    void printPlayer() {
        if (auto p = player.lock()) { // Create a weak_ptr to
        check for validity
            std::cout << "Player is still in the game\n";
        } else {
            std::cout << "Player no longer exists\n";
        }
    }

private:
    std::weak_ptr<Player> player; // Weak reference to avoid cycles
};

int main() {
    std::shared_ptr<Player> player1(new Player());
    Game game;
    game.setPlayer(player1);
    game.printPlayer(); // Output: Player is still in the game

    player1.reset(); // Destroy Player instance
    game.printPlayer(); // Output: Player no longer exists

    return 0;
}
```

In this example, the Game class holds a weak_ptr to Player, allowing it to observe the Player without extending its lifetime, thus preventing memory leaks.

Best Practices for Using Smart Pointers in Game Development

1. **Prefer std::unique_ptr for Single Ownership**: Use std::unique_ptr when you want to ensure that a resource has a single owner. It's lightweight and provides automatic cleanup.

2. **Use std::shared_ptr for Shared Resources**: When multiple parts of your game need access to the same object, opt for std::shared_ptr. Be cautious with shared_ptr to avoid performance overhead from reference counting.

3. **Avoid Cyclic References**: When using std::shared_ptr, be mindful of potential cyclic references. Use std::weak_ptr to break cycles and prevent memory leaks.

4. **Initialize Smart Pointers Immediately**: To avoid dangling pointers, always initialize smart pointers as soon as they are declared.

5. **Avoid Mixing Raw Pointers and Smart Pointers**: Be consistent in your memory management. Mixing raw pointers with smart pointers can lead to confusion and errors. Stick with one method for managing memory in a given context.

6. **Use std::make_unique and std::make_shared**: These helper functions simplify the creation of smart pointers and reduce the risk of memory leaks from mismanaged raw pointers.

Example of std::make_unique:

cpp

```cpp
#include <iostream>
#include <memory>

class Level {
public:
    Level() { std::cout << "Level created\n"; }
    ~Level() { std::cout << "Level destroyed\n"; }
};

int main() {
    auto level = std::make_unique<Level>(); // Automatically
    managed unique_ptr
    return 0; // Level is automatically destroyed here
}
```

Using std::make_unique helps ensure that memory is properly managed and reduces the chances of errors.

Smart pointers are essential tools in modern C++ programming, providing safer and more efficient memory management techniques for game development. By utilizing std::unique_ptr, std::shared_ptr, and std::weak_ptr, developers can minimize memory leaks, avoid dangling pointers, and create more robust game applications. Implementing these smart pointer strategies can significantly enhance your ability to manage resources effectively, ultimately leading to improved game performance and stability.

C++11 and Beyond: Features for Enhanced Game Development

C++ has evolved significantly since its inception, with each new standard introducing features that enhance performance, simplify code, and facilitate modern programming practices. With the arrival of C++11, followed by C++14, C++17, and the latest standards, game developers now have access to a range of powerful features that make writing efficient, maintainable, and robust game code easier. This section explores the essential features introduced in C++11 and later, focusing on how they can enhance game development.

Key Features of C++11

1. **Auto Keyword**

The auto keyword allows the compiler to automatically deduce the type of a variable from its initializer. This feature simplifies code, especially when dealing with complex data types, and enhances readability.

Example:

```cpp
cpp

#include <vector>
#include <iostream>

int main() {
    std::vector<int> scores = {10, 20, 30};

    // Using auto to simplify type declaration
    for (auto score : scores) {
        std::cout << score << " "; // Output: 10 20 30
    }
    return 0;
}
```

By using auto, developers can avoid specifying the exact type of score, making the code cleaner and less prone to errors.

2. **Range-Based For Loops**

Range-based for loops provide a more straightforward syntax for iterating through collections like arrays and containers. This feature improves code clarity and reduces the risk of off-by-one errors.

Example:

```cpp
cpp

#include <vector>
#include <iostream>

int main() {
    std::vector<int> enemies = {1, 2, 3, 4};

    for (auto enemy : enemies) {
        std::cout << "Enemy ID: " << enemy << std::endl;
    }
```

```
        return 0;
}
```

This loop simplifies iterating through the enemies vector, making it easier to read and understand.

3. Lambda Expressions

Lambda expressions are anonymous functions that can be defined inline, allowing for concise and flexible function objects. This feature is particularly useful for callbacks and short functions, enhancing code modularity.

Example:

```cpp
#include <vector>
#include <algorithm>
#include <iostream>

int main() {
    std::vector<int> scores = {100, 90, 85, 70};

    // Lambda to find scores greater than 80
    auto highScoreCount = std::count_if(scores.begin(),
    scores.end(), [](int score) {
        return score > 80;
    });

    std::cout << "Number of high scores: " << highScoreCount <<
    std::endl; // Output: 3
    return 0;
}
```

In this example, the lambda expression provides a quick way to define criteria for counting high scores without needing a separate function.

4. Smart Pointers

As discussed in the previous section, C++11 introduced smart pointers

52

(std::unique_ptr, std::shared_ptr, and std::weak_ptr). These tools help manage memory automatically, reducing memory leaks and improving overall game stability.

Features from C++14, C++17, and Beyond

While C++11 introduced significant improvements, subsequent versions added features that further enhance game development capabilities.

1. **C++14 Features**

- **Generic Lambdas**: In C++14, lambda expressions can have auto parameters, allowing them to be more versatile and generic.

Example:

```cpp
#include <vector>
#include <algorithm>
#include <iostream>

int main() {
    std::vector<int> numbers = {1, 2, 3, 4, 5};

    auto sum = [](auto a, auto b) { return a + b; };

    int total = 0;
    for (auto number : numbers) {
        total = sum(total, number);
    }

    std::cout << "Total: " << total << std::endl; // Output: 15
    return 0;
}
```

- **Return Type Deduction**: Functions can automatically deduce their return type using auto, simplifying function signatures.

2. C++17 Features

- **std::optional**: This feature allows developers to represent optional values without using pointers. It enhances safety by clearly indicating when a value may be absent.

Example:

```cpp
#include <optional>
#include <iostream>

std::optional<int> findEnemyHealth(int id) {
    if (id == 1) return 100; // Example condition
    return std::nullopt; // No enemy found
}

int main() {
    auto health = findEnemyHealth(1);

    if (health) {
        std::cout << "Enemy Health: " << *health << std::endl; //
        Output: Enemy Health: 100
    } else {
        std::cout << "Enemy not found." << std::endl;
    }

    return 0;
}
```

- **std::variant**: This feature allows for type-safe unions, enabling variables to hold one of several types. This is useful for representing entities that can take on various forms.

3. C++20 Features

- **Concepts**: Concepts are a way to specify template requirements. They enable developers to enforce type constraints on template parameters, improving code readability and reducing template errors.

Example:

```cpp
#include <iostream>
#include <concepts>

template <typename T>
concept Numeric = std::is_arithmetic_v<T>;

template <Numeric T>
T add(T a, T b) {
    return a + b;
}

int main() {
    std::cout << add(5, 3) << std::endl; // Output: 8
    // std::cout << add("Hello", "World"); // Error: not numeric
    return 0;
}
```

- **Ranges**: C++20 introduced ranges, a powerful way to work with sequences. Ranges provide a more expressive and concise syntax for working with collections, improving code clarity.

Benefits of Using Modern C++ Features in Game Development

1. **Enhanced Readability**: Features like auto, range-based for loops, and lambda expressions lead to cleaner and more readable code, making it easier to understand the intent behind code.
2. **Improved Performance**: Many modern C++ features are designed to optimize performance. For example, smart pointers reduce memory

management overhead, while features like std::variant allow efficient handling of multiple types without the pitfalls of traditional unions.

3. **Increased Safety**: The introduction of smart pointers and std::optional reduces common programming errors, such as memory leaks and null pointer dereferencing, enhancing overall application stability.

4. **Simplified Code Maintenance**: With the use of concepts and improved template handling, developers can create more maintainable code. This is especially valuable in large codebases typical in game development, where clear interfaces and type safety are crucial.

5. **Rapid Prototyping**: Modern features allow developers to quickly prototype ideas and iterate on game mechanics. Lambdas and generic programming reduce the boilerplate code needed for common tasks, enabling faster development cycles.

C++11 and beyond have introduced numerous features that significantly enhance game development. From smart pointers that automate memory management to powerful template features like concepts, these advancements empower developers to write cleaner, safer, and more efficient code. Leveraging these features not only streamlines the development process but also contributes to the creation of high-performance games that can stand out in a competitive market.

Game-Specific Programming Foundations

G ame Loops and Frame Timing for Consistent Performance
In game development, achieving consistent performance and
smooth gameplay is crucial for delivering an engaging experience.
At the heart of this performance is the game loop, a fundamental concept that
drives the execution of a game. This chapter delves into the mechanics of
game loops and frame timing, exploring how they work together to ensure a
smooth and responsive gaming experience.

Understanding the Game Loop

The game loop is the central part of a game that continuously updates the
game state and renders graphics to the screen. It is responsible for controlling
the flow of the game, processing user input, updating game entities, and
rendering graphics. The game loop typically consists of three main phases:

1. **Processing Input**: This phase captures and processes input from the
   user, such as keyboard and mouse events. It translates these inputs into
   actions that affect the game state.
2. **Updating Game State**: During this phase, the game logic is executed.
   This includes updating the positions and states of game entities, checking
   for collisions, and managing game events. This is often done at a fixed
   time step to ensure consistency in gameplay.
3. **Rendering Graphics**: In the rendering phase, the current state of the
   game is drawn to the screen. This involves rendering sprites, 3D models,
   and UI elements, ensuring that players see the most up-to-date visuals.

The Basic Structure of a Game Loop

A simple representation of a game loop can be illustrated as follows:

```cpp
#include <iostream>
#include <chrono>

int main() {
    using namespace std::chrono;

    auto previousTime = high_resolution_clock::now();
    const double targetFrameTime = 1.0 / 60.0; // 60 frames per
    second

    while (true) {
        auto currentTime = high_resolution_clock::now();
        duration<double> deltaTime = currentTime - previousTime;

        if (deltaTime.count() >= targetFrameTime) {
            previousTime = currentTime;

            // Process input
            // Update game state
            // Render graphics
        }
    }
    return 0;
}
```

In this example, the game loop checks if enough time has passed to warrant an update. If the time elapsed (deltaTime) exceeds the target frame time (approximately 16.67 milliseconds for 60 FPS), the loop processes input, updates the game state, and renders graphics.

Frame Timing

Frame timing is a critical aspect of the game loop that affects how smoothly a game runs. It ensures that updates and rendering occur at consistent intervals, resulting in a smoother experience for players. Frame timing involves two main concepts: frame rate and delta time.

Frame Rate

The frame rate (frames per second or FPS) indicates how many times the game loop runs in one second. A higher frame rate generally results in smoother gameplay. Common target frame rates for games are 30, 60, and even 120 FPS for high-performance titles.

However, simply targeting a high FPS is not always the best approach. Different hardware may run at different speeds, and capping the frame rate can help maintain a consistent experience across various systems. Many games implement a frame rate limiter to control the maximum FPS, preventing the game from running too fast on high-performance machines.

Delta Time

Delta time represents the time elapsed between the current frame and the previous frame. It is crucial for achieving consistent movement and behavior of game entities, regardless of the frame rate. Using delta time, developers can adjust movement speeds, animations, and physics calculations to ensure that gameplay remains consistent, even when the frame rate fluctuates.

Example of Using Delta Time:

```cpp
float playerSpeed = 5.0f; // Units per second
float deltaTime; // Time elapsed since last frame

// In the game loop
player.position.x += playerSpeed * deltaTime;
```

In this example, the player's position is updated based on the speed and the time elapsed. This ensures that if the frame rate drops, the player still moves at a consistent speed relative to real time.

Fixed Timestep vs. Variable Timestep

When designing a game loop, developers often face the decision of whether to use a fixed timestep or a variable timestep for updating game logic.

Fixed Timestep

A fixed timestep means that the game state updates at consistent intervals, regardless of frame rate. This approach simplifies physics calculations and results in more predictable behavior. It is especially useful for games that rely on precise physics interactions, such as platformers or simulations.

Example of a Fixed Timestep Loop:

```cpp
const double fixedTimeStep = 1.0 / 60.0; // 60 updates per second
double accumulator = 0.0;

while (true) {
    auto currentTime = high_resolution_clock::now();
    deltaTime += duration<double>(currentTime -
    previousTime).count();
    previousTime = currentTime;

    while (accumulator >= fixedTimeStep) {
        // Update game state
        accumulator -= fixedTimeStep;
    }

    // Render graphics
}
```

In this example, the game updates the state at a fixed interval of 1/60 seconds, ensuring consistent physics and behavior.

Variable Timestep

A variable timestep allows the game state to update based on the actual time elapsed. This approach can lead to smoother animations and more responsive gameplay but may introduce issues like inconsistent physics behavior if frame rates fluctuate significantly.

When using a variable timestep, developers need to carefully handle scenarios where game logic behaves differently at different frame rates. It can be more challenging to implement and requires additional considerations for physics and collision detection.

Best Practices for Game Loops and Timing

1. **Use Delta Time**: Always incorporate delta time into your calculations for movement and animations. This practice ensures that gameplay remains consistent across different frame rates.
2. **Implement a Frame Rate Limiter**: To maintain consistent performance, consider capping the frame rate. This can help prevent high-performance machines from running the game too fast and ensure a uniform experience across devices.
3. **Choose a Timestep Approach**: Decide whether a fixed or variable timestep suits your game's needs. For physics-heavy games, a fixed timestep is often preferred, while variable timesteps can work well for simpler games with less reliance on precise physics.
4. **Profile and Optimize**: Continuously profile your game loop to identify bottlenecks in performance. Optimize the code to ensure that the loop runs as efficiently as possible, especially during the rendering phase.
5. **Use VSync**: Vertical synchronization (VSync) can help prevent screen tearing by synchronizing the frame rate with the refresh rate of the monitor. However, be mindful that this may introduce input lag, so it's essential to test the impact on gameplay.

The game loop and frame timing are foundational concepts in game development that directly impact the performance and responsiveness of a game. Understanding how to implement a robust game loop, manage frame timing, and utilize delta time effectively enables developers to create smooth, engaging gameplay experiences. By adhering to best practices and choosing the right approach for the game's specific needs, developers can enhance the quality of their games and ensure players enjoy a seamless gaming experience.

Event Handling: Capturing Player Input with SDL/SFML

Effective event handling is essential in game development, as it allows developers to capture player input and translate it into in-game actions. The way a game responds to user interactions can significantly influence the overall experience, making smooth and responsive event handling a key component. This section will explore how to handle events using two popular libraries: SDL (Simple DirectMedia Layer) and SFML (Simple and Fast Multimedia Library).

Introduction to Event Handling

Event handling in game development involves listening for user inputs—such as keyboard presses, mouse movements, and joystick interactions—and responding to these events accordingly. A robust event handling system ensures that user actions are captured accurately and processed in real-time, creating an interactive and engaging gameplay experience.

In general, event handling can be broken down into several key components:

1. **Event Polling**: Continuously checking for events during each iteration of the game loop.
2. **Event Queues**: Storing incoming events in a queue for processing, allowing for organized handling of multiple events.
3. **Event Dispatching**: Routing captured events to the appropriate functions or classes that handle specific inputs or actions.

SDL Event Handling

SDL is a cross-platform multimedia library widely used for game development. It provides a powerful and flexible event handling system, making it easy to capture user inputs.

Setting Up SDL

To start using SDL for event handling, first ensure you have installed SDL on your development environment. Here's how to initialize SDL in a C++ project:

cpp

```
#include <SDL2/SDL.h>
#include <iostream>

int main(int argc, char* argv[]) {
    if (SDL_Init(SDL_INIT_VIDEO) < 0) {
        std::cerr << "Failed to initialize SDL: " <<
        SDL_GetError() << std::endl;
        return 1;
    }

    SDL_Window* window = SDL_CreateWindow("SDL Event Handling",
    SDL_WINDOWPOS_UNDEFINED, SDL_WINDOWPOS_UNDEFINED, 800, 600, 0);
    if (!window) {
        std::cerr << "Failed to create window: " << SDL_GetError()
        << std::endl;
        SDL_Quit();
        return 1;
    }

    // Main loop and event handling would go here

    SDL_DestroyWindow(window);
    SDL_Quit();
    return 0;
}
```

Polling for Events

Within the game loop, you can poll for events using the SDL_PollEvent function. Here's an example of how to capture keyboard input and window events:

```cpp
cpp

SDL_Event event;
bool running = true;

while (running) {
    while (SDL_PollEvent(&event)) {
        if (event.type == SDL_QUIT) {
            running = false; // Handle window close event
        }
        if (event.type == SDL_KEYDOWN) {
            if (event.key.keysym.sym == SDLK_ESCAPE) {
                running = false; // Handle the escape key
            }
            // Handle other key presses
        }
        if (event.type == SDL_MOUSEBUTTONDOWN) {
            if (event.button.button == SDL_BUTTON_LEFT) {
                std::cout << "Left mouse button clicked!" <<
                std::endl; // Handle mouse clicks
            }
        }
    }

    // Update game state and render here
}
```

In this example, the game loop continuously polls for events and responds to specific inputs, such as closing the window or pressing the escape key.

Handling Keyboard Input

Handling keyboard input is essential for player control. SDL allows you to check for specific key presses by examining the SDL_Keycode values. Here's how to capture movement inputs:

```cpp
cpp
```

```
if (event.type == SDL_KEYDOWN) {
    switch (event.key.keysym.sym) {
        case SDLK_UP:
            // Move player up
            break;
        case SDLK_DOWN:
            // Move player down
            break;
        case SDLK_LEFT:
            // Move player left
            break;
        case SDLK_RIGHT:
            // Move player right
            break;
        // Additional cases for other keys
    }
}
```

This structure enables intuitive player controls based on keyboard inputs, allowing players to interact with the game environment effectively.

SFML Event Handling

SFML is another popular multimedia library that simplifies graphics, audio, and input handling in C++. Its event handling system is user-friendly and efficient.

Setting Up SFML

To use SFML in your project, ensure you have installed the library and linked it correctly. Here's how to initialize SFML and create a window:

cpp

```
#include <SFML/Graphics.hpp>
#include <iostream>

int main() {
    sf::RenderWindow window(sf::VideoMode(800, 600), "SFML Event
```

```
Handling");

    // Main loop and event handling would go here

    return 0;
}
```

Polling for Events

SFML uses an event loop to capture inputs. Here's how to handle various events, including window events and keyboard inputs:

```cpp
while (window.isOpen()) {
    sf::Event event;
    while (window.pollEvent(event)) {
        if (event.type == sf::Event::Closed) {
            window.close(); // Handle window close event
        }
        if (event.type == sf::Event::KeyPressed) {
            if (event.key.code == sf::Keyboard::Escape) {
                window.close(); // Handle the escape key
            }
            // Handle other key presses
        }
        if (event.type == sf::Event::MouseButtonPressed) {
            if (event.mouseButton.button == sf::Mouse::Left) {
                std::cout << "Left mouse button clicked!" <<
                std::endl; // Handle mouse clicks
            }
        }
    }

    // Update game state and render here
}
```

In this example, the SFML event loop continuously polls for events and responds to user interactions in a straightforward manner.

Handling Player Input in SFML

SFML makes it easy to manage keyboard and mouse inputs. Here's an example of how to capture movement based on keyboard input:

cpp

```cpp
if (event.type == sf::Event::KeyPressed) {
    switch (event.key.code) {
        case sf::Keyboard::W:
            // Move player up
            break;
        case sf::Keyboard::S:
            // Move player down
            break;
        case sf::Keyboard::A:
            // Move player left
            break;
        case sf::Keyboard::D:
            // Move player right
            break;
        // Additional cases for other keys
    }
}
```

This structure allows developers to implement intuitive controls and responses based on player actions, creating a more immersive experience.

Best Practices for Event Handling

1. **Keep It Simple**: Avoid complex event handling logic within the main game loop. Instead, create dedicated functions or classes to manage events, improving code readability and maintainability.

2. **Use an Event Queue**: Consider implementing an event queue to store events that need to be processed later. This can help manage multiple events and maintain order, especially in more complex games.

3. **Implement Action Mapping**: Create a mapping system that associates keys or buttons with specific actions. This can simplify input handling

and allow for easy remapping of controls, enhancing player customization.

4. **Handle Input States**: Track the state of input devices (e.g., whether a key is currently pressed) to manage actions such as continuous movement. This can improve responsiveness and player control.

5. **Optimize for Performance**: Minimize the amount of processing done during event handling. Ensure that the event handling code is efficient to avoid bottlenecks in the game loop.

Effective event handling is crucial for creating an interactive and responsive gaming experience. Both SDL and SFML provide powerful tools for capturing player input, allowing developers to implement robust input systems. By following best practices and leveraging the features of these libraries, developers can create games that respond intuitively to player actions, enhancing overall enjoyment and immersion. In the following sections, we will explore additional programming patterns and techniques to further enhance gameplay mechanics and player engagement.

Coordinating Game States: Menus, Gameplay, and Pauses

In game development, managing different game states is essential for creating a smooth and coherent user experience. A game typically consists of several states, including menus, gameplay, and pause screens. Each state requires different handling of user input, rendering, and game logic. This section will delve into how to coordinate these various game states effectively, ensuring a seamless transition between them and maintaining a fluid gaming experience.

Understanding Game States

Game states represent distinct phases in a game's lifecycle, each with unique functionalities and user interfaces. The primary states often include:

1. **Main Menu**: The starting point of the game, where players can start a new game, load a saved game, adjust settings, or exit.
2. **Gameplay**: The active state where players engage with the game mechanics, face challenges, and progress through levels or objectives.
3. **Pause Menu**: An intermediary state that allows players to pause the game, view options, and resume or exit.

By organizing the game into these states, developers can streamline input handling, rendering processes, and game logic, leading to a more maintainable and organized codebase.

Implementing Game States

To implement game states, we can use a finite state machine (FSM) or a similar structure that defines possible states and handles transitions between them. This approach keeps the logic for each state modular and easier to manage.

Basic Structure of a State Machine

Here's a simplified structure of a state machine for managing game states in C++:

```
cpp

enum class GameState {
    MainMenu,
    Gameplay,
    Pause
};

class Game {
public:
    GameState currentState;

    Game() : currentState(GameState::MainMenu) {}

    void changeState(GameState newState) {
```

```cpp
        currentState = newState;
        // Additional logic for entering a new state can be added
        here
    }

    void update() {
        switch (currentState) {
            case GameState::MainMenu:
                handleMainMenu();
                break;
            case GameState::Gameplay:
                handleGameplay();
                break;
            case GameState::Pause:
                handlePause();
                break;
        }
    }

private:
    void handleMainMenu() {
        // Logic for the main menu (input handling, rendering)
    }

    void handleGameplay() {
        // Logic for gameplay (input handling, game mechanics)
    }

    void handlePause() {
        // Logic for the pause menu (input handling, rendering)
    }
};
```

In this structure, the game continuously updates based on the current state. The changeState method can be invoked whenever a transition is necessary.

Handling the Main Menu

The main menu is the first interaction point for players. Here's how to manage this state effectively:

Displaying the Main Menu

To display the main menu, the game should render options for starting a game, loading a saved game, and adjusting settings. This might involve creating buttons or text options that players can select.

cpp

```cpp
void Game::handleMainMenu() {
    // Render menu options
    std::cout << "1. Start Game" << std::endl;
    std::cout << "2. Load Game" << std::endl;
    std::cout << "3. Exit" << std::endl;

    // Handle input
    SDL_Event event;
    while (SDL_PollEvent(&event)) {
        if (event.type == SDL_QUIT) {
            exit(0); // Exit the game
        }
        if (event.type == SDL_KEYDOWN) {
            switch (event.key.keysym.sym) {
                case SDLK_1:
                    changeState(GameState::Gameplay);
                    break;
                case SDLK_2:
                    // Load game logic
                    break;
                case SDLK_3:
                    exit(0); // Exit the game
                    break;
            }
        }
    }
}
```

Managing Gameplay State

The gameplay state is where the core mechanics of the game occur. Players interact with the environment, make progress, and face challenges.

Gameplay Logic and Input Handling

71

In the gameplay state, the game must handle various inputs for character control, environment interaction, and other mechanics. Here's an example of how to structure this logic:

cpp

```cpp
void Game::handleGameplay() {
    // Update game state
    updateGameLogic();

    // Render game scene
    renderGame();

    // Handle input
    SDL_Event event;
    while (SDL_PollEvent(&event)) {
        if (event.type == SDL_QUIT) {
            exit(0); // Exit the game
        }
        if (event.type == SDL_KEYDOWN) {
            if (event.key.keysym.sym == SDLK_ESCAPE) {
                changeState(GameState::Pause); // Transition to
                pause
            }
            // Handle character control
        }
    }
}
```

Implementing the Pause State

The pause state provides players a moment to take a break, review options, or adjust settings without affecting the game progress.

Displaying the Pause Menu

When the game transitions to the pause state, it should display a menu with options such as "Resume," "Settings," and "Exit to Main Menu."

cpp

```cpp
void Game::handlePause() {
    // Render pause menu
    std::cout << "Paused" << std::endl;
    std::cout << "1. Resume" << std::endl;
    std::cout << "2. Settings" << std::endl;
    std::cout << "3. Exit to Main Menu" << std::endl;

    // Handle input
    SDL_Event event;
    while (SDL_PollEvent(&event)) {
        if (event.type == SDL_QUIT) {
            exit(0); // Exit the game
        }
        if (event.type == SDL_KEYDOWN) {
            switch (event.key.keysym.sym) {
                case SDLK_1:
                    changeState(GameState::Gameplay); // Resume
                    gameplay
                    break;
                case SDLK_2:
                    // Settings logic
                    break;
                case SDLK_3:
                    changeState(GameState::MainMenu); // Return to
                    main menu
                    break;
            }
        }
    }
}
```

Transitioning Between States

Managing transitions between states is critical for ensuring a smooth experience. Here are a few guidelines:

1. **Immediate Feedback**: Provide immediate feedback when a state changes, such as visually indicating a transition or playing a sound effect.

This enhances user experience by confirming their actions.

2. **Pause Game Logic**: When transitioning to the pause state, ensure all gameplay logic is paused to prevent unintended actions or calculations. This might involve disabling timers or freezing game objects.

3. **Consistent Input Handling**: Ensure input handling remains consistent across different states. For example, pressing the escape key should always transition to the pause state regardless of the gameplay context.

4. **State Initialization**: When entering a new state, initialize any necessary variables or game objects. This helps maintain clarity and prevents bugs related to uninitialized states.

Coordinating game states—menus, gameplay, and pauses—is essential for creating an engaging and user-friendly gaming experience. By implementing a finite state machine and ensuring smooth transitions, developers can effectively manage input, rendering, and game logic for each state. With a well-organized approach to state management, players can enjoy a fluid and immersive experience, keeping them engaged and eager to continue playing. In the next section, we will explore more advanced programming techniques for game development, including the use of design patterns and optimizations for performance.

Game Entity Management and Object Lifetime

Effective game entity management is crucial for ensuring that a game runs smoothly and efficiently. Game entities can include everything from player characters and enemies to items and environmental objects. Each entity in a game has its own lifecycle, requiring careful management of its creation, update, and destruction processes. This section will cover strategies for managing game entities and their lifetimes, focusing on performance optimization, memory management, and organization.

Understanding Game Entities

A game entity is any object that has a distinct presence in the game world. Entities can be classified into various categories, such as:

- **Player Characters**: The main characters controlled by players.
- **Non-Player Characters (NPCs)**: Characters that interact with players but are not directly controlled by them.
- **Items**: Collectible objects that can be used by players, such as weapons or health packs.
- **Environment Objects**: Static or dynamic elements within the game world, such as trees, buildings, and moving platforms.

Each entity typically has properties (attributes) and behaviors (methods) that define its interactions within the game. Effective entity management ensures that these interactions occur seamlessly and efficiently.

Entity Lifecycle Management

The lifecycle of a game entity typically follows these phases:

1. **Creation**: When a new entity is instantiated, it must be properly initialized with its attributes and behaviors.
2. **Update**: Entities require regular updates to manage their state, behaviors, and interactions with other entities.
3. **Destruction**: When an entity is no longer needed, it must be removed from memory to prevent resource leaks and ensure efficient memory usage.

Implementing an Entity Component System (ECS)

An effective approach to manage game entities is to use an Entity Component System (ECS) architecture. ECS separates data (components) from behavior (systems), promoting flexibility and reusability.

Components

Components are data structures that hold properties related to entities. For example:

- **PositionComponent**: Holds the entity's position in the game world (x, y coordinates).
- **VelocityComponent**: Manages the entity's movement speed and direction.
- **SpriteComponent**: Handles rendering and visual representation of the entity.

cpp

```cpp
struct PositionComponent {
    float x, y;
};

struct VelocityComponent {
    float vx, vy;
};

struct SpriteComponent {
    std::string textureID; // Identifier for the texture to render
};
```

Systems

Systems are responsible for processing entities that contain specific components. For example, a MovementSystem might update the position of all entities with PositionComponent and VelocityComponent:

cpp

```cpp
void MovementSystem(std::vector<Entity>& entities) {
    for (auto& entity : entities) {
        if (entity.hasComponent<PositionComponent>() &&
        entity.hasComponent<VelocityComponent>()) {
            auto& position =
            entity.getComponent<PositionComponent>();
            auto& velocity =
            entity.getComponent<VelocityComponent>();
```

```
        position.x += velocity.vx;
        position.y += velocity.vy;
    }
  }
}
```

Managing Object Lifetime with Smart Pointers

Memory management is critical in game development, especially for managing the lifetime of game entities. Using smart pointers in C++ simplifies memory management by automatically handling object lifetimes, thus reducing the chances of memory leaks or dangling pointers.

Unique Pointers

std::unique_ptr is a smart pointer that maintains sole ownership of an object, ensuring that the object is automatically destroyed when the unique_ptr goes out of scope. This is particularly useful for entities that are created dynamically:

cpp

```
std::unique_ptr<Entity> player = std::make_unique<Entity>();
```

Shared Pointers

std::shared_ptr allows multiple pointers to own the same object. This is useful for scenarios where multiple game systems need to access the same entity, such as in a game that supports cooperative multiplayer gameplay:

cpp

```
std::shared_ptr<Entity> enemy = std::make_shared<Entity>();
```

By using smart pointers, developers can ensure that entities are properly cleaned up when they are no longer needed, thus preventing memory leaks.

Implementing Entity Management in a Game

An effective entity management system should incorporate both the ECS pattern and smart pointers. Below is a simple implementation demonstrating how to manage entities in a game loop.

Entity Management Class

Here's an example of an EntityManager class that handles entity creation, updating, and destruction:

cpp

```cpp
class EntityManager {
public:
    void addEntity(std::unique_ptr<Entity> entity) {
        entities.push_back(std::move(entity));
    }

    void updateEntities() {
        for (auto& entity : entities) {
            if (entity) {
                entity->update(); // Call update method of the
                entity
            }
        }
    }

    void removeEntity(size_t index) {
        if (index < entities.size()) {
            entities[index] = nullptr; // Mark entity for removal
        }
    }

private:
    std::vector<std::unique_ptr<Entity>> entities; // Store
    entities
};
```

Managing Entity Creation and Destruction

To create and destroy entities, you can use factory methods that encapsulate the logic for initialization:

cpp

```cpp
class EntityFactory {
public:
    static std::unique_ptr<Entity> createPlayer(float x, float y) {
        auto player = std::make_unique<Entity>();
        player->addComponent<PositionComponent>({x, y});
        player->addComponent<VelocityComponent>({0, 0});
        player->addComponent<SpriteComponent>({"player_texture"});
        return player;
    }

    static std::unique_ptr<Entity> createEnemy(float x, float y) {
        auto enemy = std::make_unique<Entity>();
        enemy->addComponent<PositionComponent>({x, y});
        enemy->addComponent<VelocityComponent>({-1, 0}); // Move
        left
        enemy->addComponent<SpriteComponent>({"enemy_texture"});
        return enemy;
    }
};
```

Updating Entities and Handling Destruction

In the game loop, the EntityManager can be used to update entities and handle their destruction:

cpp

```cpp
void Game::update() {
    entityManager.updateEntities(); // Update all entities

    // Example of removing an entity if it goes off-screen
    for (size_t i = 0; i < entities.size(); ++i) {
        if (entities[i]->getPosition().y > SCREEN_HEIGHT) {
            entityManager.removeEntity(i); // Mark for removal
```

```
            }
        }
    }
```

Effective game entity management is vital for creating a well-structured and performant game. By using an Entity Component System architecture and leveraging smart pointers for memory management, developers can maintain a clear separation of data and behavior, making their code more modular and easier to manage. Understanding the lifecycle of game entities—from creation to destruction—enables developers to create robust and efficient games, ultimately leading to a better player experience.

In the next section, we will explore more advanced game mechanics, including collision detection and response, enhancing the overall gameplay experience.

Managing Game Assets: Loading and Optimizing Textures, Sounds, and Models

Effective asset management is crucial in game development, as the performance and quality of a game heavily rely on how well assets are loaded, optimized, and utilized. Assets include textures, sounds, models, and other media that enhance the player's experience. This section will cover best practices for loading and optimizing these assets to ensure your game runs smoothly and efficiently.

Understanding Game Assets

Game assets are the various media elements that constitute a game. They can be broadly categorized into:

- **Textures**: 2D images that are applied to 3D models to give them color and detail. Textures are essential for creating visual richness in the game world.

- **Sounds**: Audio files used for sound effects, background music, and voice acting. Sounds greatly enhance the immersive experience of a game.
- **Models**: 3D representations of objects and characters within the game. Models can be simple or complex, depending on the level of detail required.

Asset Management Strategies

Managing game assets effectively requires a well-defined approach that covers asset creation, loading, and optimization. Below are key strategies to ensure efficient asset management:

1. Asset Organization

Organizing your assets into a clear directory structure is fundamental for easy access and management. A typical directory structure might include:

```bash

/assets
    /textures
    /sounds
    /models
    /fonts

```

By categorizing assets, you can quickly locate and manage them during development.

2. Asset Loading Techniques

Efficient loading of assets is vital to ensure that the game runs smoothly, especially during the initial startup and scene transitions. Here are common asset loading techniques:

- **Synchronous Loading**: Loading assets in a blocking manner, where the game waits until an asset is fully loaded before continuing. While simple to implement, this can lead to performance issues and stuttering during gameplay.

- **Asynchronous Loading**: Loading assets in a non-blocking manner, allowing the game to continue running while assets are loaded in the background. This is often achieved using threads or coroutines. For example, using SDL or SFML, you can load textures asynchronously:

```cpp
std::future<Texture> loadTextureAsync(const std::string& filePath)
{
    return std::async(std::launch::async, [filePath]() {
        Texture texture;
        texture.loadFromFile(filePath);
        return texture;
    });
}
```

- **Streaming Assets**: Loading assets on demand, which is particularly useful for large worlds or open-world games. Assets are loaded and unloaded as the player moves through the environment.

3. Asset Optimization Techniques

Optimizing assets is essential for reducing memory usage and improving performance. Here are several optimization techniques:

- **Texture Atlases**: Combining multiple textures into a single texture atlas can reduce the number of draw calls, improving rendering performance. This technique involves packing multiple images into a single larger image and using UV coordinates to reference them.
- **Compressed Formats**: Use compressed image formats (such as PNG or DDS) and audio formats (like OGG or MP3) to reduce file sizes without significant loss of quality. Compression minimizes memory usage and

loading times.

- **Level of Detail (LOD)**: Implementing LOD techniques allows the game to use different resolutions of a model based on the distance from the camera. High-detail models can be used when close to the player, while simpler models can be used when they are farther away.
- **Occlusion Culling**: This technique ensures that objects not visible to the camera are not rendered, improving performance. For example, if a building is obstructing the view of another object, the occluded object can be culled from the rendering process.

Loading Textures Efficiently

Loading textures is a common task in game development. Here's how to do it effectively:

Load Textures into Memory: Use a texture loading function that handles loading, creating a cache for already loaded textures to avoid redundant loading.

cpp

```cpp
class TextureManager {
public:
    Texture& getTexture(const std::string& filePath) {
        // Check if texture is already loaded
        auto it = textureCache.find(filePath);
        if (it != textureCache.end()) {
            return it->second; // Return existing texture
        }
        // Load new texture
        Texture texture;
        texture.loadFromFile(filePath);
        textureCache[filePath] = texture;
        return textureCache[filePath];
    }

private:
    std::unordered_map<std::string, Texture> textureCache; //
```

```
    Texture cache
};
```

Unloading Textures: When an asset is no longer needed, ensure it is unloaded from memory to free resources. This can be done during level transitions or when an entity is destroyed.

Managing Sounds

Sound assets require similar considerations as textures. Here are essential practices for managing sounds:

- **Preload Sounds**: Load essential sound effects at the beginning of the game to minimize delays during gameplay. For example, preload background music tracks and important sound effects like jumps or collisions.

```cpp
class SoundManager {
public:
    void preloadSound(const std::string& soundID, const
    std::string& filePath) {
        SoundBuffer buffer;
        buffer.loadFromFile(filePath);
        soundBuffers[soundID] = buffer; // Cache loaded sound
    }

    void playSound(const std::string& soundID) {
        Sound sound;
        sound.setBuffer(soundBuffers[soundID]);
        sound.play(); // Play sound effect
    }

private:
    std::unordered_map<std::string, SoundBuffer> soundBuffers; //
```

```
    Sound buffer cache
};
```

- **Use Sound Pools**: Implement sound pools for frequently played sound effects (e.g., gunfire or footsteps). This involves maintaining a collection of sound objects that can be reused rather than instantiated repeatedly.

Managing 3D Models

3D models require additional considerations:

- **Model Loading**: Utilize libraries like Assimp (Open Asset Import Library) to load various 3D model formats. Assimp allows you to import and convert 3D models into a format your game engine can utilize.

```cpp
Assimp::Importer importer;
const aiScene* scene = importer.ReadFile("model.obj",
aiProcess_Triangulate | aiProcess_FlipUVs);
if (!scene) {
    // Handle error
}
```

- **Instancing**: For models that are used multiple times (like trees in a forest), consider using instancing techniques to draw multiple copies of the same model with minimal overhead. This significantly improves performance in scenes with numerous identical objects.

Managing game assets effectively is a fundamental aspect of game development that can significantly impact performance and player experience. By adopting best practices for asset organization, loading, and optimization, developers can create games that run smoothly and deliver high-quality visuals and sound. Implementing techniques like texture atlases, sound preloading, and model instancing helps ensure that the game remains responsive and engaging, providing players with an immersive experience.

Introduction to Graphics Programming

Fundamentals of 2D Graphics: Pixels, Coordinate Systems, and Rendering

Understanding 2D graphics is crucial for any game developer, as it forms the backbone of visual representation in video games. This chapter delves into the essential concepts of 2D graphics, focusing on pixels, coordinate systems, and rendering techniques that allow developers to create compelling visual experiences in their games.

Understanding Pixels

Pixels, short for "picture elements," are the smallest units of a digital image displayed on a screen. Every image you see on a computer monitor or mobile device is made up of an array of pixels, and their arrangement, color, and properties define the image's overall appearance. Here are some key points regarding pixels:

- **Pixel Composition**: Each pixel typically consists of three color components: Red, Green, and Blue (RGB). The intensity of each component determines the pixel's final color. The combination of these colors allows for a broad spectrum of hues.
- **Color Depth**: Color depth indicates how many bits are used to represent the color of a single pixel. Common formats include:
- **8-bit**: 256 colors (often using a palette).
- **16-bit**: 65,536 colors.
- **24-bit**: Over 16 million colors (standard for most images).

- **Resolution**: Resolution is the total number of pixels displayed on the screen, typically expressed as width × height (e.g., 1920 × 1080). Higher resolution allows for greater detail and clarity in images but also requires more memory and processing power.

Example of Pixels in Action

When creating a sprite for a 2D game character, each pixel's color value is carefully defined to render the character on the screen. A sprite might be a 64 × 64 pixel image, where each pixel is assigned a color value that contributes to the character's appearance.

Coordinate Systems in 2D Graphics

In 2D graphics, coordinate systems are essential for positioning and manipulating objects within the game environment. The two most common coordinate systems used in 2D graphics are:

1. Cartesian Coordinate System

The Cartesian coordinate system is widely used in 2D graphics and consists of two axes:

- **X-axis**: Typically runs horizontally (left to right).
- **Y-axis**: Runs vertically (top to bottom).

In this system, the origin (0,0) is usually located at the top-left corner of the screen. Positive X values move to the right, while positive Y values move downwards.

Example:

- A point located at (10, 20) would be 10 pixels to the right and 20 pixels down from the top-left corner of the screen.

2. Screen Coordinate System

In contrast, some frameworks and engines (like OpenGL) might use a different convention where the origin is at the center of the screen:

- **X-axis**: Positive values extend to the right, while negative values extend to the left.
- **Y-axis**: Positive values extend upwards, while negative values extend downwards.

This system allows for easier calculations when positioning objects symmetrically around a central point.

Rendering in 2D Graphics

Rendering refers to the process of generating the final image that will be displayed on the screen. The rendering process can be broken down into several steps:

1. Drawing Primitives

Rendering in 2D graphics begins with drawing basic shapes or primitives. Common primitives include:

- **Points**: Single pixels with specified coordinates.
- **Lines**: Defined by two endpoints, lines can be rendered with varying thicknesses and styles.
- **Shapes**: More complex forms, such as rectangles, circles, and polygons, can be created using a series of points.

For example, to draw a rectangle in a game using SDL, you would define the rectangle's position, width, and height and use SDL's rendering functions to display it:

cpp

```
SDL_Rect rect = { x, y, width, height };
SDL_RenderFillRect(renderer, &rect);
```

2. Textures and Sprites

Textures are images applied to 2D shapes, often referred to as sprites. To render a texture:

1. **Load the Texture**: Use image loading libraries to read texture files (like PNG or BMP).
2. **Create a Sprite**: Map the texture to a rectangular area defined by coordinates on the screen.
3. **Render the Sprite**: Draw the sprite using the rendering context.

For example, in SFML, rendering a texture involves creating a sprite object and calling the draw method:

```cpp
sf::Texture texture;
texture.loadFromFile("sprite.png");
sf::Sprite sprite(texture);
sprite.setPosition(x, y);
window.draw(sprite);
```

3. Transformation Operations

Transformations manipulate how objects are rendered in the game. Common transformations include:

- **Translation**: Moving an object from one position to another.
- **Rotation**: Rotating an object around a specified pivot point.
- **Scaling**: Changing the size of an object in proportion to its original size.

In most graphics libraries, transformations can be applied using transformation matrices, allowing for complex animations and effects.

```cpp
// Applying a transformation in SFML
sprite.setPosition(newX, newY);
sprite.setRotation(angle);
sprite.setScale(scaleX, scaleY);
```

4. Rendering Pipeline

The rendering pipeline is the sequence of operations that take place to render graphics on the screen. In 2D graphics, the pipeline typically involves:

1. **Clearing the Screen**: Before rendering a new frame, clear the previous content.
2. **Drawing Objects**: Render sprites, shapes, and text to the screen in the desired order.
3. **Presenting the Frame**: Display the rendered frame to the screen. In SDL, this is done using SDL_RenderPresent(renderer).

Example: Rendering a Simple Scene

To illustrate the concepts covered, consider a simple game scene involving a player character and a background:

```cpp
void renderScene(SDL_Renderer* renderer, Player& player,
Background& bg) {
    // Clear the screen
    SDL_RenderClear(renderer);

    // Render the background
    bg.render(renderer);

    // Render the player character
    player.render(renderer);

    // Present the back buffer to the screen
    SDL_RenderPresent(renderer);
}
```

Understanding the fundamentals of 2D graphics, including pixels, coordinate systems, and rendering techniques, is essential for developing engaging and visually appealing games. By mastering these concepts, developers can create rich graphics that enhance gameplay and deliver memorable player experiences.

Working with SDL and SFML for 2D Game Development

In the realm of 2D game development, two of the most popular libraries are **SDL (Simple DirectMedia Layer)** and **SFML (Simple and Fast Multimedia Library)**. Both libraries provide a wealth of features that facilitate graphics rendering, input handling, audio management, and more. This section will explore the strengths, features, and differences between SDL and SFML, and guide you through setting up a simple game using each library.

Overview of SDL

SDL is a low-level multimedia library designed to provide a simple interface to various multimedia components. It is highly portable and supports various platforms, including Windows, macOS, Linux, and mobile devices. SDL is widely used in both indie and professional game development, as it gives developers access to hardware-accelerated graphics through OpenGL and Direct3D.

Key Features of SDL

- **Graphics Rendering**: SDL provides a powerful 2D rendering engine and allows integration with 3D graphics APIs like OpenGL and Direct3D.
- **Audio Playback**: SDL can handle audio playback through its SDL_mixer extension, making it easy to manage sound effects and music.
- **Input Handling**: It supports various input devices, including keyboard, mouse, and game controllers, enabling responsive control schemes.
- **Cross-Platform Compatibility**: Write your code once and deploy it on multiple platforms without significant changes.

- **Extensible**: SDL supports a variety of extensions and libraries, such as SDL_image for image loading and SDL_ttf for font rendering.

Setting Up SDL

To get started with SDL, follow these steps:

Install SDL:

- Download SDL from the official website (libsdl.org).
- Install the library according to the instructions for your platform (Windows, macOS, Linux).

Create a New Project:

- Set up a new C++ project in your chosen IDE (e.g., Visual Studio, Code::Blocks).
- Link the SDL library to your project settings.

Basic SDL Program: Here's a simple SDL program that creates a window and displays a colored background:

cpp

```cpp
#include <SDL.h>

int main(int argc, char* argv[]) {
    SDL_Init(SDL_INIT_VIDEO);  // Initialize SDL
    SDL_Window* window = SDL_CreateWindow("SDL 2D Game",
    SDL_WINDOWPOS_CENTERED, SDL_WINDOWPOS_CENTERED, 800, 600,
    SDL_WINDOW_SHOWN);
    SDL_Renderer* renderer = SDL_CreateRenderer(window, -1,
    SDL_RENDERER_ACCELERATED);

    // Main loop
    bool isRunning = true;
    while (isRunning) {
```

```
    SDL_Event event;
    while (SDL_PollEvent(&event)) {
        if (event.type == SDL_QUIT) {
            isRunning = false;
        }
    }

    // Clear the screen
    SDL_SetRenderDrawColor(renderer, 0, 0, 0, 255); // Set
    color to black
    SDL_RenderClear(renderer);

    // Render (you can add drawing functions here)

    // Present the back buffer
    SDL_RenderPresent(renderer);
    }

    SDL_DestroyRenderer(renderer);
    SDL_DestroyWindow(window);
    SDL_Quit();  // Clean up
    return 0;
}
```

Overview of SFML

SFML is a high-level multimedia library that offers a simpler and more user-friendly interface compared to SDL. It provides easy access to graphics, audio, and network functionalities, making it a popular choice for beginners and those seeking rapid development cycles. SFML is particularly well-suited for 2D game development.

Key Features of SFML

- **Simple and Intuitive API**: SFML is designed to be easy to use, with a clear and consistent API that minimizes boilerplate code.
- **Object-Oriented Design**: The library follows an object-oriented approach, making it more approachable for developers familiar with C++ classes and objects.

- **Integrated Audio Support**: SFML includes audio capabilities, allowing developers to manage sounds and music effortlessly.
- **Window Management**: SFML handles window creation, events, and graphics rendering in a straightforward manner.
- **Cross-Platform**: Like SDL, SFML is cross-platform, enabling deployment on various operating systems.

Setting Up SFML

To begin with SFML, follow these steps:

Install SFML:

- Download SFML from the official website (sfml-dev.org).
- Install the library based on your platform.

Create a New Project:

- Set up a new C++ project in your preferred IDE.
- Link the SFML libraries to your project.

Basic SFML Program: Below is a simple SFML program that creates a window and fills it with a color:

```cpp
#include <SFML/Graphics.hpp>

int main() {
    sf::RenderWindow window(sf::VideoMode(800, 600), "SFML 2D
    Game");

    // Main loop
    while (window.isOpen()) {
        sf::Event event;
        while (window.pollEvent(event)) {
            if (event.type == sf::Event::Closed)
```

```
            window.close();
        }

        // Clear the window with black color
        window.clear(sf::Color::Black);

        // Render (you can add drawing functions here)

        // Display the contents of the window
        window.display();
    }

    return 0;
}
```

Comparing SDL and SFML

Both SDL and SFML have their strengths and weaknesses, making them suitable for different types of projects and developers. Here's a brief comparison:

FeatureSDLSFML

Feature	SDL	SFML
Complexity	Low-level, more control	High-level, simpler interface
Learning Curve	Steeper	More beginner-friendly
Graphics Handling	Requires integration with OpenGL	Built-in graphics support
Audio Support	Requires SDL_mixer	Integrated audio support
Object-Oriented	C-style procedural	Object-oriented design
Documentation	Comprehensive	User-friendly

Choosing Between SDL and SFML

The choice between SDL and SFML largely depends on your project requirements and personal preferences:

- **Choose SDL if**:
- You need more control over lower-level graphics and multimedia operations.
- You are familiar with OpenGL or wish to integrate with it for 3D graphics.
- You plan to develop games that may require advanced features not supported by higher-level libraries.
- **Choose SFML if**:
- You prefer a simpler, more user-friendly API that allows for rapid development.
- You are developing primarily 2D games and want to minimize boilerplate code.
- You value object-oriented programming and want a modern C++ experience.

Both SDL and SFML are excellent choices for 2D game development, each offering unique advantages. By understanding their features and use cases, you can select the library that best aligns with your project's goals and your development style.

Introduction to 3D Graphics Programming: OpenGL Basics

3D graphics programming is a complex yet rewarding domain within game development, enabling developers to create immersive worlds and experiences. OpenGL (Open Graphics Library) is one of the most widely used APIs for rendering 2D and 3D vector graphics. Its cross-platform capabilities make it a popular choice for both commercial and indie games. This section provides an overview of the fundamentals of OpenGL, its architecture, essential concepts, and how to get started with creating your first 3D graphics application.

What is OpenGL?

OpenGL is a low-level graphics API that provides a wide range of functionalities for rendering 2D and 3D graphics. It is designed to be hardware-independent, allowing developers to write code that can run on various platforms without modification. OpenGL is managed by the Khronos Group, which maintains its specifications and updates.

Key Features of OpenGL

- **Cross-Platform Compatibility**: OpenGL works on various operating systems, including Windows, macOS, and Linux, making it an excellent choice for developers aiming for a broad audience.
- **Hardware Acceleration**: OpenGL interfaces directly with the GPU, enabling efficient rendering and high-performance graphics.
- **Extensive Functionality**: OpenGL supports a wide range of features, including textures, shaders, lighting, blending, and more, allowing developers to create visually stunning graphics.
- **Rich Ecosystem**: Numerous libraries and frameworks are built around OpenGL, enhancing its capabilities and simplifying development.

OpenGL Architecture

Understanding the architecture of OpenGL is crucial for effectively utilizing the API. The main components of OpenGL include:

Rendering Pipeline: The rendering pipeline is the sequence of steps that OpenGL takes to convert 3D models into 2D images displayed on the screen. The pipeline consists of several stages, including:

- **Vertex Processing**: In this stage, vertex data (position, color, texture coordinates, normals) is processed. Vertex shaders, written in GLSL (OpenGL Shading Language), are used to manipulate vertex attributes and transform them into clip space.
- **Primitive Assembly**: After vertex processing, vertices are grouped into primitives (triangles, lines, etc.).
- **Rasterization**: This stage converts the primitives into fragments, which are potential pixels on the screen.
- **Fragment Processing**: In this stage, fragment shaders are applied to calculate the final color of each pixel, considering lighting and texturing.

- **Framebuffer Operations**: The final step involves writing the pixel data to the framebuffer, which is displayed on the screen.

OpenGL Context: An OpenGL context is an environment where OpenGL operates. It holds all the state information related to rendering. Each context is independent, meaning changes to one context do not affect others.

State Machine: OpenGL operates as a state machine, meaning it maintains a set of states that control how rendering occurs. These states can include settings for depth testing, blending modes, and shaders. Changing a state can significantly affect the rendering results.

Getting Started with OpenGL

To start working with OpenGL, you'll need to set up your development environment. The following steps will guide you through the process:

Install OpenGL:

- OpenGL is usually included with graphics drivers, so you may already have it installed on your system. However, you may need additional libraries for creating a window and handling context. Two popular libraries are **GLFW** (for window management) and **GLEW** (for managing OpenGL extensions).

Create a New Project:

- Set up a new C++ project in your IDE (e.g., Visual Studio, Code::Blocks) and link the necessary libraries (GLFW, GLEW, and OpenGL).

Basic OpenGL Program: Below is a simple OpenGL program that initializes a window and renders a colored triangle:

cpp

```cpp
#include <GL/glew.h>
#include <GLFW/glfw3.h>
#include <iostream>

// Vertex data for a triangle
GLfloat vertices[] = {
    0.0f,  0.5f, 0.0f, // Top vertex
   -0.5f, -0.5f, 0.0f, // Bottom left vertex
    0.5f, -0.5f, 0.0f  // Bottom right vertex
};

void error_callback(int error, const char* description) {
    std::cerr << "Error: " << description << std::endl;
}

int main() {
    glfwSetErrorCallback(error_callback);
    if (!glfwInit()) {
        return -1;
    }

    GLFWwindow* window = glfwCreateWindow(800, 600, "OpenGL
    Triangle", NULL, NULL);
    if (!window) {
        glfwTerminate();
        return -1;
    }
    glfwMakeContextCurrent(window);
    glewInit();

    GLuint VBO;
    glGenBuffers(1, &VBO);
    glBindBuffer(GL_ARRAY_BUFFER, VBO);
    glBufferData(GL_ARRAY_BUFFER, sizeof(vertices), vertices,
    GL_STATIC_DRAW);

    while (!glfwWindowShouldClose(window)) {
        glClear(GL_COLOR_BUFFER_BIT);
```

```
        glEnableClientState(GL_VERTEX_ARRAY);
        glVertexPointer(3, GL_FLOAT, 0, (void*)0);
        glDrawArrays(GL_TRIANGLES, 0, 3);
        glDisableClientState(GL_VERTEX_ARRAY);

        glfwSwapBuffers(window);
        glfwPollEvents();
    }

    glDeleteBuffers(1, &VBO);
    glfwDestroyWindow(window);
    glfwTerminate();
    return 0;
}
```

Understanding Shaders in OpenGL

OpenGL uses shaders to control the rendering pipeline. Shaders are small programs that run on the GPU and allow for advanced graphical effects. The two primary types of shaders used in OpenGL are:

1. **Vertex Shader**: The vertex shader processes each vertex and transforms its position in 3D space to 2D screen coordinates. You can also pass additional data, such as colors and texture coordinates, through the vertex shader.
2. **Fragment Shader**: The fragment shader computes the color of each pixel that will be drawn to the screen. This shader is where most of the visual effects, like lighting and texturing, are applied.

Writing a Simple Shader

Here's an example of a basic vertex shader written in GLSL:

glsl

```
#version 330 core
layout(location = 0) in vec3 position;
```

```
void main() {
    gl_Position = vec4(position, 1.0);
}
```

And a basic fragment shader:

```glsl
glsl

#version 330 core
out vec4 color;

void main() {
    color = vec4(1.0, 0.5, 0.2, 1.0); // Orange color
}
```

OpenGL is a powerful and versatile API for 3D graphics programming, providing developers with the tools to create stunning visuals in their games. Understanding its architecture, rendering pipeline, and basic concepts is essential for mastering 3D graphics. As you continue your journey into game development, you'll find that mastering OpenGL will enable you to create more complex and engaging 3D experiences.

Texturing, Animation, and Basic Shading Techniques

As game development continues to evolve, the importance of high-quality visuals and smooth animations cannot be overstated. Texturing, animation, and shading techniques play crucial roles in bringing 3D models to life and creating immersive game environments. This section explores these essential elements in-depth, providing a foundation for creating visually appealing graphics in your games.

Texturing in 3D Graphics

Texturing is the process of applying surface details to 3D models, enhancing their realism and visual appeal. By mapping 2D images (textures) onto 3D surfaces, developers can simulate various materials such as wood, metal, and fabric. This section will cover the fundamentals of texturing, including texture mapping methods, UV mapping, and the use of texture coordinates.

Texture Mapping Methods

1. **Diffuse Mapping**: The most common form of texturing, diffuse mapping applies a 2D texture to a 3D surface to represent its base color. This method does not account for lighting or reflections.

2. **Specular Mapping**: Specular maps are used to define the shininess and highlight color of a surface. By using grayscale values, developers can control how shiny or dull a surface appears when light hits it.

3. **Normal Mapping**: Normal maps create the illusion of additional surface detail without adding more geometry. By altering the normal vectors of a surface, developers can simulate complex features such as bumps, grooves, and wrinkles.

4. **Bump Mapping**: Similar to normal mapping, bump mapping modifies the surface's appearance by adjusting its height information. However, it uses a grayscale height map instead of altering normals.

5. **Displacement Mapping**: This technique modifies the actual geometry of the model based on a height map, creating real surface detail rather than just an illusion.

UV Mapping

UV mapping is the process of projecting a 2D texture onto a 3D model. Each vertex of the model is assigned a corresponding point on the 2D texture, referred to as UV coordinates. This technique allows developers to define how textures are applied to complex shapes.

- **Creating UV Maps**: UV maps are created using 3D modeling software (like Blender or Maya). Artists unwrap the 3D model into a 2D representation, allowing textures to be applied accurately.

- **Texture Atlases**: To optimize rendering, developers often use texture atlases, which combine multiple textures into a single image. This approach reduces the number of texture bindings, improving performance.

Animation Techniques

Animation breathes life into game characters and environments, creating dynamic and engaging experiences for players. In this section, we will explore the fundamentals of animation techniques, including skeletal animation and keyframe animation.

Skeletal Animation

Skeletal animation is a widely used method for animating 3D characters. It involves creating a "skeleton" structure, made up of bones and joints, that drives the movement of a 3D model.

- **Rigging**: Rigging is the process of creating a skeleton for a 3D model. Bones are added to the model, and vertices are weighted to these bones, allowing for smooth movements.
- **Animation Blending**: Developers can combine multiple animations, such as walking and jumping, to create fluid transitions. Techniques like linear interpolation and spherical linear interpolation (SLERP) can be used to blend animations seamlessly.

Keyframe Animation

Keyframe animation involves defining specific points (keyframes) in an animation timeline, specifying the position, rotation, and scale of objects at those points. The software interpolates the movement between keyframes to create smooth animations.

- **Creating Keyframes**: In most animation software, developers set keyframes for various properties, allowing for precise control over the animation process.
- **Easing Functions**: Easing functions are used to create more natural

animations by controlling the speed and acceleration between keyframes. Common easing types include linear, quadratic, cubic, and exponential.

Basic Shading Techniques

Shading techniques are essential for simulating how light interacts with surfaces, adding depth and realism to 3D graphics. Understanding basic shading concepts and how to implement them using shaders is crucial for game development.

Flat Shading

Flat shading is the simplest shading technique, where each polygon is assigned a single color based on its normal and the light source. This approach results in a faceted appearance, as there is no smooth transition between adjacent faces.

Gouraud Shading

Gouraud shading calculates vertex colors based on the light source and interpolates these colors across the polygon's surface. This technique produces smoother transitions than flat shading but may result in a loss of detail, especially on small highlights.

Phong Shading

Phong shading is a more advanced technique that provides realistic lighting by calculating the color of each pixel based on the surface normal and the light source. This method considers ambient, diffuse, and specular components, resulting in a more dynamic and visually appealing outcome.

- **Ambient Lighting**: Represents the general light in the scene, affecting all surfaces equally. It simulates indirect light and helps prevent dark areas in the scene.
- **Diffuse Lighting**: Simulates the light scattered on rough surfaces, calculated based on the angle between the light source and the surface normal.

- **Specular Lighting**: Represents shiny highlights on surfaces, calculated based on the viewer's position, the light source, and the surface normal.

Implementing Shaders for Lighting

Shaders are crucial for implementing shading techniques in OpenGL. Below is an example of a simple Phong shading fragment shader:

```glsl
glsl

#version 330 core
in vec3 Normal; // Interpolated normal from the vertex shader
in vec3 FragPos; // Fragment position in world space
out vec4 color;

uniform vec3 lightPos; // Light source position
uniform vec3 viewPos; // Camera position
uniform vec3 lightColor; // Light color
uniform vec3 objectColor; // Object color

void main() {
    // Ambient
    float ambientStrength = 0.1;
    vec3 ambient = ambientStrength * lightColor;

    // Diffuse
    vec3 norm = normalize(Normal);
    vec3 lightDir = normalize(lightPos - FragPos);
    float diff = max(dot(norm, lightDir), 0.0);
    vec3 diffuse = diff * lightColor;

    // Specular
    float specularStrength = 0.5;
    vec3 viewDir = normalize(viewPos - FragPos);
    vec3 reflectDir = reflect(-lightDir, norm);
    float spec = pow(max(dot(viewDir, reflectDir), 0.0), 32);
    vec3 specular = specularStrength * spec * lightColor;

    // Final color
    vec3 finalColor = (ambient + diffuse + specular) * objectColor;
```

```
    color = vec4(finalColor, 1.0);
}
```

Texturing, animation, and shading are foundational components in 3D graphics programming, playing a critical role in creating visually compelling games. By mastering these techniques, developers can produce rich and immersive experiences that captivate players.

In the next section, we will explore advanced techniques in lighting and shadows, further enhancing the realism and depth of your 3D environments. Understanding these concepts will be crucial as you continue your journey in game development.

Camera Systems: Implementing Scrolling, Zooming, and 3D Perspectives

Camera systems are an integral part of any game, serving as the player's viewpoint within the virtual world. A well-designed camera can greatly enhance gameplay by providing the right perspective and framing the action effectively. This section delves into the various types of camera systems used in game development, focusing on scrolling, zooming, and 3D perspectives.

Understanding Camera Fundamentals

A camera in a game engine is essentially a transformation that dictates how objects in the scene are viewed. The camera's position, orientation, and perspective affect what the player sees and how they interact with the game world. Understanding the core concepts of camera systems is crucial for creating engaging gameplay experiences.

Camera Coordinate Systems

1. **World Space**: The global coordinate system where all objects in the game world exist. The camera's position and orientation can be defined

relative to this space.

2. **View Space**: Also known as camera space, this is the coordinate system in which the camera is positioned at the origin, looking down the negative Z-axis. All objects are transformed to this space for rendering.

3. **Projection Space**: The coordinate system used for rendering the 3D scene onto a 2D display. This can be achieved using different projection methods, such as orthographic or perspective projection.

Implementing Scrolling Cameras

Scrolling cameras are commonly used in 2D games, side-scrollers, and platformers. These cameras move horizontally or vertically to follow the player, creating a sense of motion and exploration. Implementing a scrolling camera involves the following key concepts:

Basic Scrolling Implementation

To implement a basic scrolling camera, you need to track the player's position and adjust the camera's position accordingly. Below is a simple example of how to achieve this in a 2D game using C++ and SDL:

```cpp
class Camera {
public:
    SDL_Rect camera; // Camera rectangle to define viewport
    int worldWidth, worldHeight; // Size of the world

    Camera(int width, int height) {
        camera.x = 0; // Starting X position
        camera.y = 0; // Starting Y position
        camera.w = width; // Width of the viewport
        camera.h = height; // Height of the viewport
    }

    void update(int playerX, int playerY) {
        // Center the camera on the player
        camera.x = playerX - (camera.w / 2);
        camera.y = playerY - (camera.h / 2);
```

```cpp
    // Clamp camera position to world bounds
    if (camera.x < 0) {
        camera.x = 0;
    }
    if (camera.y < 0) {
        camera.y = 0;
    }
    if (camera.x + camera.w > worldWidth) {
        camera.x = worldWidth - camera.w;
    }
    if (camera.y + camera.h > worldHeight) {
        camera.y = worldHeight - camera.h;
    }
    }

    SDL_Rect getCamera() {
        return camera;
    }
};
```

Smooth Camera Movement

For a more polished experience, consider implementing smooth camera movement. This can be done by interpolating the camera's position towards the player's position over time, creating a "lagging" effect. Here's how you might implement this:

cpp

```cpp
void update(float deltaTime, int playerX, int playerY) {
    int targetX = playerX - (camera.w / 2);
    int targetY = playerY - (camera.h / 2);

    camera.x += (targetX - camera.x) * deltaTime * smoothingFactor;
    camera.y += (targetY - camera.y) * deltaTime * smoothingFactor;
}
```

Implementing Zooming Functionality

Zooming allows players to change their perspective within the game, either pulling back for a broader view or zooming in for detailed action. This feature is particularly useful in strategy games, RPGs, and games with vast landscapes.

Basic Zoom Implementation

To implement zooming, you can adjust the camera's viewport size based on player input. For instance, you can use the mouse wheel or buttons to increase or decrease the camera's size:

```cpp
void zoom(float zoomFactor) {
    camera.w *= zoomFactor;
    camera.h *= zoomFactor;

    // Clamp zoom to avoid extreme values
    if (camera.w < minWidth) {
        camera.w = minWidth;
    }
    if (camera.h < minHeight) {
        camera.h = minHeight;
    }
    if (camera.w > maxWidth) {
        camera.w = maxWidth;
    }
    if (camera.h > maxHeight) {
        camera.h = maxHeight;
    }
}
```

Zooming with Smooth Transitions

For a more engaging experience, consider implementing smooth zoom transitions. This can be achieved by interpolating the camera size over time, providing a gradual zoom effect:

cpp

```cpp
void updateZoom(float deltaTime) {
    camera.w += (targetWidth - camera.w) * deltaTime *
    zoomSmoothingFactor;
    camera.h += (targetHeight - camera.h) * deltaTime *
    zoomSmoothingFactor;
}
```

3D Camera Perspectives

In 3D game development, camera perspectives are essential for creating immersive environments. There are primarily two types of projections used: **orthographic** and **perspective**.

Orthographic Projection

Orthographic projection is used for 2D games and certain types of 3D games where depth perception is less critical. In this projection, objects are rendered without perspective distortion, meaning they maintain their size regardless of distance from the camera.

- **Use Cases**: Ideal for puzzle games, strategy games, and certain platformers.

Perspective Projection

Perspective projection simulates how the human eye perceives depth. Objects appear smaller as they move farther away from the camera, creating a realistic depth effect.

- **Field of View (FOV)**: The angle of the camera's view, typically measured in degrees. A wider FOV creates a more expansive view but can cause distortion at the edges.
- **Aspect Ratio**: The ratio of the viewport's width to its height, ensuring that objects are displayed correctly regardless of screen size.
- **Near and Far Clipping Planes**: These planes define the distance range

111

in which objects are rendered. Objects closer than the near plane or farther than the far plane will not be visible.

Implementing a 3D Camera in OpenGL

To implement a 3D camera using perspective projection in OpenGL, you can use the following basic setup:

```cpp
cpp

glm::mat4 view;
glm::mat4 projection;

// Set camera position and direction
glm::vec3 cameraPosition(0.0f, 0.0f, 3.0f);
glm::vec3 cameraTarget(0.0f, 0.0f, 0.0f);
glm::vec3 upVector(0.0f, 1.0f, 0.0f);

// Create view matrix
view = glm::lookAt(cameraPosition, cameraTarget, upVector);

// Create projection matrix
float fov = glm::radians(45.0f); // Field of view in radians
float aspectRatio = width / height; // Aspect ratio
float nearPlane = 0.1f; // Near clipping plane
float farPlane = 100.0f; // Far clipping plane
projection = glm::perspective(fov, aspectRatio, nearPlane,
farPlane);
```

Implementing effective camera systems is essential for enhancing gameplay experiences in both 2D and 3D games. Scrolling and zooming features provide dynamic perspectives, while understanding and applying camera coordinate systems allows developers to create engaging and immersive environments.

Physics and Collision Detection

Physics Basics: Newtonian Mechanics in Games

Physics plays a crucial role in video game development, allowing developers to create realistic environments and interactions that enhance the gameplay experience. Among the various physics models, Newtonian mechanics stands out as the foundation for simulating motion, collision, and other physical phenomena in games. This chapter delves into the core principles of Newtonian mechanics and how they are applied in game development, enabling developers to create compelling and immersive experiences.

Understanding Newtonian Mechanics

Newtonian mechanics, formulated by Sir Isaac Newton in the 17th century, is a set of physical laws that describe the motion of objects. These laws provide a framework for predicting how objects will behave when subjected to forces, making them particularly useful in game development. The three key laws of motion are:

1. **Newton's First Law (Law of Inertia)**: An object at rest remains at rest, and an object in motion continues in motion with the same speed and in the same direction unless acted upon by a net external force. This principle emphasizes the concept of inertia and the need for force to change an object's state of motion.
2. **Newton's Second Law (F=ma)**: The acceleration of an object is directly proportional to the net force acting on it and inversely proportional

to its mass. This law provides the fundamental equation for motion in physics, enabling developers to calculate how forces affect an object's acceleration and velocity.

3. **Newton's Third Law (Action and Reaction)**: For every action, there is an equal and opposite reaction. This law highlights the interaction between objects, ensuring that forces exerted by one object on another result in corresponding forces in the opposite direction.

Applying Newtonian Mechanics in Game Development

In game development, implementing Newtonian mechanics involves creating a physics engine or leveraging existing ones to simulate realistic motion and interactions. Here are the primary components to consider:

1. Forces and Motion

In games, forces are used to manipulate the motion of objects. To apply Newton's second law, the basic equation is:

F=m·aF = m \cdot aF=m·a

Where:

- FFF is the net force applied to the object,
- mmm is the mass of the object,
- aaa is the acceleration produced by the force.

Developers must define forces such as gravity, friction, and user inputs to calculate how they influence an object's movement. For instance, when a character jumps, the force applied must counteract gravity to achieve upward motion.

Example: Applying Gravity

In many games, gravity is a constant force acting on objects. Here's a simple example of how gravity can be applied in a game loop:

```cpp
// Constants
const float GRAVITY = -9.81f; // Acceleration due to gravity
const float TIME_STEP = 0.016f; // Time step for simulation (60
FPS)

// GameObject structure
struct GameObject {
    float mass;
    float velocity; // Velocity in the vertical direction
    float position; // Vertical position
};

void updatePhysics(GameObject& obj) {
    // Apply gravity
    float force = obj.mass * GRAVITY; // Calculate gravitational
    force
    obj.velocity += (force / obj.mass) * TIME_STEP; // Update
    velocity
    obj.position += obj.velocity * TIME_STEP; // Update position
}
```

2. Collision Detection

Collision detection is essential for understanding when two objects in the game interact. Accurately detecting collisions allows for realistic responses based on Newton's laws. There are various methods for collision detection, including:

- **Bounding Volume Methods**: Use simple geometric shapes (like spheres or boxes) to approximate complex shapes, allowing for quick collision checks.
- **Pixel Perfect Collision**: A more precise method that checks for collisions at the pixel level, though computationally more expensive.
- **Spatial Partitioning**: Techniques such as quad-trees or octrees divide the game space into smaller regions, improving efficiency by limiting the number of collision checks.

Example: AABB Collision Detection

Axis-Aligned Bounding Box (AABB) collision detection is a common technique for rectangular objects:

```cpp
struct AABB {
    float x, y; // Position of the box
    float width, height; // Dimensions of the box
};

bool checkCollision(const AABB& box1, const AABB& box2) {
    return (box1.x < box2.x + box2.width &&
            box1.x + box1.width > box2.x &&
            box1.y < box2.y + box2.height &&
            box1.y + box1.height > box2.y);
}
```

3. Collision Response

Once a collision is detected, the next step is to respond to it. The response must respect Newton's third law, ensuring that forces are applied appropriately. Common responses include:

- **Elastic Collision**: Objects bounce off each other, conserving kinetic energy.
- **Inelastic Collision**: Objects stick together upon collision, conserving momentum but not energy.

Example: Elastic Collision Response

For elastic collisions, the velocities of two objects after a collision can be calculated as follows:

```cpp
void resolveCollision(GameObject& obj1, GameObject& obj2) {
    // Calculate new velocities based on conservation of momentum
```

```
float newVelocity1 = (obj1.velocity * (obj1.mass - obj2.mass)
+ (2 * obj2.mass * obj2.velocity)) / (obj1.mass + obj2.mass);
float newVelocity2 = (obj2.velocity * (obj2.mass - obj1.mass)
+ (2 * obj1.mass * obj1.velocity)) / (obj1.mass + obj2.mass);

obj1.velocity = newVelocity1;
obj2.velocity = newVelocity2;
}
```

Advanced Topics in Newtonian Physics

While the fundamental concepts of Newtonian mechanics provide a solid foundation for game physics, there are advanced topics that can enhance realism:

1. Rigid Body Dynamics

Rigid body dynamics involve the simulation of solid objects that do not deform. Implementing rigid body physics requires understanding rotational motion, angular velocity, and torque. In games, this allows for realistic interactions between objects, such as spinning and tumbling.

2. Friction and Drag

Friction is a force that opposes the relative motion of surfaces in contact. Implementing friction in games involves defining coefficients of static and kinetic friction and calculating how they affect motion. Similarly, drag is a force that slows objects down, particularly in aerial or underwater environments.

3. Damping

Damping is a technique used to reduce oscillations or vibrations in moving objects. In games, damping can smooth out motion, making interactions feel more natural. Developers can implement linear damping for velocity and angular damping for rotation.

Understanding and implementing the principles of Newtonian mechanics is crucial for creating realistic physics in games. By leveraging these foundational concepts, developers can simulate believable interactions that enhance gameplay. From applying forces and detecting collisions to managing responses and incorporating advanced techniques, mastering Newtonian mechanics opens the door to creating immersive and engaging gaming experiences.

Implementing Gravity, Friction, and Momentum in 2D Games

Incorporating realistic physics in 2D games not only enhances the player experience but also adds depth to gameplay mechanics. Gravity, friction, and momentum are fundamental concepts that can significantly influence how objects move and interact within a game world. This section will explore how to effectively implement these concepts in a 2D game environment, using practical examples and code snippets to illustrate the principles in action.

Gravity in 2D Games

Gravity is a force that pulls objects toward the ground, influencing their vertical motion. In most games, gravity is simulated as a constant downward force, affecting the velocity of objects over time.

Basic Gravity Implementation

To implement gravity in a 2D game, you typically define a gravitational constant and apply it to the vertical velocity of your game objects each frame. Here's a simple implementation:

cpp

```cpp
const float GRAVITY = 9.81f; // Acceleration due to gravity
(pixels per second squared)

struct GameObject {
    float mass;
    float velocityY; // Vertical velocity
    float positionY; // Vertical position
};

void updateGravity(GameObject& obj, float deltaTime) {
    // Apply gravity to the object's vertical velocity
    obj.velocityY += GRAVITY * deltaTime; // Increase velocity by
    gravity
    obj.positionY += obj.velocityY * deltaTime; // Update position
    based on new velocity
}
```

In this example, the updateGravity function calculates the new vertical velocity by adding the gravitational force (scaled by the time step, deltaTime) to the current velocity. The position is then updated based on this new velocity.

Ground Detection

To make gravity more realistic, you need to detect when an object is on the ground. This can be achieved using collision detection:

cpp

```cpp
bool isGrounded(const GameObject& obj) {
    // Check if the object's position is at or below ground level
    (assuming ground is at y=0)
    return obj.positionY <= 0.0f;
}
```

When the object is on the ground, you can reset its vertical velocity:

cpp

```
if (isGrounded(obj)) {
    obj.positionY = 0.0f; // Reset position to ground level
    obj.velocityY = 0.0f; // Reset vertical velocity
}
```

Friction in 2D Games

Friction is a force that opposes the motion of an object. In 2D games, it typically affects the horizontal movement of objects. There are two types of friction to consider:

- **Static Friction**: Prevents an object from starting to move when a force is applied.
- **Kinetic Friction**: Opposes the motion of an object already in motion.

Implementing Friction

To simulate friction, you can define a coefficient of friction for your objects. The frictional force can then be calculated and applied to the object's velocity.

cpp

```
const float STATIC_FRICTION = 0.5f; // Coefficient of static
friction
const float KINETIC_FRICTION = 0.3f; // Coefficient of kinetic
friction

void applyFriction(GameObject& obj, float deltaTime) {
    if (isGrounded(obj)) {
        // Check if the object is moving
        if (obj.velocityY == 0.0f) {
            // Apply static friction
            obj.velocityY *= (1.0f - STATIC_FRICTION); // Slow down
        } else {
```

```
            // Apply kinetic friction
            obj.velocityY *= (1.0f - KINETIC_FRICTION); // Slow
            down more aggressively
        }
    }
}
```

In this code, the applyFriction function modifies the object's vertical velocity based on whether it is moving or at rest. The amount by which the velocity is reduced is determined by the friction coefficients.

Momentum in 2D Games

Momentum is the quantity of motion an object has, which is the product of its mass and velocity. Implementing momentum in your game can create more realistic movement, particularly in response to forces.

Calculating Momentum

To calculate momentum, you can create a simple function:

cpp

```
float calculateMomentum(const GameObject& obj) {
    return obj.mass * obj.velocityY; // Simple momentum calculation
}
```

Using momentum in gameplay can involve simulating collisions where momentum is conserved. For example, when two objects collide, the momentum before the collision can be compared to the momentum afterward to determine their new velocities.

Example: Collision Response Using Momentum

When two objects collide, you can resolve their velocities based on the conservation of momentum:

```cpp
cpp

void resolveCollision(GameObject& obj1, GameObject& obj2) {
    float totalMomentum = calculateMomentum(obj1) +
    calculateMomentum(obj2);
    float totalMass = obj1.mass + obj2.mass;

    // Calculate new velocities based on momentum conservation
    obj1.velocityY = (totalMomentum * (obj1.mass / totalMass)) /
    obj1.mass;
    obj2.velocityY = (totalMomentum * (obj2.mass / totalMass)) /
    obj2.mass;
}
```

In this example, after a collision, the velocities of both objects are adjusted based on their masses and the total momentum of the system.

Putting It All Together

Implementing gravity, friction, and momentum in a 2D game requires integrating these concepts within your game loop. A basic example of how these elements work together might look like this:

```cpp
cpp

void gameLoop(float deltaTime) {
    GameObject player;
    player.mass = 1.0f;
    player.positionY = 100.0f;
    player.velocityY = 0.0f;

    while (gameRunning) {
        // Update gravity
        updateGravity(player, deltaTime);

        // Apply friction
        applyFriction(player, deltaTime);
```

```
    // Check for ground contact
    if (isGrounded(player)) {
        // Reset player position and velocity if on ground
        player.positionY = 0.0f;
        player.velocityY = 0.0f;
    }

    // Render the player, update other game logic, etc.
    }
}
```

This code snippet shows a simplified game loop where gravity, friction, and ground detection are applied to the player object each frame, allowing for dynamic and realistic movement.

By understanding and implementing gravity, friction, and momentum, you can create more engaging and lifelike physics in your 2D games. These concepts are fundamental to simulating realistic movements and interactions, contributing to the overall player experience. As you continue to develop your game, consider how these physical laws can enhance gameplay mechanics and offer players a more immersive experience.

Collision Detection: Bounding Boxes, Circles, and Pixel-Perfect Methods

Collision detection is a critical component of game physics, enabling games to respond dynamically to interactions between game objects. Accurate collision detection not only enhances gameplay experience but also ensures that the game logic behaves as expected. This section will delve into various methods of collision detection, including bounding boxes, circles, and pixel-perfect techniques.

Bounding Box Collision Detection

Bounding boxes are one of the simplest and most commonly used methods for collision detection. They provide a rectangular area that encapsulates a game object. By checking if two bounding boxes overlap, you can quickly determine if a collision has occurred.

Axis-Aligned Bounding Boxes (AABB)

Axis-aligned bounding boxes (AABBs) are defined by two points: the minimum and maximum corners of the rectangle. They are called "axis-aligned" because their edges are aligned with the coordinate axes.

Implementation of AABB Collision Detection

Here's how to implement AABB collision detection:

```cpp
cpp

struct AABB {
    float minX, minY; // Minimum corner
    float maxX, maxY; // Maximum corner
};

bool checkAABBCollision(const AABB& box1, const AABB& box2) {
    return (box1.minX < box2.maxX && box1.maxX > box2.minX &&
            box1.minY < box2.maxY && box1.maxY > box2.minY);
}
```

In this function, checkAABBCollision checks for overlaps between two AABBs. If they overlap in both the x and y directions, a collision is detected.

Benefits and Limitations

- **Benefits**: AABB collision detection is computationally inexpensive and easy to implement, making it ideal for many 2D games.
- **Limitations**: It can produce false positives for objects that are not actually colliding. This occurs because the bounding box may encompass areas that do not represent the shape of the object accurately.

Circle Collision Detection

For circular objects, a more natural approach is to use circular collision detection. This method checks the distance between the centers of two circles to determine if they are colliding.

Implementing Circle Collision Detection

The collision detection for two circles is straightforward: if the distance between their centers is less than the sum of their radii, a collision has occurred.

```cpp
struct Circle {
    float centerX, centerY; // Center coordinates
    float radius; // Radius of the circle
};

bool checkCircleCollision(const Circle& circle1, const Circle&
circle2) {
    float dx = circle1.centerX - circle2.centerX;
    float dy = circle1.centerY - circle2.centerY;
    float distanceSquared = dx * dx + dy * dy; // Calculate
    distance squared

    float radiusSum = circle1.radius + circle2.radius;
    return distanceSquared < (radiusSum * radiusSum); // Check if
    circles overlap
}
```

In this code, checkCircleCollision calculates the distance between the centers and compares it to the sum of the radii to determine if a collision has occurred.

Benefits and Limitations

- **Benefits**: Circle collision detection is efficient and avoids the complexities associated with bounding boxes for round objects.
- **Limitations**: Like AABBs, this method can lead to false positives when circles represent complex shapes.

Pixel-Perfect Collision Detection

While bounding boxes and circles provide efficient methods for collision detection, they can be imprecise for irregularly shaped objects. Pixel-perfect collision detection offers a solution by evaluating the actual pixels that overlap between two sprites.

Implementing Pixel-Perfect Collision Detection

Pixel-perfect collision detection involves comparing the alpha values of pixels in the overlapping areas of two sprites. If both sprites have opaque pixels at the same coordinates, a collision is detected.

Step-by-Step Implementation:

1. **Get the bounding box of both objects** using AABB or circle detection to limit the area for pixel checks.
2. **Check each pixel in the overlapping area** to see if both pixels are opaque.

Here's a basic implementation:

```cpp
cpp

bool checkPixelPerfectCollision(const Sprite& sprite1, const
Sprite& sprite2, const AABB& box1, const AABB& box2) {
    // Calculate overlapping bounding box
    AABB overlapBox;
    overlapBox.minX = std::max(box1.minX, box2.minX);
    overlapBox.minY = std::max(box1.minY, box2.minY);
    overlapBox.maxX = std::min(box1.maxX, box2.maxX);
    overlapBox.maxY = std::min(box1.maxY, box2.maxY);

    // Check each pixel in the overlapping area
    for (int y = overlapBox.minY; y < overlapBox.maxY; ++y) {
        for (int x = overlapBox.minX; x < overlapBox.maxX; ++x) {
            if (sprite1.getPixel(x, y) && sprite2.getPixel(x, y))
            { // Assuming getPixel returns true for opaque pixels
                return true; // Collision detected
            }
        }
    }
```

```
    }
    return false; // No collision
}
```

In this example, checkPixelPerfectCollision first calculates the overlapping bounding box and then checks the pixels within that box for opacity in both sprites.

Benefits and Limitations

- **Benefits**: Provides accurate collision detection for complex shapes, ensuring that collisions only occur when actual visual elements overlap.
- **Limitations**: It is computationally expensive, especially for high-resolution sprites, and can lead to performance issues in games with many overlapping objects.

Choosing the Right Collision Detection Method

The choice of collision detection method often depends on the specific requirements of your game:

- **Use AABBs** when you need quick and efficient collision checks for rectangular objects or when performance is critical.
- **Use Circle detection** for round objects or where shapes naturally fit into circular forms.
- **Use Pixel-perfect detection** for precise collisions in games with irregular shapes, where accuracy is paramount.

In many cases, a hybrid approach is used—starting with bounding box or circle detection to quickly rule out non-colliding objects and then refining the results with pixel-perfect checks only for potential collisions.

Effective collision detection is vital for creating an engaging gameplay experience. By understanding the different methods—bounding boxes, circles, and pixel-perfect detection—you can choose the best approach for your game's needs. Balancing performance with accuracy will enhance your game's responsiveness and realism, ensuring that players have an immersive and enjoyable experience. As you advance through your game development journey, integrating these collision detection methods will be essential for building a robust game engine and achieving realistic interactions within your game world.

Collision Resolution and Response

Collision resolution is a vital aspect of game physics that follows collision detection. Once a collision has been identified between two or more game objects, it is essential to determine how these objects should respond to avoid unrealistic interactions and maintain the integrity of the game world. This section will explore collision resolution strategies, including physics-based responses and game logic-based resolutions.

Understanding Collision Response

When two objects collide in a game, their interaction can lead to various responses, including:

- **Elastic collisions**, where objects bounce off each other.
- **Inelastic collisions**, where objects stick together or deform.
- **Sliding**, where objects slide against each other without penetrating.
- **Stopping**, where an object comes to a complete stop after impact.

The type of response depends on the physical properties of the objects involved, such as mass, velocity, and friction.

Basic Principles of Collision Resolution

The principles of collision resolution can be boiled down to a few core ideas:

1. **Separation**: After a collision, objects must be separated to prevent them from overlapping. This often involves calculating the minimum translation vector (MTV) required to move the objects apart.
2. **Adjustment of Velocities**: The velocities of the objects may need to be adjusted to simulate realistic reactions. This adjustment can involve reversing or altering the direction of movement.
3. **Application of Physics Laws**: Use Newton's laws of motion to calculate the effects of collisions based on the physical properties of the objects involved.

Implementing Collision Resolution
1. Minimum Translation Vector (MTV)

The Minimum Translation Vector is the shortest distance needed to separate two colliding objects. Once you have determined the collision and identified the MTV, you can apply it to resolve the collision.

Here's a basic implementation:

```cpp
Vector2D calculateMTV(const AABB& box1, const AABB& box2) {
    float overlapX = std::min(box1.maxX - box2.minX, box2.maxX -
    box1.minX);
    float overlapY = std::min(box1.maxY - box2.minY, box2.maxY -
    box1.minY);

    // Choose the smallest overlap to resolve collision
    if (overlapX < overlapY) {
        return Vector2D(overlapX, 0); // Resolve in x direction
    } else {
        return Vector2D(0, overlapY); // Resolve in y direction
    }
}
```

This function computes the overlap in both the x and y directions and returns the vector representing the minimum translation required to separate the two boxes.

2. Adjusting Object Positions

Once you have the MTV, you can adjust the positions of the colliding objects to separate them. Here's how to implement that:

```cpp
cpp

void resolveCollision(AABB& box1, AABB& box2) {
    Vector2D mtv = calculateMTV(box1, box2);

    // Adjust the positions based on MTV
    box1.minX += mtv.x * 0.5f; // Move box1 out of collision
    box1.maxX += mtv.x * 0.5f;
    box1.minY += mtv.y * 0.5f;
    box1.maxY += mtv.y * 0.5f;

    box2.minX -= mtv.x * 0.5f; // Move box2 out of collision
    box2.maxX -= mtv.x * 0.5f;
    box2.minY -= mtv.y * 0.5f;
    box2.maxY -= mtv.y * 0.5f;
}
```

In this function, resolveCollision adjusts the positions of both boxes based on the MTV, ensuring that they no longer overlap.

Handling Velocities and Rebounds

To create realistic responses, the velocities of colliding objects must be modified based on physical principles:

1. **Elastic Collision Response:** For a perfectly elastic collision, use the laws of conservation of momentum and kinetic energy. The following equations can be applied:

$$v_{1\_final} = \frac{(m_1 - m_2)v_{1\_initial} + 2m_2 v_{2\_initial}}{m_1 + m_2}$$

$$v_{2\_final} = \frac{(m_2 - m_1)v_{2\_initial} + 2m_1 v_{1\_initial}}{m_1 + m_2}$$

2. **Inelastic Collision Response:** For inelastic collisions, where the objects stick together, the final velocity can be computed as follows:

$$v_{final} = \frac{m_1 v_{1\_initial} + m_2 v_{2\_initial}}{m_1 + m_2}$$

Example of Elastic Collision Resolution

cpp

```cpp
void resolveElasticCollision(GameObject& obj1, GameObject& obj2) {
    Vector2D relativeVelocity = obj2.velocity - obj1.velocity;
    Vector2D collisionNormal = (obj1.position -
    obj2.position).normalize();

    float velocityAlongNormal =
    relativeVelocity.dot(collisionNormal);

    // Only resolve if objects are moving towards each other
    if (velocityAlongNormal > 0) {
        return; // No collision resolution needed
    }

    // Coefficients of restitution for elasticity
    float e = 0.8f; // Restitution coefficient, 1 is perfectly
    elastic

    // Calculate impulse scalar
    float impulseScalar = -(1 + e) * velocityAlongNormal;
    impulseScalar /= (1 / obj1.mass + 1 / obj2.mass);

    // Apply impulse to the objects
    obj1.velocity += impulseScalar * collisionNormal / obj1.mass;
    obj2.velocity -= impulseScalar * collisionNormal / obj2.mass;
}
```

In this function, resolveElasticCollision calculates the new velocities for both objects after a collision based on their masses and restitution coefficient.

Handling Game Logic in Collision Response

Beyond physics, collision resolution can involve game logic responses, such as:

- **Triggering events**: A collision might trigger events, such as scoring points, displaying messages, or playing sound effects.
- **State changes**: Collision responses can change the states of game objects, like destroying an enemy upon collision with a player or transitioning to a different game state.

Example of Game Logic Integration

cpp

```cpp
void handleCollision(GameObject& obj1, GameObject& obj2) {
    resolveElasticCollision(obj1, obj2);

    // Implement game-specific responses
    if (obj1.type == "player" && obj2.type == "enemy") {
        // Handle player collision with enemy
        obj1.health -= 1; // Decrease health
        // Trigger game over if health is zero
        if (obj1.health <= 0) {
            gameState = GameState::GAME_OVER;
        }
    } else if (obj1.type == "bullet" && obj2.type == "enemy") {
        // Handle bullet collision with enemy
        obj2.health -= 1; // Decrease enemy health
        if (obj2.health <= 0) {
            obj2.isAlive = false; // Mark enemy as dead
        }
    }
}
```

In this example, the handleCollision function not only resolves the physics of the collision but also implements game logic to update the health of the involved game objects.

Collision resolution and response are crucial for creating a realistic and engaging gameplay experience. By understanding the principles of separation, adjustment of velocities, and integrating game logic, developers can ensure that game interactions feel responsive and meaningful. The techniques outlined in this section will empower you to create more dynamic and engaging games, leading to an overall improved player experience. In the next chapter, we will delve into advanced topics such as integrating physics engines and optimizing collision detection for complex game worlds.

Introduction to Rigid Body Dynamics and Advanced Physics Engines

In the realm of game development, creating lifelike interactions between objects is crucial for engaging gameplay. Rigid body dynamics and advanced physics engines play a pivotal role in simulating realistic object behavior. This section will provide an overview of rigid body dynamics, explain the fundamentals of physics engines, and explore how they can be leveraged to enhance gameplay.

Understanding Rigid Body Dynamics

Rigid body dynamics refers to the study of the motion and interactions of solid objects that do not deform under stress. In the context of games, this means that the shape and volume of an object remain constant, allowing developers to predict how objects will move and react to forces.

Key Concepts of Rigid Body Dynamics

1. **Rigid Bodies**: A rigid body is an idealized solid object where the distance between any two points on the object remains unchanged regardless of the forces acting on it. This simplification allows for efficient calculations in physics simulations.

2. **Forces and Torques**: Rigid body dynamics are governed by Newton's laws of motion, which describe how forces (pushes or pulls) and torques (rotational forces) affect an object's motion. Key equations include:

- $F=m{\cdot}aF = m \cdot aF=m{\cdot}a$ (Newton's second law of motion, where FFF is the net force, mmm is the mass, and aaa is the acceleration)
- $\tau=I{\cdot}\alpha\tau = I \cdot \alpha\tau=I{\cdot}\alpha$ (where $\tau\tau\tau$ is torque, III is the moment of inertia, and $\alpha\alpha\alpha$ is angular acceleration)

Collisions and Constraints: Rigid bodies interact through collisions, which require calculating the impact forces and resolving the resulting motion. Constraints, such as joints and hinges, are also employed to connect rigid bodies, allowing them to interact in specific ways.

Momentum and Energy Conservation: When two rigid bodies collide, both momentum and energy must be conserved (in elastic collisions). Understanding how to calculate these quantities is essential for realistic collision responses.

Physics Engines: Tools for Simulating Dynamics

Physics engines are specialized libraries that provide the necessary functionality to simulate the behavior of rigid bodies and other physical phenomena in games. These engines abstract the complexities of physics calculations, allowing developers to focus on gameplay rather than the underlying mathematics.

Popular Physics Engines

1. **Box2D**: A widely-used 2D physics engine that supports rigid body dynamics, collisions, and various constraints. It is suitable for games with a focus on 2D graphics and simple physics interactions.
2. **Bullet Physics**: A robust physics engine designed for 3D simulations. Bullet supports rigid body dynamics, soft body dynamics, and collision detection. It is commonly used in various game engines and applications,

including Unreal Engine and Blender.

3. **Havok Physics**: A powerful physics engine known for its high performance and advanced features. Havok is frequently used in AAA games and provides sophisticated collision detection, character physics, and vehicle dynamics.

4. **Unity's Built-in Physics**: Unity incorporates both 2D and 3D physics engines (Box2D for 2D and PhysX for 3D). Unity makes it easy for developers to implement physics by using predefined components, which handle collisions, rigid body behaviors, and other physics interactions.

Implementing Rigid Body Dynamics in Your Game

To implement rigid body dynamics effectively, follow these key steps:

Defining Rigid Bodies: Create a rigid body class that encapsulates properties such as position, velocity, mass, and moment of inertia. This class will serve as a foundation for all game objects that interact with physics.

```cpp
class RigidBody {
public:
    Vector2D position;
    Vector2D velocity;
    float mass;
    float angularVelocity;
    float momentOfInertia;

    RigidBody(float m) : mass(m), velocity(0, 0),
    angularVelocity(0) {}

    // Update method to apply forces and update position
    void update(float deltaTime) {
        position += velocity * deltaTime;
    }
};
```

Applying Forces and Torques: Implement methods for applying forces and torques to rigid bodies. Use Newton's laws to update velocities and positions based on these inputs.

```cpp
void applyForce(RigidBody& body, const Vector2D& force) {
    Vector2D acceleration = force / body.mass;
    body.velocity += acceleration; // Update linear velocity
}

void applyTorque(RigidBody& body, float torque) {
    body.angularVelocity += torque / body.momentOfInertia; //
    Update angular velocity
}
```

1. **Handling Collisions**: Integrate collision detection and resolution mechanisms using a physics engine or custom algorithms. Ensure that rigid bodies respond realistically to collisions based on their physical properties.

2. **Optimizing Performance**: Physics simulations can be computationally intensive. Optimize your implementation by minimizing the number of collision checks, using spatial partitioning techniques (e.g., quad-trees or grids), and simplifying the geometry of rigid bodies where possible.

Integrating Advanced Physics Features

Beyond basic rigid body dynamics, advanced physics engines offer a range of features to enhance gameplay:

1. **Soft Body Dynamics**: Some engines support soft body physics, allowing objects to deform under stress. This can be used for effects like cloth, jelly-like surfaces, or character animations.

2. **Fluid Dynamics**: Simulating fluid behavior can add realism to water surfaces, smoke, and other liquids. Advanced engines can incorporate particle systems to represent fluids accurately.

3. **Vehicle Physics**: Many physics engines provide specialized support for

vehicle dynamics, enabling realistic handling, traction, and suspension behaviors for cars, trucks, and other vehicles.

4. **Character Controllers**: Physics engines often include character controller components that handle player movement and interactions with the environment. This allows for more fluid movement and realistic character interactions.

Rigid body dynamics and advanced physics engines are essential for creating realistic and engaging gameplay experiences. By understanding the principles of rigid body motion and effectively utilizing physics engines, developers can simulate lifelike interactions between objects, enhance player immersion, and create dynamic game worlds. In the next chapter, we will explore the intricacies of sound and music integration in games, further enriching the player experience.

Artificial Intelligence for Game Characters

Introduction to Game AI: Finite State Machines and Behavior Trees
Artificial Intelligence (AI) is a core component of game development, enabling dynamic and responsive behaviors for non-playable characters (NPCs) and other in-game entities. AI techniques such as Finite State Machines (FSMs) and Behavior Trees (BTs) help simulate decision-making processes, allowing characters to respond intelligently to player actions and environmental changes.

This section introduces game AI, explaining how FSMs and BTs work, their strengths and limitations, and how to implement them effectively in a game setting.

The Role of AI in Game Development

In games, AI drives the behavior of NPCs, creating challenges, aiding immersion, and enriching gameplay. Whether it's an enemy soldier reacting to the player's movements or a friendly companion assisting in a mission, AI techniques add depth and realism to the gaming experience. By implementing AI systems, game developers can design characters that act based on defined rules, objectives, and in-game stimuli.

Key AI Requirements in Game Development

1. **Realism**: AI should behave in ways that match the game's setting and objectives, offering a natural and believable interaction for players.

2. **Performance**: Since games often involve multiple AI agents, performance efficiency is critical to maintaining real-time responsiveness.

3. **Modularity**: AI logic must be adaptable and easy to extend, allowing developers to add or modify behaviors without extensive rework.

4. **Scalability**: As games grow in complexity, AI systems should scale to accommodate additional agents and more nuanced behaviors.

Finite State Machines (FSMs)

Finite State Machines (FSMs) are among the simplest and most commonly used AI architectures in game development. An FSM consists of a finite number of states and transitions between those states, allowing characters to switch behaviors based on conditions.

How FSMs Work

In an FSM, each state represents a unique behavior or mode, and transitions between states occur based on specific events or conditions. For example, an enemy NPC might have states like Patrolling, Chasing, and Attacking. When certain conditions are met, such as detecting the player, the enemy can transition from Patrolling to Chasing.

Example Structure of an FSM

Consider a basic FSM structure for a guard NPC:

- **States**:
- **Idle**: The guard stands in place, waiting or watching.
- **Patrol**: The guard moves along a predefined route.
- **Alert**: The guard searches an area after detecting suspicious activity.
- **Chase**: The guard actively pursues the player.
- **Transitions**:
- **Idle → Patrol**: If idle time is over, begin patrolling.
- **Patrol → Alert**: If suspicious sound or visual cue is detected.
- **Alert → Chase**: If the player is directly observed.
- **Chase → Idle**: If the player is lost, return to idle after a cooldown.

Benefits of FSMs

- **Simplicity**: FSMs are easy to design, implement, and understand, making them suitable for straightforward NPC behaviors.
- **Predictability**: Since FSMs follow explicit transitions, their behavior is highly predictable and easy to debug.
- **Performance**: FSMs are lightweight and don't require complex computations, making them suitable for real-time applications.

Limitations of FSMs

- **Scalability Issues**: As more states and transitions are added, FSMs can become complex, making them harder to manage and maintain.
- **Rigid Behavior**: FSMs operate in predefined patterns, which can make NPC behavior feel repetitive or robotic, especially in complex games.

Implementing FSMs in C++

cpp

```cpp
enum GuardState { Idle, Patrol, Alert, Chase };

class GuardAI {
public:
    GuardState state;

    void update() {
        switch(state) {
            case Idle:
                handleIdle();
                break;
            case Patrol:
                handlePatrol();
                break;
            case Alert:
                handleAlert();
```

```
                break;
            case Chase:
                handleChase();
                break;
        }
    }

    void handleIdle() {
        // Logic for Idle state
    }

    void handlePatrol() {
        // Logic for Patrol state
    }

    // Additional state handlers...
};
```

Behavior Trees (BTs)

Behavior Trees (BTs) offer a modular, scalable alternative to FSMs, ideal for implementing more complex and flexible AI. Originally developed for robotics, BTs are widely used in games to manage hierarchical, goal-oriented behaviors.

How Behavior Trees Work

A behavior tree consists of nodes that represent tasks or actions. Nodes are organized hierarchically, and execution flows from parent nodes to child nodes based on conditions or requirements. This structure allows for more flexible, goal-oriented decision-making.

Structure of a Behavior Tree

- **Root Node**: The starting point of the tree, from which all decisions flow.
- **Composite Nodes**: Branching nodes that manage other nodes based on logical operations (e.g., sequence, selector).
- **Decorator Nodes**: Conditional nodes that check specific criteria and control whether a child node is executed.

- **Leaf Nodes**: End nodes representing actions or tasks that characters perform.

Example Behavior Tree for a Guard NPC

1. **Root Node**: "Guard Behavior"

- **Sequence**: "Patrol Routine"
- **Action**: Move to waypoint.
- **Condition**: Check for player proximity.
- **Selector**: "Alert State"
- **Sequence**: Search for player.
- **Action**: Engage in chase if player is found.

Types of Composite Nodes

- **Sequence Nodes**: Execute child nodes in sequence; if any node fails, the sequence stops.
- **Selector Nodes**: Execute child nodes in order until one succeeds; if all fail, the selector node fails.

Benefits of Behavior Trees

- **Modularity**: BTs allow easy organization and modification of individual behaviors without affecting the entire tree structure.
- **Flexibility**: Nodes can be reused across different characters, making BTs suitable for complex AI needs.
- **Scalability**: BTs handle a large number of actions and conditions more effectively than FSMs.

Limitations of Behavior Trees

- **Complexity**: While modular, BTs require a good understanding of the hierarchical structure, making them more complex to implement initially.

- **Debugging Challenges**: BTs can become challenging to debug, especially when dealing with numerous conditional nodes and actions.

Implementing Behavior Trees in C++

```cpp
class Node {
public:
    virtual bool execute() = 0;
// Abstract function to execute node
};

class SequenceNode : public Node {
    std::vector<Node*> children;
public:
    bool execute() override {
        for (Node* child : children) {
            if (!child->execute()) return false;
// Stop on failure
        }
        return true;
    }
};

class PatrolNode : public Node {
public:
    bool execute() override {
        // Logic for patrolling action
        return true;
    }
};
```

When to Use FSMs vs. Behavior Trees

Choosing between FSMs and BTs depends on the complexity of the game and the desired flexibility:

- **FSMs** are suitable for simpler games with fewer states and predictable behaviors, where performance and simplicity are essential.
- **Behavior Trees** excel in games requiring complex decision-making and flexible, modular behaviors, particularly for NPCs with varied or goal-oriented actions.

Finite State Machines and Behavior Trees are foundational AI structures in game development, each offering unique advantages. FSMs provide a straightforward, efficient method for implementing simple AI behaviors, while BTs support more complex, modular, and flexible behaviors. Selecting the right approach depends on the game's requirements, with FSMs being ideal for simpler behaviors and BTs for more intricate, layered decision-making.

Pathfinding Algorithms: A*, Dijkstra, and Grid-Based Navigation

Pathfinding algorithms are integral to game AI, enabling NPCs and other agents to navigate complex environments intelligently. In game development, these algorithms help characters find the shortest or most optimal path from one location to another, factoring in obstacles, terrain types, and other dynamic factors. Two widely-used algorithms in pathfinding are A* (A-star) and Dijkstra's algorithm, both of which provide effective solutions for navigating grid-based and node-based maps.

The Role of Pathfinding in Games

Pathfinding is essential for creating responsive and realistic behaviors in NPCs, particularly in games involving exploration, combat, or resource gathering. Effective pathfinding allows characters to move smoothly across the game world, evade obstacles, and respond dynamically to changes, adding depth and realism to gameplay.

Key Requirements for Pathfinding in Games

1. **Efficiency**: The algorithm must be capable of computing paths quickly to support real-time movement, especially when multiple agents are involved.
2. **Accuracy**: NPCs should find the most effective route that meets their objectives, whether it's the shortest path or one that avoids specific obstacles.
3. **Adaptability**: The pathfinding system should handle dynamic environments, adjusting paths as conditions change (e.g., new obstacles or moving targets).
4. **Scalability**: Pathfinding solutions must work efficiently in large or open-world environments with complex terrains and large numbers of agents.

Dijkstra's Algorithm

Dijkstra's Algorithm is a foundational pathfinding algorithm known for calculating the shortest path from a start node to all other nodes in a graph. It's highly reliable for cases where all path lengths are positive, making it an excellent choice for games with static, grid-based maps.

How Dijkstra's Algorithm Works

1. **Initialization**: Start at the source node, setting its distance to zero and all other nodes to infinity.
2. **Exploration**: For each unvisited node, consider all its unvisited neighbors, updating their distances if a shorter path is found.
3. **Selection**: Mark the node with the smallest tentative distance as visited, then repeat the process.
4. **Termination**: The algorithm completes once all nodes have been visited or when the destination node's shortest path is found.

Advantages of Dijkstra's Algorithm

- **Accuracy**: Dijkstra's reliably finds the shortest path for any given node in the graph.

- **Simplicity**: It's straightforward to implement and understand, making it suitable for static environments.

Limitations of Dijkstra's Algorithm

- **Computationally Heavy**: Dijkstra's examines all nodes, which can be inefficient in large or complex maps.
- **Lack of Heuristic**: It's a blind search without any heuristic guidance, which limits its performance compared to heuristic-based algorithms like A*.

Implementing Dijkstra's Algorithm in C++

```cpp
cpp

#include <vector>
#include <queue>
#include <limits>

const int INF = std::numeric_limits<int>::max();

void dijkstra(int start, std::vector<std::vector<std::pair<int,
int>>> &graph, std::vector<int> &dist) {
    dist[start] = 0;
    std::priority_queue<std::pair<int, int>> pq;
    pq.push({0, start});

    while (!pq.empty()) {
        int current = pq.top().second;
        int distance = -pq.top().first;
        pq.pop();

        if (distance > dist[current]) continue;

        for (auto &neighbor : graph[current]) {
            int next = neighbor.first;
            int weight = neighbor.second;
```

```
if (dist[current] + weight < dist[next]) {
    dist[next] = dist[current] + weight;
    pq.push({-dist[next], next});
}
        }
    }
}
```

A* Algorithm

The A* (A-star) algorithm builds upon Dijkstra's by adding a heuristic to prioritize nodes that are closer to the target, drastically improving efficiency in pathfinding, especially in grid-based games with obstacles.

How A* Works

1. **Initialization**: Each node in the grid has two values: G (distance from start to the current node) and H (heuristic estimate from the current node to the destination).
2. **Heuristic Calculation**: A* typically uses the Manhattan or Euclidean distance for its heuristic, guiding the search toward the target more directly.
3. **Exploration**: From the starting node, A* explores the neighbors, calculating F = G + H for each, prioritizing nodes with the lowest F.
4. **Termination**: The algorithm continues until the destination node is reached or no viable path exists.

Advantages of A*

- **Efficiency**: The heuristic component reduces unnecessary searches, making A* faster than Dijkstra's for many cases.
- **Optimality**: A* guarantees the shortest path if the heuristic is admissible (i.e., it never overestimates the actual cost).

Limitations of A*

- **Heuristic Dependency**: The effectiveness of A* depends on a well-chosen heuristic, which may vary based on the game environment.
- **Higher Memory Usage**: A* often consumes more memory due to storing the G, H, and F values for each node.

Implementing A* Algorithm in C++

```cpp
cpp

#include <vector>
#include <queue>
#include <cmath>

struct Node {
    int x, y;
    int g, h;
    Node* parent;

    int f() const { return g + h; }
};

int heuristic(const Node& a, const Node& b) {
    return abs(a.x - b.x) + abs(a.y - b.y);  // Manhattan distance
    for grid-based games
}

void a_star(Node start, Node goal,
std::vector<std::vector<int>>& grid) {
    // Code to initialize, implement
 A*, and store optimal path
}
```

Grid-Based Navigation

Grid-based navigation is a common pathfinding technique for 2D games, where the game world is divided into a matrix of cells or nodes. This simplifies pathfinding as algorithms like A* and Dijkstra's can treat each cell as a node, making it easy to calculate paths based on cell adjacency.

Setting Up Grid-Based Navigation

1. **Define the Grid**: The game environment is divided into a 2D grid, with each cell representing a node that can either be passable or an obstacle.
2. **Assigning Costs**: Cells can be assigned movement costs based on terrain types (e.g., grass, water, sand), allowing for more realistic pathfinding.
3. **Neighbor Identification**: For each cell, neighboring cells are defined, typically up, down, left, right, and optionally diagonals.

Advantages of Grid-Based Navigation

- **Simplicity**: Grid-based systems are easy to implement and visualize.
- **Compatibility**: They work well with algorithms like A* and Dijkstra's, which rely on node-based structures.

Optimizing Grid-Based Navigation

To improve efficiency, developers can use optimizations like hierarchical pathfinding, which groups clusters of nodes, or influence maps, where cells hold dynamic data such as danger zones or preferred paths.

Choosing the Right Algorithm for Your Game

The choice between Dijkstra's, A*, and grid-based navigation depends on the specific game requirements:

- **Use Dijkstra's Algorithm** for scenarios where all paths are of equal importance, such as games where NPCs must explore or traverse all nodes.
- *Use A Algorithm** when efficiency and directed pathfinding are critical, such as real-time games with frequent path recalculations.
- **Use Grid-Based Navigation** for 2D games or grid-structured maps where simplicity and visualization ease are essential.

Pathfinding algorithms like Dijkstra's and A*, combined with grid-based navigation, form the backbone of NPC movement in games. Understanding these algorithms and their implementation allows for precise, adaptable, and performant AI-driven navigation. In the next section, we will dive into **Advanced AI Techniques**, where we'll look into adaptive algorithms, decision-making models, and more sophisticated ways to simulate human-like intelligence in NPCs. This step will further enhance the depth and realism of AI behavior, adding another layer of engagement to gameplay.

Steering Behaviors: Flocking, Evading, and Pursuing

Steering behaviors give NPCs (non-player characters) fluid and lifelike movements, particularly in dynamic game environments where agents need to interact, evade, or collaborate with one another. These behaviors are widely used in games to simulate group movement (flocking), defensive tactics (evading), and aggressive pursuits, creating a realistic and engaging player experience.

Steering behaviors are particularly effective in games featuring crowds, animals, enemies, and other group-based AI units, as they offer a balance between realism and computational efficiency.

Core Concepts of Steering Behaviors

Unlike pathfinding algorithms, which are used primarily to compute an optimal path between two points, steering behaviors continuously adjust an agent's direction and speed in response to nearby objects or agents. This responsiveness allows NPCs to adapt fluidly to the environment, producing natural, unscripted movement patterns. Steering behaviors are typically combined to produce complex interactions, each behavior contributing to the final vector that controls the NPC's movement.

Key Factors in Steering Behaviors

1. **Separation**: Keeping distance from neighboring agents to avoid collisions.

2. **Cohesion**: Moving toward the average position of a group or cluster.
3. **Alignment**: Matching the velocity or direction of nearby agents.
4. **Arrival**: Slowing down as an NPC reaches a destination or target.
5. **Avoidance**: Reacting to obstacles to prevent collisions.

By blending these components, we can create a range of behaviors that produce responsive and natural-looking AI in different scenarios.

Flocking Behavior

Flocking is a complex behavior derived from the combination of **separation**, **alignment**, and **cohesion**. This behavior, inspired by animals like birds or fish, allows agents to move in a cohesive group, maintaining both unity and dynamic interaction.

Implementing Flocking Behavior

1. **Separation**: Each agent steers to avoid colliding with its neighbors, ensuring that each has enough space within the group. This is especially important in tight areas or densely packed groups.
2. **Alignment**: Each agent tries to match its velocity vector with those of nearby agents, creating smooth and unified group movement.
3. **Cohesion**: Each agent steers toward the average position of its local group, helping keep the group together as a single unit.

These sub-behaviors can be weighted differently depending on the desired effect. For example, an increased weight on cohesion will cause the flock to group closer together, while a stronger separation weight will make each agent more independent.

Example Code Snippet: Simple Flocking Algorithm

```cpp
cpp

#include <vector>
#include <cmath>
```

```
// Pseudo-code for a simplified flocking algorithm
class Boid {
public:
    Vector2 position, velocity;

    Vector2 computeSeparation
(const std::vector<Boid>& neighbors) {
        Vector2 separationForce;
        for (const auto& neighbor : neighbors) {
            if (distance(position, neighbor.position) <
            separationRadius) {
                separationForce +=
(position - neighbor.position);
            }
        }
        return separationForce;
    }

    Vector2 computeAlignment
(const std::vector<Boid>& neighbors) {
        Vector2 averageVelocity;
        for (const auto& neighbor : neighbors) {
            averageVelocity += neighbor.velocity;
        }
        averageVelocity /= neighbors.size();
        return (averageVelocity - velocity);
    }

    Vector2 computeCohesion
(const std::vector<Boid>& neighbors) {
        Vector2 centerOfMass;
        for (const auto& neighbor : neighbors) {
            centerOfMass += neighbor.position;
        }
        centerOfMass /= neighbors.size();
        return (centerOfMass - position);
    }

    void update(const std::vector<Boid>& neighbors) {
```

```cpp
        Vector2 separation = computeSeparation(neighbors) *
        separationWeight;
        Vector2 alignment = computeAlignment(neighbors) *
        alignmentWeight;
        Vector2 cohesion = computeCohesion(neighbors) *
        cohesionWeight;

        velocity += separation + alignment + cohesion;
        position += velocity;
    }
};
```

Evading Behavior

Evading allows NPCs to avoid a pursuer or avoid entering specific danger zones. This behavior is frequently combined with pathfinding to dynamically steer away from threats, adding depth to AI decision-making. Evading can be used for stealth games, fleeing mechanics, or creating intelligent and evasive opponents.

How Evading Works

Evading involves predicting the pursuer's future position based on its current velocity and steering away from that position. The evading agent calculates where it anticipates the pursuer will be and adjusts its own trajectory to avoid that area. This results in realistic defensive movement patterns that feel more challenging and less predictable to the player.

Example Code Snippet: Basic Evasion Algorithm

```cpp
cpp

class Evader {
public:
    Vector2 position, velocity;

    Vector2 evade(const Vector2& pursuerPos, const Vector2&
    pursuerVelocity) {
        Vector2 futurePursuerPos =
```

```cpp
pursuerPos + pursuerVelocity * predictionFactor;
        Vector2 escapeVector =
 position - futurePursuerPos;
        return normalize(escapeVector) * maxSpeed;
    }

    void update(const Vector2& pursuerPos, const Vector2&
    pursuerVelocity) {
        Vector2 evasionForce = evade
(pursuerPos, pursuerVelocity);
        velocity += evasionForce;
        position += velocity;
    }
};
```

Pursuing Behavior

Pursuing is the inverse of evading, in which an agent seeks to catch or reach another target. This behavior is essential for creating AI opponents that chase the player or other NPCs, enhancing the sense of engagement in gameplay. Pursuing can be implemented by estimating the target's future position and adjusting the pursuer's trajectory accordingly.

How Pursuing Works

The pursuer predicts where the target will be in the near future based on its current velocity, adjusting its movement to intercept that point. This approach prevents the pursuer from merely trailing behind the target and instead intercepts it dynamically, making the AI feel more adaptive and challenging.

Example Code Snippet: Pursuit Algorithm

```cpp
cpp

class Pursuer {
public:
    Vector2 position, velocity;
```

```
    Vector2 pursue(const Vector2&
targetPos, const Vector2& targetVelocity) {
        Vector2 futureTargetPos =
targetPos + targetVelocity * predictionFactor;
        Vector2 pursuitVector = futureTargetPos - position;
        return normalize(pursuitVector) * maxSpeed;
    }

    void update(const Vector2& targetPos, const Vector2&
    targetVelocity) {
        Vector2 pursuitForce =
 pursue(targetPos, targetVelocity);
        velocity += pursuitForce;
        position += velocity;
    }
};
```

Combining Steering Behaviors

In many games, AI characters need to exhibit multiple behaviors simul-taneously, such as pursuing while avoiding obstacles or flocking while steering toward a specific goal. By blending multiple steering behaviors with appropriate weighting, we can create complex AI systems that simulate real-life behavior.

Weighted Blending of Behaviors

Each steering behavior can be assigned a weight based on the current situation, allowing the NPC to prioritize certain actions over others. For example:

- **Pursuit with Avoidance**: Combining pursuit with an obstacle avoidance behavior.
- **Flocking with Cohesion**: Weighing alignment and cohesion equally while reducing separation to create tightly-knit groups.
- **Evade and Wander**: Blending evasion with random wandering to create unpredictable evasive behavior.

155

Steering behaviors like flocking, evading, and pursuing add a layer of realistic movement and interaction to game AI, creating a compelling, immersive environment. By mastering these foundational techniques, developers can design characters that respond intelligently to their surroundings and provide a more challenging, engaging experience for players. In the next section, we'll delve into advanced AI decision-making techniques such as adaptive behaviors, goal-driven actions, and dynamic obstacle handling to further enrich NPC interactions in complex game environments.

AI for Real-Time Strategy Games: Decision Making and Resource Management

Real-time strategy (RTS) games pose unique AI challenges due to their complexity and the need for quick, adaptive decision-making. RTS AI must handle multiple tasks simultaneously, from managing resources to making strategic and tactical decisions. Unlike other genres, RTS games demand AI systems that can efficiently allocate resources, evaluate complex battlefield situations, and plan and adapt to ever-evolving game conditions in real-time.

This section covers essential aspects of RTS game AI, including decision-making frameworks, resource management, tactical and strategic planning, and adaptive responses.

Core Concepts in RTS AI

AI in RTS games functions on multiple layers, each focused on a specific type of task. These tasks can be broken down as follows:

1. **Strategic Decision-Making**: High-level, long-term planning focused on achieving overall objectives, such as conquering territories, building bases, and expanding control.
2. **Tactical Decision-Making**: Mid-level, short-term planning based on battlefield conditions, such as deploying troops, choosing formations, and executing attacks.
3. **Resource Management**: Collecting, allocating, and using resources

156

(like gold, energy, or food) to sustain and grow the player's or AI's empire or base.

4. **Micro-Management**: Fine control over individual units, such as dodging attacks or positioning units optimally within battles.

5. **Adaptive Behavior**: Reacting to the player's strategy and altering tactics accordingly, including defense and counter-strategies.

In implementing these tasks, AI for RTS games often employs state machines, rule-based systems, behavior trees, and increasingly, machine learning for complex adaptive behaviors.

Strategic Decision-Making: Goal-Oriented Action Planning (GOAP)

For AI to make informed, high-level strategic decisions, it uses Goal-Oriented Action Planning (GOAP), a decision-making framework that allows it to pursue and prioritize multiple objectives based on changing circumstances. GOAP enables AI to set goals such as expanding territory, defending bases, or acquiring resources and then plan sequences of actions to accomplish these goals efficiently.

Key Aspects of GOAP

- **Goal Selection**: AI prioritizes goals based on their importance, choosing actions that best support overall objectives. For instance, if resources are scarce, it may prioritize mining over building a new base.
- **Action Planning**: AI evaluates the sequence of actions required to achieve each goal and selects actions that yield the highest benefit.
- **Dynamic Adjustment**: AI can adjust its goals based on player actions, such as redirecting resources to defense if under attack.

GOAP in RTS games allows the AI to remain flexible and responsive, adapting its strategies based on battlefield conditions and resource availability.

Tactical Decision-Making: Real-Time Unit Deployment and Combat Strategy

While strategic decision-making focuses on long-term goals, tactical decision-making deals with real-time battlefield management, including unit deployment, positioning, and combat tactics.

Implementing Tactical AI

1. **Positioning and Formation**: AI positions units effectively to maximize their strengths. For example, placing archers behind infantry provides a defensive advantage while keeping vulnerable units out of close combat.
2. **Target Selection**: AI prioritizes high-value targets based on the situation, such as attacking enemy artillery first to minimize damage.
3. **Flanking and Ambushing**: The AI plans maneuvers to outmaneuver enemies by flanking or ambushing, increasing the effectiveness of its attacks and lowering vulnerability.
4. **Retreat and Regroup**: When necessary, AI units will retreat and regroup to minimize losses, allowing them to recover and prepare for another attack.

Effective tactical AI requires constant monitoring of battlefield conditions and the ability to adapt formations and strategies to counter the player's moves.

Resource Management: Gathering, Allocation, and Optimization

Resource management is one of the core mechanics of any RTS game, impacting both the player's and AI's growth and military power. An AI that effectively manages resources will build stronger bases, field larger armies, and maintain better defense systems.

Key Resource Management Techniques

1. **Resource Gathering**: AI identifies and prioritizes resource collection points, assigning workers to gather necessary materials. Efficient gathering ensures that the AI can produce units and structures without interruption.
2. **Resource Allocation**: AI allocates resources to different tasks based on

priorities, like producing units, constructing buildings, or researching technology.

3. **Economic Balance**: To avoid over-investing in one aspect (such as military production at the cost of infrastructure), the AI balances economic growth with defensive and offensive capabilities.

4. **Optimization and Upgrades**: AI invests in technology upgrades and enhancements to improve the efficiency of resource collection and unit production.

Example Code Snippet: Simplified Resource Management

```cpp
class ResourceManager {
public:
    int food, gold, energy;

void gatherResource(ResourceType type, int amount) {
        switch (type) {
case ResourceType::Food: food += amount; break;
case ResourceType::Gold: gold += amount; break;
case ResourceType::Energy: energy += amount; break;
        }
    }

    void allocateResources(UnitType unit) {
        if (canAfford(unit)) {
            produceUnit(unit);
            consumeResources(unit);
        }
    }

private:
    bool canAfford(UnitType unit)
{ /* Check if resources are sufficient */ }
    void consumeResources(UnitType unit)
{ /* Deduct resources */ }
```

```
    void produceUnit(UnitType unit)
{ /* Create unit */ }
};
```

This code structure enables basic resource management and unit production based on available resources.

Adaptive AI: Learning from Player Behavior

Adaptive AI, also known as dynamic difficulty adjustment, allows the game AI to respond to the player's tactics and change strategies accordingly. This adaptability makes RTS AI more challenging and realistic, as it keeps the player engaged and prevents repetitive gameplay.

Techniques for Adaptive AI

1. **Pattern Recognition**: AI identifies patterns in the player's behavior (e.g., frequent use of specific units) and adjusts its strategy to counter those tactics.
2. **Difficulty Scaling**: Based on the player's skill level or success rate, AI can dynamically adjust its own difficulty by increasing resources, enhancing unit production rates, or applying more advanced tactics.
3. **Counter Strategies**: If the player frequently attacks with air units, for example, the AI will allocate more resources to anti-air defenses.
4. **Predictive Modeling**: Advanced AI can use predictive algorithms to anticipate the player's moves, giving it an advantage in forming counterattacks or defensive responses.

Example Adaptive Behavior: Countering Unit Types

Suppose the player often deploys a large number of heavy infantry. The AI may recognize this pattern and begin investing more heavily in artillery or anti-infantry units, creating a more challenging encounter for the player. Adaptive responses can also occur at the strategic level, such as increasing defenses or upgrading technologies that counter specific player tendencies.

Micro-Management for Enhanced Control

Micro-management refers to the fine-grained control of individual units, which is crucial in high-stakes battles or when managing special unit abilities. Effective micro-management enables AI to dodge attacks, maximize unit positioning, and use abilities efficiently.

1. **Dodging and Evading**: AI-controlled units dodge incoming attacks to minimize damage.
2. **Ability Usage**: AI strategically deploys special abilities at optimal moments, such as healing units in critical health or using crowd control abilities on groups of enemy units.
3. **Targeted Attacks**: AI prioritizes high-value targets and vulnerable units, focusing fire on key players to maximize its advantage.

Micro-management contributes to the overall depth of RTS AI, especially when coupled with adaptive strategies and efficient resource management.

RTS games require a sophisticated AI system that can manage resources, execute strategic and tactical decisions, and adapt to the player's evolving tactics. By combining these elements, RTS AI can provide players with challenging and dynamic gameplay that adapts to their strategies. This chapter covered the core aspects of decision-making and resource management for RTS AI, setting the foundation for creating intelligent, responsive, and competitive opponents. In the next section, we'll explore further advanced techniques, including real-time adaptation, advanced decision trees, and machine learning applications in game AI.

Optimizing AI for Performance: Multithreading and Efficient Data Structures

In games, especially real-time strategy (RTS) and other simulation-heavy genres, efficient AI performance is critical to maintain smooth gameplay without bottlenecks. Complex decision-making, pathfinding, and real-time event handling can place a heavy load on the CPU. To meet these demands, AI optimization relies on multithreading and the use of efficient data structures. These approaches enable the AI to perform numerous calculations simultaneously, distribute workloads, and retrieve data faster, enhancing both performance and responsiveness.

This section explores the importance of multithreading for concurrent AI tasks, introduces common concurrency patterns, and delves into data structures that allow for faster computation and memory management.

Multithreading for Concurrent AI Tasks

Multithreading allows the AI to distribute its workload across multiple CPU cores, which is essential for real-time games where the AI must make fast decisions without interrupting the main game loop. By breaking down AI tasks into threads, game performance can remain consistent, even under high computational load.

Key Components for Multithreading AI:

1. **Threading Model**: Choose a threading model that balances ease of implementation and performance requirements. Common models include task-based threading, thread pools, and worker threads.

2. **Concurrency Patterns**: Implement concurrency patterns such as the Producer-Consumer pattern, where one thread generates tasks (e.g., pathfinding) and another thread processes them. This approach reduces bottlenecks in task-intensive AI.

3. **Thread Synchronization**: Use synchronization mechanisms like mutexes and semaphores to manage data shared across threads. Ensuring thread-safe data access is crucial to avoid race conditions and maintain accurate AI responses.

Example: Multithreaded Pathfinding

Pathfinding can be computationally expensive, especially when multiple units navigate the map simultaneously. By multithreading pathfinding calculations, the AI can handle numerous pathfinding requests in parallel.

```cpp
#include <thread>
#include <mutex>
#include <queue>

std::queue<PathRequest> pathRequests;
std::mutex queueMutex;

void pathfindingWorker() {
    while (true) {
        std::unique_lock<std::mutex> lock(queueMutex);
        if (!pathRequests.empty()) {
            PathRequest request = pathRequests.front();
            pathRequests.pop();
            lock.unlock();

            // Process pathfinding request
            calculatePath(request.start, request.end);
        } else {
            lock.unlock();
            std::this_thread::sleep_for
(std::chrono::milliseconds(10));
        }
    }
}

void submitPathRequest(const PathRequest& request) {
    std::lock_guard<std::mutex> lock(queueMutex);
    pathRequests.push(request);
}
```

In this example, a dedicated pathfinding thread continually checks a queue for path requests, calculates paths independently, and reduces the workload on the main game loop.

Common Concurrency Patterns in AI

Concurrency patterns help manage multiple tasks by defining clear workflows that prevent conflicts and optimize efficiency. Here are several patterns frequently applied in AI for games:

1. **Producer-Consumer Pattern**: Separates task generation (producer) from task execution (consumer), ideal for handling multiple simultaneous requests like pathfinding or collision checks.
2. **Thread Pool**: A pool of reusable threads executes multiple tasks, avoiding the overhead of creating and destroying threads repeatedly. Commonly used for frequent AI calculations, such as steering behaviors or target selection.
3. **Fork-Join Pattern**: Splits large tasks into smaller sub-tasks, processes them in parallel, and then combines the results. Useful for pathfinding on large maps where paths can be split into segments.
4. **Double Buffering**: Maintains two sets of data structures, so one is always available to the AI while the other updates, minimizing waiting time and data conflicts.

Using these patterns enables the AI to work efficiently within the game's performance constraints.

Data Structures for Fast Access and Minimal Memory Overhead

Choosing the right data structures can have a profound impact on AI performance. By using structures optimized for fast access and minimal memory overhead, AI systems can quickly retrieve and manipulate data, making calculations more efficient.

Optimized Data Structures in Game AI:

1. **Spatial Partitioning**: Structures like quadtrees and grids divide space into sections, allowing the AI to efficiently locate objects and units within a region. This setup is especially useful for collision detection and range queries.
2. **Hash Maps**: Hash maps enable fast data retrieval based on keys, reducing the time spent on searching for specific game entities or states. They're useful in AI for caching frequently accessed data.
3. **Priority Queues**: Used in pathfinding algorithms like A*, priority

queues ensure that AI considers the most relevant nodes first, optimizing processing order and pathfinding speed.

4. **Graphs and Adjacency Lists**: Representing maps and movement networks as graphs allows AI to perform pathfinding and connectivity checks efficiently. Adjacency lists are especially memory-efficient for large maps.

5. **Octrees**: For 3D games, octrees are an advanced version of quadtrees, breaking space into cubes instead of squares. They allow efficient handling of spatial data in 3D environments for tasks like raycasting and collision detection.

Example: Using Spatial Partitioning for Efficient Collision Checks

By organizing objects within a grid or quadtree, the AI can quickly determine which objects are near each other, reducing the number of collision checks required.

```cpp
class Quadtree {
    Rect boundary;
    std::vector<Entity*> entities;
    Quadtree* children[4] =
{nullptr, nullptr, nullptr, nullptr};

public:
    void insert(Entity* entity) {
        if (!boundary.contains(entity->position)) return;

        if (entities.size()
< MAX_ENTITIES && !children[0]) {
            entities.push_back(entity);
        } else {
            if (!children[0]) subdivide();
            for (int i = 0; i < 4; i++)
  children[i]->insert(entity);
        }
```

```
    }

    void subdivide() {
        // Split the region into four quadrants
    }
};
```

This structure enables the game to handle thousands of entities in complex scenes without performance drops.

Memory Management Techniques for Performance

Memory management is a significant concern in performance optimization, particularly in large-scale games. Inefficient memory handling can lead to fragmentation, slowdowns, and crashes. Here are a few best practices:

1. **Object Pooling**: Reuses objects rather than creating and destroying them repeatedly, which conserves memory and minimizes allocation overhead.
2. **Memory Alignment**: Ensures that data is stored at memory addresses that optimize access speed, which can be critical in CPU-bound AI tasks.
3. **Caching Frequently Accessed Data**: Caching allows the AI to store commonly accessed data in memory, reducing the need to recompute or reload data.
4. **Efficient Data Layout**: Structures of Arrays (SoA) can often outperform Arrays of Structures (AoS) for AI because SoA improves cache utilization, allowing faster access to specific properties.

Optimizing AI for performance requires a combination of multithreading and careful data structure selection. By distributing tasks across multiple threads, the AI can handle complex tasks concurrently, maintaining a smooth and responsive gaming experience. Meanwhile, choosing efficient data structures enhances data access speed and memory management, reducing the risk of performance bottlenecks. As AI becomes increasingly complex in modern games, employing these optimization techniques becomes essential to achieving high-performance AI capable of handling real-time, adaptive decision-making at scale.

Audio Integration and Management

Audio Basics: Sound Effects, Music, and Audio Buffers
Audio is a critical element in game development, shaping player experience through immersive soundscapes, enhancing the atmosphere, and providing cues that improve gameplay. Effective audio design requires an understanding of how sounds are produced, managed, and optimized for real-time playback in games. This section delves into the basics of game audio, covering sound effects, background music, and the technicalities of handling audio buffers.

Understanding the Components of Game Audio

Game audio can generally be divided into three main types:

1. **Sound Effects (SFX)**: Short, event-triggered sounds like footsteps, gunshots, or explosions. These sounds are usually loaded into memory for quick access and can be manipulated based on game context.
2. **Background Music**: Looped or continuous tracks that set the tone of a game level or scene. Music often uses longer, streamed audio files that play in the background without the need for complex event-based manipulation.
3. **Voice Acting (optional)**: Spoken lines or character dialogue that require specific playback timing, and often necessitate high-fidelity sound. This can include environmental cues, narration, or character-driven dialogue.

Sound effects and music are typically the primary focus in most games, as they influence a player's perception, emotional engagement, and immersion in the game world.

Sound Effects (SFX) in Games

Sound effects add depth to in-game interactions, helping players perceive and interpret gameplay cues more intuitively. Effective use of sound effects involves understanding their timing, spatial location, and intensity.

1. **Event-Driven Playback**: Game engines trigger sound effects based on in-game events. For example, a footstep sound is triggered each time a player's character takes a step.

2. **Spatial Audio**: Many games place sound effects spatially within the game's 3D environment, allowing players to sense direction and distance based on sound alone. Techniques like stereo panning and 3D positional audio are used to make sounds appear as though they're coming from specific directions.

3. **Dynamic Sound Effects**: Game events can adjust the properties of sound effects to match the context. For example, a footstep sound may vary in volume or pitch depending on the character's speed, surface type, or intensity of the action.

Background Music and Game Atmosphere

Background music creates emotional resonance in games and is instrumental in setting the mood. Whether it's a tense orchestral track in a survival horror game or a relaxing melody in a simulation, the role of music is essential in reinforcing the intended emotional response.

1. **Looping Music**: Many games use looping tracks for background music, especially for long scenes or open-world environments. Loops are created to blend seamlessly, maintaining immersion without abrupt stops or transitions.

2. **Dynamic Music Systems**: Advanced games use adaptive music that shifts based on game events. For example, background music might

become faster or more intense during combat sequences and slow down during exploration.

3. **Memory Management**: Music files are often larger than sound effects and are commonly streamed from disk rather than preloaded into memory to avoid performance bottlenecks.

Audio Buffers: Essential Components in Game Sound Processing

Audio buffers are crucial for audio playback in games, holding segments of audio data temporarily as it moves from storage to output devices. Understanding how to work with audio buffers is essential for smooth and efficient sound integration.

1. **Definition and Purpose**: An audio buffer is a small, fixed-size segment of memory that holds audio data during playback. Buffers ensure that sound plays continuously, without interruptions, by preloading data in chunks before it's needed.

2. **Buffer Management**: Efficient buffer management is critical for preventing audio dropouts or delays. Buffers need to be replenished (filled with audio data) before they run out, typically using a streaming or double-buffering approach.

3. **Latency and Performance**: Buffer size can affect latency—larger buffers reduce the likelihood of audio dropouts but may introduce delay. Smaller buffers decrease latency but require frequent refilling, which can be resource-intensive.

4. **Streaming Audio**: Streaming allows large audio files to be played back in real-time without consuming large amounts of memory. Music and ambient soundtracks are commonly streamed to avoid loading them into memory all at once.

Example: Loading and Playing Sound with SDL

Using libraries like SDL, developers can manage audio by loading sounds into buffers and controlling playback with the SDL mixer. Here's a brief example of loading and playing a sound effect:

```cpp
#include <SDL2/SDL.h>
#include <SDL2/SDL_mixer.h>

void playSoundEffect(const char* filePath) {
    if (SDL_Init(SDL_INIT_AUDIO) < 0) return;
    if (Mix_OpenAudio(44100, MIX_DEFAULT_FORMAT, 2, 2048) < 0)
    return;

    Mix_Chunk* soundEffect = Mix_LoadWAV(filePath);
    if (soundEffect != nullptr) {
        Mix_PlayChannel(-1, soundEffect, 0);
    }
    Mix_FreeChunk(soundEffect);
    Mix_CloseAudio();
    SDL_Quit();
}
```

In this example, SDL_Init and Mix_OpenAudio initialize SDL's audio system. A sound effect is loaded from a file and stored in memory, ready for playback. Mix_PlayChannel plays the sound, allowing control over channels and repeating options.

Sound File Formats and Compression

Choosing the correct audio file format impacts quality, performance, and memory usage. Different formats serve distinct purposes in game audio:

1. **WAV (Waveform Audio File)**: Uncompressed, high-quality audio format, commonly used for short sound effects due to its minimal processing requirements.
2. **MP3 (MPEG Audio Layer III)**: Compressed, lossy format suitable for background music, where storage and memory efficiency are prioritized over sound quality.
3. **OGG Vorbis**: Open-source, compressed format similar to MP3 but

offering slightly better quality at comparable file sizes. Widely used for background music in games.

In game development, it's common to balance file size with quality by choosing compressed formats for longer audio (like music) and uncompressed formats for shorter, critical sounds (like UI sounds or character actions).

Integrating Audio Libraries and APIs

Game engines often provide built-in audio support, but some projects use standalone libraries for more flexibility. Here are a few widely used audio libraries and APIs in game development:

1. **OpenAL**: An open-source, cross-platform audio API often used for 3D audio. OpenAL supports spatial audio and effects, making it a good choice for realistic soundscapes.
2. **FMOD**: A robust audio engine with extensive tools for audio mixing, DSP effects, and spatial audio. FMOD is widely used in both AAA and indie games due to its ease of integration and versatility.
3. **SDL Mixer**: A simple library built on top of SDL for handling sound effects and music. SDL Mixer supports WAV, MP3, and OGG formats, and is ideal for simpler 2D games or applications where full audio control isn't required.

Optimizing Audio Performance and Memory Usage

For real-time audio processing, maintaining performance is essential. Several strategies can help balance audio quality and processing power requirements:

1. **Sample Rate Reduction**: Lowering the sample rate reduces memory usage and processing demands. Background audio can often be set at a lower sample rate without noticeable quality loss.
2. **Asset Compression**: Compressing audio assets (e.g., using OGG instead

of WAV) minimizes memory usage, especially for background tracks.

3. **Audio Culling**: Dynamic audio culling reduces active sounds based on priority and distance. For example, sounds outside the player's hearing range or non-critical background sounds can be paused to save processing power.

Understanding and applying core audio concepts is essential for creating an engaging game environment. By integrating sound effects, music, and managing audio buffers effectively, you can enhance the player's experience and ensure smooth, immersive gameplay. Whether it's the subtle background ambiance or the satisfying crunch of an in-game action, well-crafted audio brings a game to life, making it memorable and impactful. As development progresses, optimizing and balancing audio quality with performance becomes crucial, ensuring that sound design enhances the overall game experience without straining system resources.

Adding Sound with OpenAL and SDL_Mixer

Integrating sound in games is made more flexible and powerful through libraries like OpenAL and SDL_Mixer, each providing a variety of audio functionalities. OpenAL is highly effective for 3D spatial audio and is favored for games that require complex soundscapes. SDL_Mixer, on the other hand, is ideal for simpler 2D games or projects with more basic audio needs, offering straightforward playback for music and sound effects. Here's a deep dive into utilizing both libraries to handle audio in game development, from setup to playback.

OpenAL: Basics and Usage

OpenAL (Open Audio Library) is an open-source API designed for cross-platform 3D audio. It's particularly well-suited for creating immersive audio environments with realistic spatial effects, allowing sounds to appear from specific locations in the game's 3D space.

Setting Up OpenAL

1. **Install OpenAL**: On Windows, the OpenAL installer is typically required, while on Linux/macOS, OpenAL is usually available through package managers. The OpenAL SDK contains libraries, headers, and sample code.
2. **Linking OpenAL**: In your project settings, link OpenAL32.lib (Windows) or libopenal.a (Linux/macOS), and include AL/al.h and AL/alc.h headers in your code.

Playing Sound with OpenAL

OpenAL's sound system is built around three core components: **buffers**, **sources**, and **listeners**.

1. **Buffers**: Store the sound data in memory, loaded from audio files (usually in .wav format).
2. **Sources**: Play sounds by pulling data from buffers. Sources can be positioned in 3D space.
3. **Listeners**: Represent the player's position and orientation in the game, affecting how sounds are heard.

Example: Loading and Playing Sound in OpenAL

```cpp
cpp

#include <AL/al.h>
#include <AL/alc.h>
#include <iostream>

void playSound(const char* filename) {
    ALCdevice* device = alcOpenDevice(nullptr);  // Open the
    default device
    ALCcontext* context = alcCreateContext(device, nullptr);
    alcMakeContextCurrent(context);

    ALuint buffer, source;
```

```
alGenBuffers(1, &buffer);
alGenSources(1, &source);

// Load your audio data into the buffer (typically .wav data)
// Set the buffer data using alBufferData() after loading
alSourcei(source, AL_BUFFER, buffer);
alSourcePlay(source);

// Clean up
alDeleteSources(1, &source);
alDeleteBuffers(1, &buffer);
alcMakeContextCurrent(nullptr);
alcDestroyContext(context);
alcCloseDevice(device);
}
```

In this example, an **OpenAL context** is created for audio playback. The sound buffer is linked to the source, and alSourcePlay initiates the playback. Once completed, resources are cleaned up to avoid memory leaks.

Adding 3D Spatial Effects

OpenAL can position audio sources in 3D space, making it ideal for scenarios where sounds need to come from specific directions:

```cpp
cpp

alSource3f(source, AL_POSITION, x, y, z);   // Sets position in 3D
space
alListener3f(AL_POSITION, playerX, playerY, playerZ);   // Sets
listener position
```

This approach makes OpenAL ideal for first-person or third-person games, where accurate spatial sound improves immersion.

SDL_Mixer: Simple Audio Integration for 2D Games

SDL_Mixer is an audio library that works on top of SDL, offering straight-forward functionalities for handling sound effects and music. SDL_Mixer supports popular formats like WAV, MP3, and OGG and simplifies audio handling with easy-to-use functions for loading, playing, and controlling audio assets.

Setting Up SDL_Mixer

To use SDL_Mixer, install it using package managers or build it from source. Link SDL_mixer.h in your project, and ensure that SDL2_mixer.lib or the equivalent library is included in the linker settings.

Playing Sound Effects and Music

SDL_Mixer loads sound effects as Mix_Chunk objects and music as Mix_Music. Here's how to set up and play both sound types:

1. **Initialize SDL_Mixer**: Call Mix_OpenAudio() to initialize SDL_Mixer with specified frequency and format settings.
2. **Load and Play Audio**:

- Use Mix_LoadWAV() for short sounds (sound effects).
- Use Mix_LoadMUS() for longer music files.

Example: Loading and Playing a Sound Effect with SDL_Mixer

```cpp
cpp

#include <SDL2/SDL.h>
#include <SDL2/SDL_mixer.h>
#include <iostream>

void playSoundEffect(const char* filePath) {
    if (Mix_OpenAudio(44100, MIX_DEFAULT_FORMAT, 2, 2048) < 0)
        return;

    Mix_Chunk* soundEffect = Mix_LoadWAV(filePath);
    if (soundEffect != nullptr) {
        Mix_PlayChannel(-1, soundEffect, 0);
    }
```

```cpp
    Mix_FreeChunk(soundEffect);
    Mix_CloseAudio();
}
```

Here, Mix_OpenAudio initializes the audio device, and Mix_LoadWAV loads a .wav file. Mix_PlayChannel plays the sound on a free channel, allowing for multiple sounds to play simultaneously. Finally, Mix_FreeChunk frees the sound's memory.

Example: Playing Background Music with SDL_Mixer

cpp

```cpp
#include <SDL2/SDL_mixer.h>

void playBackgroundMusic(const char* musicPath) {
    if (Mix_OpenAudio(44100, MIX_DEFAULT_FORMAT, 2, 2048) < 0)
        return;

    Mix_Music* music = Mix_LoadMUS(musicPath);
    if (music != nullptr) {
        Mix_PlayMusic(music, -1);  // -1 to loop indefinitely
    }

    // Free resources when done
    Mix_FreeMusic(music);
    Mix_CloseAudio();
}
```

This example plays music on a loop until manually stopped. Music is loaded via Mix_LoadMUS and played with Mix_PlayMusic.

Choosing Between OpenAL and SDL_Mixer

- **Use OpenAL** when developing 3D games that require immersive spatial audio. OpenAL excels in positioning sounds in 3D, supporting complex environments like open-world games or simulations.
- **Use SDL_Mixer** for simpler 2D games, where audio needs are basic, and

3D spatialization isn't required. SDL_Mixer is lightweight and offers rapid setup and deployment for straightforward sound playback.

Integrating sound effectively involves choosing the right library and understanding the specific needs of your game. OpenAL and SDL_Mixer each offer unique advantages; mastering both provides flexibility to develop audio-rich environments for a wide range of gaming experiences. With knowledge of loading, playing, and optimizing sound, you can craft an immersive audio experience tailored to your game's style and scope.

3D Positional Audio: Adding Depth to Game Sounds

In modern game development, the auditory experience significantly enhances immersion and realism. 3D positional audio is a crucial component that allows players to perceive sound not just as an abstract element but as a spatial cue that interacts with the game world. This section will explore the principles of 3D audio, how to implement it using OpenAL and SDL_Mixer, and its importance in gameplay dynamics.

Understanding 3D Positional Audio

3D positional audio refers to the technique of simulating sound in a three-dimensional space, allowing players to hear sounds as if they are coming from specific locations within the game environment. This enhances realism by mimicking how sound travels and is perceived in real life, considering factors like distance, direction, and obstacles.

Key aspects of 3D audio include:

1. **Sound Positioning**: The ability to place sounds at specific coordinates in the game world, allowing players to perceive where the sound originates.

2. **Distance Attenuation**: Sounds diminish in volume and quality as they

move farther away from the listener, simulating real-world physics.

3. **Doppler Effect**: This effect alters the perceived frequency of a sound based on the relative motion of the source and listener, which is particularly useful in racing or action games.

Implementing 3D Positional Audio with OpenAL

OpenAL is designed with 3D audio in mind. Here's how to effectively implement 3D positional audio in your game using OpenAL:

Set Up Audio Environment: Initialize OpenAL, create buffers and sources, and set the listener's position and orientation.

cpp

```
ALCdevice* device = alcOpenDevice(nullptr);
ALCcontext* context = alcCreateContext(device, nullptr);
alcMakeContextCurrent(context);
```

Create and Load Sound Buffers: Load your sound files into buffers and generate sources for playback.

cpp

```
ALuint buffer;
alGenBuffers(1, &buffer);
// Load audio data into the buffer (e.g., from a WAV file)
// alBufferData(buffer, AL_FORMAT_MONO16, audioData, dataSize,
frequency);
```

Positioning the Listener: Set the listener's position and orientation to match the player's position in the game.

cpp

```
ALfloat listenerPos[] = { playerX, playerY, playerZ };
ALfloat listenerOri[] = { 0.0f, 0.0f, -1.0f, 0.0f, 1.0f, 0.0f };
```

```
// Forward and Up vectors
alListenerfv(AL_POSITION, listenerPos);
alListenerfv(AL_ORIENTATION, listenerOri);
```

Positioning Sound Sources: Each sound source can be positioned in the 3D space relative to the listener.

cpp

```
ALuint source;
alGenSources(1, &source);
alSourcei(source, AL_BUFFER, buffer);
alSource3f(source, AL_POSITION, soundX, soundY, soundZ);
```

Playing Sounds: When the game is played, sounds will automatically adjust in volume and spatialization based on their distance from the listener.

cpp

```
alSourcePlay(source);
```

Example: 3D Positional Sound Implementation

Consider a scenario in a first-person shooter (FPS) game where players can hear footsteps or gunfire coming from different directions. Using OpenAL, the following implementation would provide realistic audio cues:

cpp

```
// Update listener position based on player's current location
ALfloat playerPosition[] = { playerX, playerY, playerZ };
alListenerfv(AL_POSITION, playerPosition);

// Load footstep sound
ALuint footstepBuffer;
alGenBuffers(1, &footstepBuffer);
```

```
// Load footstep sound data
// alBufferData(footstepBuffer, AL_FORMAT_MONO16, footstepData,
footstepDataSize, footstepFrequency);

// Create a source for footstep sound
ALuint footstepSource;
alGenSources(1, &footstepSource);
alSourcei(footstepSource, AL_BUFFER, footstepBuffer);

// Set source position (where the sound comes from)
alSource3f(footstepSource, enemyX, enemyY, enemyZ);

// Play the footstep sound when an enemy moves
alSourcePlay(footstepSource);
```

In this code, the listener's position is updated to match the player's coordinates, allowing for dynamic sound positioning based on movement.

Implementing 3D Positional Audio with SDL_Mixer

SDL_Mixer, while primarily focused on 2D audio, can still simulate basic 3D audio effects. However, its 3D audio capabilities are limited compared to OpenAL. To implement a simple 3D audio effect with SDL_Mixer, you will need to manually adjust the volume based on distance from the listener.

Initialize SDL and SDL_Mixer:

cpp

```
if (Mix_OpenAudio(44100, MIX_DEFAULT_FORMAT, 2, 2048) < 0) {
    // Handle error
}
```

Load Sounds:

cpp

```
Mix_Chunk* soundEffect = Mix_LoadWAV("sound.wav");
```

Calculate Volume Based on Distance:

You can simulate the distance effect by modifying the volume of the sound based on its distance from the listener.

cpp

```
void playSoundAtPosition(Mix_Chunk* soundEffect, float soundX,
float soundY, float listenerX, float listenerY) {
    float distance = sqrt(pow(soundX - listenerX, 2) + pow(soundY
    - listenerY, 2));
    int volume = std::max(0, 128 - static_cast<int>(distance)); //
    Volume range: 0 to 128
    Mix_VolumeChunk(soundEffect, volume);
    Mix_PlayChannel(-1, soundEffect, 0);
}
```

In this implementation, the volume of the sound effect decreases as the distance from the listener increases, creating a basic sense of 3D audio.

Benefits of 3D Positional Audio

1. **Enhanced Immersion**: Players experience a more engaging environment, feeling as though they are part of the game world rather than just observers.
2. **Improved Gameplay Mechanics**: 3D audio can provide critical gameplay feedback, such as alerts to nearby enemies or environmental cues (e.g., distant explosions).
3. **Realistic Sound Experience**: Mimicking real-world sound propagation creates a more believable atmosphere, increasing player satisfaction.

Implementing 3D positional audio in games significantly enriches the auditory experience. Whether through OpenAL's sophisticated spatialization capabilities or simpler approaches using SDL_Mixer, adding depth to game sounds can transform how players interact with and perceive your game. By accurately placing audio in a 3D space, you can create an immersive experience that draws players deeper into the game world, enhancing engagement and enjoyment. As you develop your game, consider how sound can not only complement visuals but also serve as a vital gameplay mechanic, guiding players through their adventures.

Managing Audio Assets and Optimizing for Performance

In game development, managing audio assets effectively and optimizing their performance are crucial for delivering a seamless and immersive player experience. Proper audio management can significantly enhance the overall quality of the game while minimizing memory usage and processing overhead. This section delves into best practices for organizing, loading, and optimizing audio assets, as well as techniques to ensure efficient audio performance.

Organizing Audio Assets

A well-structured organization of audio assets not only simplifies the development process but also ensures that your game can handle audio effectively during runtime. Here are some strategies to consider:

Asset Directory Structure: Create a clear directory structure for your audio assets. A typical organization might include:

```bash
/audio
    /sfx            // Sound effects
        /footsteps
        /explosions
        /weapons
    /music          // Background music
    /dialogues      // Voiceovers and dialogues
```

Consistent Naming Conventions: Use consistent and descriptive naming for your audio files. This practice makes it easier to identify and reference audio assets in the code. For example, name sound effects with prefixes indicating their type:

- sfx_footstep_grass.wav
- sfx_explosion_large.wav
- music_battle_theme.mp3

Metadata Files: Consider using metadata files to describe audio assets, such as duration, volume levels, and looping requirements. This information can be loaded at runtime to optimize audio playback.

Loading and Unloading Audio Assets

Efficiently loading and unloading audio assets is essential for maintaining performance, especially in resource-constrained environments. Here are some best practices:

1. **Preload Critical Assets**: Load essential audio assets at the start of the game or level to minimize loading times during gameplay. This approach is particularly useful for background music or key sound effects that are frequently used.
2. **Load on Demand**: For less critical audio assets, consider loading them

on demand when needed. For example, load sound effects for specific enemy types only when the player encounters them for the first time.

3. **Unloading Unused Assets**: Release memory by unloading audio assets that are no longer needed. This practice is particularly important in games with multiple levels or environments. Use appropriate functions provided by your audio library, such as Mix_FreeChunk in SDL_Mixer.

4. **Streaming Audio**: For large audio files, such as background music or ambient sounds, consider streaming them instead of loading them entirely into memory. Streaming allows you to play audio in segments, reducing memory usage. SDL_mixer supports streaming through the Mix_LoadMUS function.

Optimizing Audio Performance

To ensure that audio playback does not hinder the game's performance, implement the following optimization strategies:

1. **Audio Compression**: Use compressed audio formats (e.g., MP3, Ogg Vorbis) for background music and large sound effects. Compression reduces file sizes and memory usage, although you should balance this with the quality requirements of your game.

2. **Limit Concurrent Sounds**: Manage the number of simultaneous sounds that can be played at once. Limiting concurrent sound effects can prevent audio overload and reduce CPU usage. For example, you can allow a maximum of 16 simultaneous sound effects while managing the playback of others using a queue system.

3. **Volume Control and Mixing**: Implement dynamic volume control and mixing to balance different audio sources. This practice allows you to reduce the volume of background music when sound effects are played, ensuring that important audio cues are not drowned out.

4. **Use Audio Pools**: For frequently used sound effects, implement an audio pool where a set number of audio sources are pre-created and reused. This approach avoids the overhead of creating and destroying audio sources repeatedly, enhancing performance.

```cpp
const int POOL_SIZE = 10;
ALuint soundPool[POOL_SIZE];
int nextSourceIndex = 0;

// Initialize audio sources in the pool
for (int i = 0; i < POOL_SIZE; i++) {
    alGenSources(1, &soundPool[i]);
}

// Function to play sound from pool
void playFromPool(ALuint buffer) {
    alSourcei(soundPool[nextSourceIndex], AL_BUFFER, buffer);
    alSourcePlay(soundPool[nextSourceIndex]);
    nextSourceIndex = (nextSourceIndex + 1) % POOL_SIZE; // Loop
    back to the start
}
```

Profiling and Monitoring: Regularly profile your game's audio performance using profiling tools. Monitor the CPU and memory usage of audio processing to identify potential bottlenecks. Adjust the loading strategy, asset management, and playback methods based on profiling results.

Managing audio assets and optimizing their performance is vital in creating a high-quality gaming experience. By organizing audio files efficiently, implementing effective loading strategies, and optimizing playback performance, developers can ensure that audio contributes positively to gameplay without compromising performance. Prioritizing audio management not only enhances player immersion but also creates a smoother and more enjoyable gaming experience overall. As you refine your game's audio system, keep in mind the delicate balance between quality, performance, and player engagement.

Real-Time Audio Effects: Dynamic Sound Manipulation

In modern game development, creating an immersive audio experience goes beyond simply playing sound files; it requires dynamic sound manipulation and real-time audio effects. This allows developers to enhance gameplay through adaptive soundscapes that respond to player actions and environmental changes. In this section, we will explore various real-time audio effects, their implementation, and best practices for using them effectively in games.

Understanding Real-Time Audio Effects

Real-time audio effects involve altering audio signals as they are played back, allowing for interactive sound design that can change in response to gameplay conditions. This dynamic manipulation can include effects such as reverb, echo, pitch shifting, and audio filtering, which can significantly enhance the atmosphere and emotional impact of a game.

Key Types of Real-Time Audio Effects:

1. **Reverb**: Simulates the natural reflections of sound in an environment, creating a sense of space. Different reverb settings can be applied based on the game's environment, such as a small room versus an open field.
2. **Echo**: Delays the audio signal, creating repetitions of sound that can add depth and a sense of distance. This effect is often used in larger spaces to simulate sound bouncing off distant surfaces.
3. **Pitch Shifting**: Alters the frequency of the audio signal, changing its pitch without affecting its speed. This can be used to create unique sound effects or to adapt audio cues based on in-game events.
4. **Filters**: Modify the frequency response of audio signals, allowing for the enhancement or attenuation of certain frequencies. Common filters include high-pass, low-pass, and band-pass filters, which can be used to simulate various environments or effects.

Implementing Real-Time Audio Effects

To implement real-time audio effects, developers can use audio libraries that support DSP (Digital Signal Processing) capabilities. Two popular libraries for this purpose are **OpenAL** and **FMOD**. Below are examples of how to implement common audio effects using these libraries.

1. Reverb with OpenAL:

OpenAL provides a simple way to apply reverb effects using environmental parameters. Here's how to set up a basic reverb effect:

cpp

```
// Enable EAX (Environmental Audio Extensions) effects
ALCdevice* device = alcOpenDevice(NULL);
ALCcontext* context = alcCreateContext(device, NULL);
alcMakeContextCurrent(context);

// Set up reverb properties
ALfloat reverb_params[] = {
    AL_EAXREVERB_DENSITY, 0.5f,
    AL_EAXREVERB_DIFFUSION, 0.5f,
    AL_EAXREVERB_GAIN, 0.5f,
    AL_EAXREVERB_GAINHF, -0.5f,
    AL_EAXREVERB_DECAY_TIME, 1.5f,
    AL_EAXREVERB_DECAY_HFRATIO, 0.5f,
    AL_EAXREVERB_REFLECTIONS_GAIN, 0.5f,
    AL_EAXREVERB_REFLECTIONS_DELAY, 0.01f,
    AL_EAXREVERB_LATE_REVERB_GAIN, 0.5f,
    AL_EAXREVERB_LATE_REVERB_DELAY, 0.1f,
    AL_EAXREVERB_AIR_ABSORPTION_GAINHF, 0.5f,
    AL_EAXREVERB_FLAGS, AL_TRUE
};

// Apply reverb effect
alEAXSetProperties(AL_EFFECT_EAXREVERB, reverb_params);
```

2. Echo Effect with FMOD:

FMOD is a versatile audio library that provides an easy-to-use API for applying various audio effects. Here's an example of adding an echo effect to a sound:

188

```cpp
FMOD::System* system;
FMOD::Sound* sound;
FMOD::Channel* channel;

// Create a system and load a sound
FMOD::System_Create(&system);
system->init(512, FMOD_INIT_NORMAL, 0);
system->createSound("sound.wav", FMOD_DEFAULT, 0, &sound);

// Create an echo effect
FMOD::DSP* echoDSP;
system->createDSPByType(FMOD_DSP_TYPE_ECHO, &echoDSP);
echoDSP->setParameterFloat(FMOD_DSP_ECHO_DELAY, 500.0f); // Delay
in milliseconds
echoDSP->setParameterFloat(FMOD_DSP_ECHO_FEEDBACK, 0.5f); //
Feedback level

// Add the effect to the sound channel
channel->addDSP(0, echoDSP);
channel->setVolume(1.0f); // Set volume to full
sound->setMode(FMOD_LOOP_NORMAL); // Loop the sound
channel->setPaused(false); // Start playing the sound
```

Best Practices for Dynamic Sound Manipulation

To effectively utilize real-time audio effects in your game, consider the following best practices:

1. **Contextual Audio Effects**: Apply audio effects based on the game context. For example, increase reverb in enclosed spaces and decrease it in open areas. This practice enhances immersion and provides auditory feedback to the player.

2. **Performance Considerations**: Real-time audio effects can be CPU-intensive. Profile your audio performance regularly to ensure that adding effects does not negatively impact gameplay. Consider using

simpler effects or reducing the number of concurrent effects when performance issues arise.

3. **Dynamic Adjustment**: Allow for dynamic adjustments of audio effects based on gameplay events. For instance, if a player enters a cave, you might increase the reverb intensity. Such changes create a more engaging audio landscape.

4. **Testing in Different Environments**: Always test your audio effects in various environments to ensure that they provide the desired impact without causing distortion or overwhelming other sounds. Make adjustments as necessary based on player feedback.

5. **Balancing Effects**: Carefully balance the volume and intensity of audio effects with other audio elements in the game. Ensuring that sound effects complement music and dialogue without overpowering them is essential for a cohesive audio experience.

Dynamic sound manipulation through real-time audio effects is a powerful tool in game development. By applying various effects such as reverb, echo, and filtering, developers can create a rich and immersive auditory experience that enhances gameplay. Implementing these effects requires a sound understanding of audio libraries and performance considerations, but the result can significantly elevate the overall quality of a game. As players become increasingly attuned to audio nuances, effectively utilizing dynamic sound manipulation will become ever more essential in creating engaging and memorable gaming experiences.

Advanced Memory Management for Games

U nderstanding Memory Allocation Patterns in Games
Effective memory management is a cornerstone of high-performance game development. As games become more complex, the way memory is allocated, used, and deallocated can significantly impact performance, stability, and overall user experience. Understanding various memory allocation patterns is essential for developers looking to optimize their games and manage resources efficiently. This chapter will delve into different memory allocation patterns used in game development, exploring their benefits, drawbacks, and practical applications.

The Importance of Memory Management in Game Development

In game development, memory management refers to the process of allocating and deallocating memory in an efficient manner. Poor memory management can lead to various issues, including:

- **Memory Leaks**: Unused memory that is not released can accumulate over time, eventually leading to crashes or slowdowns.
- **Fragmentation**: Over time, memory can become fragmented, leading to inefficient use of resources and potential performance degradation.
- **Slow Performance**: Inefficient memory allocation patterns can lead to performance bottlenecks, especially in real-time applications where every millisecond counts.
- **Increased Load Times**: If memory is not managed correctly, it can slow

down the loading of assets, leading to a negative user experience.

Understanding how to effectively manage memory is essential for maintaining performance and delivering a seamless gaming experience.

Memory Allocation Patterns

Game developers typically employ several common memory allocation patterns. Each has its own use cases, advantages, and disadvantages. Below are some of the most prevalent memory allocation patterns in game development:

1. Stack Allocation

Overview: Stack allocation involves allocating memory for variables in a contiguous block, typically on the call stack. This method is managed automatically; memory is allocated when a function is called and released when the function returns.

Advantages:

- **Speed**: Stack allocation is generally faster than heap allocation because it simply moves the stack pointer.
- **Automatic Management**: Developers do not need to manually release memory, which minimizes the risk of memory leaks.

Disadvantages:

- **Limited Lifetime**: Variables allocated on the stack are only valid within the function scope. Once the function exits, the memory is released.
- **Size Limitations**: The size of the stack is limited, which can lead to stack overflow if too much memory is allocated.

Use Cases: Stack allocation is ideal for small, temporary objects that are used within a limited scope, such as local variables and small structures.

2. Heap Allocation

Overview: Heap allocation allows for dynamic memory allocation, where memory is allocated from a pool known as the heap. Developers explicitly request memory allocation and must also manage its deallocation.

Advantages:

- **Flexibility**: Heap allocation allows developers to allocate memory as needed, which is useful for creating objects of varying sizes.
- **Lifetime Control**: Developers have complete control over the lifespan of objects, which can exist beyond the scope of a function.

Disadvantages:

- **Fragmentation**: Over time, frequent allocations and deallocations can lead to memory fragmentation, reducing efficiency.
- **Performance Overhead**: Allocating memory from the heap can be slower than stack allocation due to the overhead of managing the heap.

Use Cases: Heap allocation is suitable for larger objects or those with unpredictable lifetimes, such as game entities, levels, and assets.

3. Object Pooling

Overview: Object pooling is a technique where a pool of reusable objects is maintained, minimizing the need for frequent memory allocation and deallocation. When an object is no longer needed, it is returned to the pool instead of being deleted.

Advantages:

- **Performance Optimization**: Reduces the overhead of memory allocation, leading to smoother performance, especially during gameplay.
- **Reduced Fragmentation**: Since memory is reused, fragmentation is minimized.

Disadvantages:

- **Complexity**: Managing an object pool adds complexity to the codebase, requiring careful handling of object states.
- **Memory Overhead**: If not managed properly, object pools can consume more memory than necessary.

Use Cases: Object pooling is commonly used for frequently created and destroyed objects, such as bullets in a shooting game, enemies, or particle effects.

4. Memory Mapping

Overview: Memory mapping involves mapping a file directly into the memory address space of a process. This allows for efficient access to file data as if it were part of the program's memory.

Advantages:

- **Fast Access**: Memory mapping allows for quick access to large data files without loading them entirely into RAM.
- **Efficient Use of Resources**: Reduces memory overhead, as only the required portions of a file are loaded.

Disadvantages:

- **Complexity**: Implementing memory mapping can be more complex than traditional methods, requiring careful handling of file I/O operations.
- **Platform Dependence**: The implementation of memory mapping can vary between platforms, leading to potential compatibility issues.

Use Cases: Memory mapping is useful for loading large asset files, such as textures and models, particularly in open-world games where many assets are needed simultaneously.

5. Chunk Allocation

Overview: Chunk allocation involves dividing memory into fixed-size blocks (chunks) and allocating these blocks to objects as needed. This approach minimizes fragmentation and allows for efficient memory usage.

Advantages:

- **Reduced Fragmentation**: Fixed-size chunks lead to more predictable memory usage and reduced fragmentation.
- **Simplicity**: Allocating and freeing chunks can be simpler than managing individual memory requests.

Disadvantages:

- **Wasted Space**: If objects do not perfectly fit the chunk size, there can be wasted memory.
- **Overhead for Small Objects**: For small objects, the overhead of chunk management can outweigh the benefits.

Use Cases: Chunk allocation is suitable for scenarios where many small objects of similar size are created and destroyed frequently, such as in level streaming or terrain generation.

Best Practices for Memory Management in Games

To ensure optimal memory management in games, developers should adhere to several best practices:

1. **Profile and Monitor Memory Usage**: Regularly profile memory usage to identify potential leaks, fragmentation, and bottlenecks. Tools such as Valgrind, Visual Studio's Memory Profiler, and built-in profiling tools can help track memory performance.
2. **Minimize Heap Usage**: Use stack allocation for small, short-lived objects whenever possible. Reserve heap allocation for larger, more complex objects that require dynamic memory.

3. **Implement Object Pools**: Use object pooling for frequently created and destroyed objects. This reduces the overhead of allocation and helps maintain consistent performance during gameplay.

4. **Avoid Unnecessary Copies**: Use references or pointers to avoid unnecessary copies of large objects, which can be costly in terms of memory and performance.

5. **Clean Up Resources**: Always release memory that is no longer needed, and implement proper cleanup mechanisms to prevent memory leaks. Use smart pointers when applicable to automate memory management.

6. **Test on Target Hardware**: Test memory performance on the target hardware to ensure that memory management strategies are effective across various platforms and configurations.

7. **Optimize Asset Management**: Use efficient methods for loading and unloading assets, such as lazy loading or streaming, to minimize memory usage during gameplay.

Understanding memory allocation patterns is crucial for creating efficient, high-performing games. By leveraging stack and heap allocation, implementing object pooling, utilizing memory mapping, and adopting chunk allocation strategies, developers can optimize memory usage and minimize performance issues. Adhering to best practices in memory management ensures that games not only run smoothly but also provide a seamless experience for players. As the complexity of games continues to grow, mastering memory management will remain a vital skill for developers in the industry.

Custom Memory Allocators and Pools

In game development, performance is critical, and memory management plays a vital role in achieving that efficiency. While standard memory allocation techniques such as stack and heap allocation suffice for many applications, there are scenarios where custom memory allocators and pools can significantly enhance performance and reduce overhead. This section delves into custom memory allocators and pools, their implementation, and their advantages and disadvantages in the context of game development.

What are Custom Memory Allocators?

Custom memory allocators are specialized systems designed to handle memory allocation in a way that optimizes performance for specific use cases. Instead of relying on the default memory management provided by languages like C++, developers create their own allocation mechanisms tailored to the unique needs of their game.

Key Characteristics:

- **Specialized Behavior**: Custom allocators can implement specific allocation strategies, such as fixed-size blocks or varying sizes, based on the expected usage patterns of game objects.
- **Performance Optimization**: They can minimize fragmentation, reduce allocation time, and enhance cache performance by organizing memory layouts more effectively.
- **Control**: Developers have complete control over how memory is allocated, managed, and deallocated, allowing for more efficient use of resources.

Benefits of Custom Memory Allocators
Performance Improvements:

- Custom allocators can provide faster allocation and deallocation times compared to standard heap allocators, especially for frequently created and destroyed objects.
- They can minimize cache misses by organizing memory in a way that keeps related data close together, improving access times.

Reduced Fragmentation:

- By using strategies such as pooling and fixed-size allocations, custom allocators can significantly reduce memory fragmentation, leading to more efficient use of memory over time.

Tailored to Game Needs:

- Custom allocators can be designed to meet the specific requirements of a game, such as the expected lifetime of objects and their sizes, enabling better overall performance and memory management.

Memory Tracking and Debugging:

- Developers can implement tracking within custom allocators to monitor memory usage, helping identify leaks and fragmentation issues more easily.

Implementing Custom Memory Allocators

The implementation of a custom memory allocator typically involves creating a class or structure that encapsulates the allocation logic. Below are the steps and components involved in creating a simple custom memory allocator:

1. **Memory Pool Initialization**

To begin, allocate a large block of memory that will serve as the pool from which smaller allocations will be made. This can be done using standard heap allocation initially.

```cpp
class MemoryPool {
private:
    char* pool;              // Pointer to the memory pool
    size_t poolSize;         // Size of the memory pool
    size_t blockSize;        // Size of each block
    bool* freeBlocks;        // Array to track free blocks
```

```cpp
public:
    MemoryPool(size_t poolSize, size_t blockSize);
    ~MemoryPool();
    void* allocate();
    void deallocate(void* ptr);
};
```

2. Allocation Logic

The allocation function should find a free block within the pool, mark it as used, and return a pointer to the memory. If no blocks are free, the function can return nullptr or implement an expansion strategy.

cpp

```cpp
void* MemoryPool::allocate() {
    for (size_t i = 0; i < poolSize / blockSize; ++i) {
        if (!freeBlocks[i]) {  // If the block is free
            freeBlocks[i] = true;  // Mark as used
            return (void*)(pool + i * blockSize);  // Return the
            block
        }
    }
    return nullptr;  // No available blocks
}
```

3. Deallocation Logic

The deallocation function should mark a block as free, allowing it to be reused for future allocations.

cpp

```cpp
void MemoryPool::deallocate(void* ptr) {
    size_t blockIndex = ((char*)ptr - pool) / blockSize;
    if (blockIndex < poolSize / blockSize) {
        freeBlocks[blockIndex] = false;  // Mark as free
    }
```

```
}
```

4. Destructor to Free Memory Pool

Ensure that the destructor properly frees the memory pool and any associated resources.

```cpp
MemoryPool::~MemoryPool() {
    delete[] pool;  // Release the memory pool
    delete[] freeBlocks;  // Release the tracking array
}
```

Use Cases for Custom Memory Allocators

Custom memory allocators are particularly beneficial in scenarios where:

- **High Object Turnover**: Games with frequent creation and destruction of objects, such as projectiles or particle effects, can benefit from object pools to optimize memory management.
- **Real-Time Performance**: In real-time applications where latency is crucial, custom allocators can reduce the overhead of standard memory management.
- **Predictable Memory Usage**: When developers can predict the memory usage patterns, they can design custom allocators that align closely with those patterns, minimizing waste and improving performance.

Memory Pools

Memory pools are a specific type of custom memory allocator that pre-allocates a large chunk of memory and divides it into smaller, fixed-size blocks. This technique is particularly effective in games where many objects of similar size are frequently created and destroyed.

Benefits of Memory Pools
Fast Allocation and Deallocation:

- Allocating memory from a pool is typically much faster than heap allocation since it involves simply returning a pointer to a free block.

Reduced Fragmentation:

- By reusing a fixed number of blocks, memory pools help maintain a more contiguous memory usage pattern, which can lead to fewer fragmentation issues.

Predictable Memory Usage:

- Memory pools provide a predictable memory footprint, which is beneficial for performance-critical applications.

Ease of Management:

- With a limited number of objects managed, tracking and debugging memory usage becomes simpler.

Implementing Memory Pools

The implementation of memory pools follows similar principles as custom allocators but focuses on managing fixed-size blocks:

1. **Define the Pool Size**: Choose an appropriate size for the memory pool based on expected usage.
2. **Create Fixed-Size Blocks**: Allocate the pool and manage it as a series of fixed-size blocks.
3. **Track Free and Used Blocks**: Maintain a structure (e.g., a linked list or an array) to keep track of which blocks are free and which are in use.

Example Implementation of a Simple Memory Pool

```cpp
cpp

class SimpleMemoryPool {
private:
    std::vector<void*> freeBlocks;
    char* pool;
    size_t blockSize;
    size_t poolSize;

public:
    SimpleMemoryPool(size_t blockSize, size_t poolSize) {
        this->blockSize = blockSize;
        this->poolSize = poolSize;
        pool = new char[poolSize]; // Allocate the memory pool
        for (size_t i = 0; i < poolSize / blockSize; ++i) {
            freeBlocks.push_back(pool + i * blockSize); //
            Initialize free blocks
        }
    }

    ~SimpleMemoryPool() {
        delete[] pool; // Free the memory pool
    }

    void* allocate() {
        if (freeBlocks.empty()) {
            return nullptr; // No free blocks available
        }
        void* block = freeBlocks.back(); // Get a block from the
        back
        freeBlocks.pop_back(); // Remove from the free list
        return block; // Return the allocated block
    }

    void deallocate(void* block) {
        freeBlocks.push_back(block); // Add the block back to the
        free list
    }
};
```

Custom memory allocators and pools provide powerful tools for managing memory in game development, allowing developers to optimize performance and minimize fragmentation. By creating specialized allocation mechanisms tailored to the unique demands of a game, developers can enhance the overall efficiency of their applications, ensuring smooth gameplay and an enjoyable user experience. As games continue to grow in complexity, the importance of mastering memory management strategies cannot be overstated.

Object Pooling for Reusable Entities

In game development, object pooling is an effective design pattern used to manage the allocation and reuse of objects, especially when dealing with high-frequency instantiation and destruction. This approach is particularly beneficial for entities that are frequently created and destroyed during gameplay, such as projectiles, enemies, and particle effects. Object pooling helps to mitigate the overhead associated with dynamic memory allocation, leading to improved performance and reduced garbage collection overhead. This section explores the principles of object pooling, its implementation, and its advantages and challenges in game development.

What is Object Pooling?

Object pooling is a design pattern that involves creating a fixed number of objects at the beginning of a game (or a level) and reusing them throughout the game's runtime, instead of continuously creating and destroying instances. When an object is no longer needed, instead of being destroyed, it is returned to the pool for later use.

Key Characteristics of Object Pooling:

- **Pre-allocation**: A predefined number of objects are created and stored in a pool at the start, based on expected gameplay requirements.
- **Reusability**: Instead of creating new instances, the game fetches inactive objects from the pool, modifies them as needed, and returns them to the pool when done.
- **Performance Optimization**: Reduces the overhead associated with fre-

quent memory allocations and deallocations, minimizing fragmentation and improving cache performance.

Benefits of Object Pooling
Performance Gains:

- Reduces the number of allocations and deallocations, which can be expensive operations, especially in high-performance scenarios.
- Minimizes the time spent in garbage collection by reusing objects instead of creating new ones.

Predictable Memory Usage:

- By limiting the number of active instances, developers can predict memory usage more accurately, leading to better performance tuning.

Reduced Latency:

- Helps maintain a consistent frame rate by preventing frame drops caused by frequent memory allocation operations during gameplay.

Improved Cache Locality:

- Reusing a fixed set of objects leads to better cache performance as frequently accessed objects remain close in memory, reducing cache misses.

Implementing Object Pooling
The implementation of an object pool generally involves creating a class that manages the pool of objects. The following steps outline a simple approach to creating an object pool in C++.
1. Define the Object Pool Class
The object pool class should manage the creation, reuse, and destruction

of pooled objects. Below is an example of how to define such a class.

```cpp
template <typename T>
class ObjectPool {
private:
    std::vector<T*> pool; // Vector to hold the pool of objects
    std::vector<bool> used; // Vector to track usage of objects
    size_t poolSize; // Total number of objects in the pool

public:
    ObjectPool(size_t size);
    ~ObjectPool();

    T* acquire(); // Acquire an object from the pool
    void release(T* object); // Release an object back to the pool
};
```

2. Constructor and Destructor

In the constructor, allocate the required number of objects and initialize the used vector to track their availability.

```cpp
template <typename T>
ObjectPool<T>::ObjectPool(size_t size) : poolSize(size) {
    for (size_t i = 0; i < poolSize; ++i) {
        pool.push_back(new T()); // Allocate a new object
        used.push_back(false); // Mark all objects as unused
    }
}

template <typename T>
ObjectPool<T>::~ObjectPool() {
    for (auto obj : pool) {
        delete obj; // Clean up allocated objects
    }
}
```

```
}
```

3. **Acquire Method**

The acquire method should find an unused object in the pool, mark it as used, and return it. If all objects are in use, it can return nullptr or handle the situation as needed.

cpp

```cpp
template <typename T>
T* ObjectPool<T>::acquire() {
    for (size_t i = 0; i < poolSize; ++i) {
        if (!used[i]) { // Find an unused object
            used[i] = true; // Mark it as used
            return pool[i]; // Return the object
        }
    }
    return nullptr; // No available objects
}
```

4. **Release Method**

The release method should mark an object as unused, allowing it to be reused in the future.

cpp

```cpp
template <typename T>
void ObjectPool<T>::release(T* object) {
    for (size_t i = 0; i < poolSize; ++i) {
        if (pool[i] == object) {
            used[i] = false; // Mark the object as unused
            break;
        }
    }
}
```

Example Use Case: Bullet Pooling

To illustrate the use of an object pool, consider a simple example involving a bullet pool for a shooting game:

cpp

```cpp
class Bullet {
public:
    void initialize(); // Reset bullet properties
    void update(); // Update bullet logic
    void draw(); // Draw the bullet
};

class BulletPool : public ObjectPool<Bullet> {
public:
    BulletPool(size_t size) : ObjectPool<Bullet>(size) {}
};
```

In the game loop, when the player shoots, instead of creating a new bullet, the game would acquire one from the BulletPool, set its position, and activate it. Once the bullet goes off-screen or hits an object, it would be released back to the pool.

Challenges of Object Pooling
Memory Overhead:

- While pooling reduces allocation overhead, it can lead to unused memory if the pool is larger than necessary or if objects are not reused effectively.

Complexity:

- Implementing an object pool adds complexity to the codebase, requiring careful management of object lifetimes and states.

Limitations on Object Lifetimes:

- Objects in the pool must be reset or reinitialized before reuse, which can complicate object management, especially for complex entities.

Best Practices for Object Pooling
Size Estimation:

- Estimate the required pool size based on gameplay mechanics to minimize wasted resources and ensure that sufficient objects are available when needed.

Dynamic Resizing:

- Implement functionality to grow the pool dynamically if all objects are in use, or allow the pool to shrink during quieter gameplay periods to optimize memory usage.

Initialize Objects Properly:

- Ensure that objects are properly initialized and reset when acquired from the pool to prevent unintended state carryover.

Monitor Performance:

- Regularly profile memory usage and performance to fine-tune the pool size and object management strategies based on actual gameplay behavior.

Object pooling is a powerful technique in game development that enhances performance by minimizing the overhead associated with frequent memory allocation and deallocation. By reusing objects instead of creating new ones, developers can optimize resource usage and improve the responsiveness of their games. While implementing an object pool requires careful design considerations, the benefits it provides make it an essential practice in modern game programming. As games continue to evolve in complexity, mastering object pooling can lead to a significant improvement in gameplay experience and overall application performance.

Cache Optimization and Avoiding Memory Fragmentation

In game development, performance is critical, especially when aiming for smooth graphics and responsive gameplay. One of the most significant factors affecting performance is how efficiently the game uses memory. Cache optimization and avoiding memory fragmentation are crucial techniques for ensuring that a game runs smoothly and effectively. This section will explore the principles of cache optimization, memory fragmentation, and best practices for minimizing these issues in game development.

Understanding Caches and Memory Hierarchy

Before diving into optimization techniques, it's essential to understand how caches work. Modern CPUs use a memory hierarchy consisting of registers, cache levels (L1, L2, and L3), main memory (RAM), and secondary storage (like SSDs). Caches store copies of frequently accessed data to speed up access times.

- **L1 Cache**: The smallest and fastest cache, located closest to the CPU. It typically holds data and instructions that the CPU uses most often.
- **L2 and L3 Caches**: Larger but slower than L1, these caches store data that may not fit in L1. They still provide faster access than main memory.

Effective cache usage can significantly improve the performance of a game, as accessing data from cache is orders of magnitude faster than fetching it from main memory.

Cache Optimization Techniques
Data Locality:

- **Spatial Locality**: Refers to the tendency of programs to access data that are located close to each other in memory. To take advantage of spatial locality, structure your data so that related elements are stored together. This is particularly important for arrays and structures where elements that are used together are stored contiguously.
- **Temporal Locality**: This refers to the tendency to access the same

memory locations repeatedly within a short time frame. By keeping frequently accessed objects or data in a readily accessible location, you can reduce cache misses.

Cache-Friendly Data Structures:

- Choose data structures that fit well into cache lines. For example, using arrays instead of linked lists can enhance cache performance, as arrays store elements contiguously, enabling better spatial locality.
- Consider using structures of arrays (SoA) rather than arrays of structures (AoS) for frequently accessed properties. For instance, if you have a GameObject with position, rotation, and scale, storing all positions in one array, all rotations in another, and so on can improve cache usage.

Memory Alignment:

- Ensuring that data structures are aligned to cache line boundaries can help optimize cache usage. Misaligned data can lead to cache line splits, where accessing a single piece of data requires multiple cache lines, thus slowing down access.

Prefetching:

- Use prefetching techniques to load data into the cache before it is needed. This can be done manually in some cases, or modern compilers may optimize for this automatically. Anticipating which data will be accessed next and loading it can reduce wait times.

Minimize Cache Thrashing:

- Cache thrashing occurs when multiple threads or processes compete for cache lines, leading to frequent eviction and loading of data. To mitigate this, organize data access patterns and ensure that your threads operate on distinct data sets whenever possible.

Avoiding Memory Fragmentation

Memory fragmentation occurs when free memory is divided into small, non-contiguous blocks, making it difficult to allocate large contiguous blocks of memory. This can lead to performance degradation and increased memory usage, especially in long-running applications like games.

Types of Fragmentation:

- **Internal Fragmentation**: This occurs when memory blocks are larger than requested, wasting space inside allocated memory chunks.
- **External Fragmentation**: This happens when free memory is scattered throughout, preventing allocation of large blocks even though enough total memory is available.

Pooling:

- As discussed in the previous section on object pooling, using a pool of preallocated objects can significantly reduce fragmentation by reusing the same memory blocks throughout the game's lifetime. By allocating objects in a contiguous block, you can minimize external fragmentation.

Memory Management Strategies:

Implement custom memory allocators designed to handle specific patterns of allocation and deallocation. For instance, you might create a simple memory manager that allocates fixed-size blocks for objects that have similar lifetimes.

- Use allocation strategies such as buddy allocation, which splits memory into blocks of varying sizes while minimizing external fragmentation by combining free blocks of the same size when they are returned to the pool.

Periodic Compaction:

- Although more complex and often unnecessary for games, memory compaction can be used to reorganize memory blocks, consolidating free space to avoid fragmentation. This is more common in environments where memory usage patterns are unpredictable.

Memory Profiling and Analysis:

- Regularly profile your memory usage during development. Tools like Valgrind, AddressSanitizer, and custom profiling scripts can help identify fragmentation issues and inefficiencies in your memory allocation strategy.

Best Practices for Cache Optimization and Memory Management Profiling and Benchmarking:

- Regularly test the performance of your game, focusing on areas where caching and memory management play a significant role. Utilize profiling tools to identify bottlenecks related to memory usage.

Understand Access Patterns:

- Analyze how your game accesses data. Understanding access patterns can help you optimize data structures and memory layout to align better with CPU caching strategies.

Experiment with Different Data Structures:

- Evaluate different data structures and layouts to find the best fit for your game's needs. Sometimes, a seemingly minor change in data organization can lead to significant performance improvements.

Design for the Future:

- Consider how your game might evolve over time. While developing for current needs, anticipate future requirements and design your memory management system to accommodate potential growth without significant redesign.

Avoid Premature Optimization:

- While it's crucial to consider caching and fragmentation from the outset, avoid making overly complex optimizations early in development. Focus on building a functional game first, and optimize as needed based on profiling results.

Cache optimization and avoiding memory fragmentation are essential for ensuring high-performance game development. By leveraging data locality, cache-friendly data structures, and effective memory management strategies like object pooling, developers can create more efficient and responsive games. Understanding the intricacies of cache usage and fragmentation will empower developers to make informed decisions that lead to smoother gameplay experiences and better resource utilization. As games continue to grow in complexity and scale, mastering these concepts will become increasingly important in the pursuit of optimal performance.

Debugging and Profiling Memory Usage in Games

Debugging and profiling memory usage is a crucial part of game development, as it helps identify inefficiencies, leaks, and fragmentation issues that can adversely affect performance. By understanding how memory is allocated, used, and freed during the lifecycle of a game, developers can optimize their applications for speed and efficiency. This section delves into effective techniques and tools for debugging and profiling memory usage in games.

Importance of Memory Debugging and Profiling

Memory-related bugs, such as leaks, fragmentation, and corruption, can lead to crashes, performance degradation, and a poor user experience. Detecting these issues early in the development process can save time and resources, ensuring a stable game at launch. Moreover, effective memory profiling helps maintain optimal performance by:

- **Identifying Memory Leaks**: Detecting objects that are no longer needed but have not been deallocated.
- **Tracking Memory Usage Patterns**: Understanding how much memory is being used and where.
- **Optimizing Resource Management**: Ensuring that memory is used efficiently throughout the game.
- **Improving Performance**: Reducing overhead from memory operations can enhance frame rates and responsiveness.

Common Memory Issues in Games

1. **Memory Leaks**: Occur when memory that is no longer needed is not properly released, leading to increasing memory consumption over time.
2. **Dangling Pointers**: Happen when a pointer references a memory location that has been freed, potentially causing crashes or corrupted data.
3. **Fragmentation**: Both internal and external fragmentation can make it difficult to allocate large contiguous memory blocks, affecting performance.
4. **Uninitialized Memory Access**: Accessing memory that has not been initialized can lead to undefined behavior and crashes.

Tools for Memory Debugging and Profiling

Valgrind: A powerful tool for memory debugging, memory leak detection, and profiling. It can help find memory leaks and illegal memory accesses. Valgrind's Memcheck tool is particularly useful for detecting memory leaks, buffer overflows, and use of uninitialized memory. To use Valgrind effectively:

- Compile your game with debug symbols enabled (-g flag in GCC or Clang).
- Run your game under Valgrind to analyze memory usage.
- Review the output, which will provide detailed reports on memory allocations, leaks, and errors.

AddressSanitizer: A fast memory error detector that can identify out-of-bounds accesses and use-after-free errors. It works as a compiler flag in both GCC and Clang:

- Compile with the -fsanitize=address flag.
- AddressSanitizer will automatically detect and report memory issues at runtime.

Visual Studio Diagnostics Tools: For developers using Visual Studio, the built-in diagnostics tools provide comprehensive memory analysis features. The Memory Usage tool can help:

- Take snapshots of memory usage at different points in time.
- Compare snapshots to identify memory growth and leaks.

Google's gperftools: This set of tools includes a heap profiler that can help visualize memory usage patterns over time. It can assist in identifying memory hotspots and leaks by providing detailed reports.

Custom Memory Managers: Implementing custom memory managers that log allocations and deallocations can provide insights into memory usage patterns. By tracking memory allocation calls, developers can identify problematic areas in their code.

Techniques for Effective Memory Debugging

1. **Use Debug Builds**: Always use debug builds when profiling memory. Debug builds include additional checks and symbols that can provide more information about memory usage and help identify issues more quickly.
2. **Run Stress Tests**: Perform stress tests that simulate the worst-case scenarios for memory usage in your game. This can help reveal memory leaks and performance bottlenecks.
3. **Analyze Memory Allocation Patterns**: Monitor how memory is allocated and freed during gameplay. Identify any patterns that may indicate excessive allocations or deallocations that could lead to fragmentation.
4. **Regularly Review Code**: Conduct code reviews focusing on memory management practices. Look for common pitfalls such as unnecessary allocations, poor use of pointers, and failure to deallocate.
5. **Utilize Logging**: Implement logging to track memory allocations and deallocations in critical areas of your game. This can help identify where memory leaks may occur and how memory usage changes over time.

Best Practices for Memory Management

1. **Minimize Dynamic Memory Allocation**: Where possible, use stack allocation instead of heap allocation. Dynamic allocations can lead to fragmentation and are generally slower than stack allocations.
2. **Use RAII (Resource Acquisition Is Initialization)**: This C++ principle helps manage resource lifetimes. By tying resource management to object lifetimes, you can reduce the likelihood of memory leaks.
3. **Implement Object Pooling**: As discussed previously, object pooling can help minimize dynamic allocations by reusing existing objects rather than frequently allocating and deallocating memory.
4. **Limit Use of Global Variables**: Global variables can complicate memory management and make debugging harder. Use local variables and pass them as parameters when possible.
5. **Consider Memory Alignment**: Properly align memory allocations to prevent performance issues related to cache line boundaries.

Debugging and profiling memory usage is vital for successful game development. By employing a combination of tools, techniques, and best practices, developers can identify and resolve memory-related issues early in the development process. Understanding the intricacies of memory management will not only help in maintaining performance but also contribute to a more stable and enjoyable gaming experience. As games continue to evolve in complexity, the importance of efficient memory management will remain a cornerstone of effective game development.

Concurrency and Parallelism in Game Programming

ntroduction to Multithreading in C++

In the ever-evolving landscape of game development, performance optimization is paramount. As modern games become increasingly complex, the demand for efficient resource management and responsiveness grows. One of the most effective strategies to achieve this is through multithreading. This chapter delves into the fundamentals of multithreading in C++, exploring its importance, core concepts, and practical implementation techniques that empower developers to create high-performance games.

Understanding Multithreading

Multithreading refers to the ability of a CPU (or a single core in a multi-core processor) to provide multiple threads of execution concurrently. In simpler terms, it allows a program to perform multiple tasks simultaneously, enhancing overall efficiency and responsiveness. This capability is particularly beneficial in game development, where various processes such as rendering, physics calculations, and input handling need to occur concurrently without stalling the game's main loop.

Benefits of Multithreading in Game Development

1. **Improved Performance**: By distributing workloads across multiple threads, developers can leverage the full power of multi-core processors,

leading to improved frame rates and smoother gameplay.

2. **Enhanced Responsiveness**: Multithreading allows background tasks, such as loading assets and processing input, to run independently of the main game loop. This ensures that the game remains responsive even during resource-intensive operations.

3. **Better Resource Utilization**: With the increasing prevalence of multi-core systems, multithreading allows developers to optimize CPU usage, preventing bottlenecks that can arise when tasks are processed sequentially.

Key Concepts in Multithreading

To effectively utilize multithreading in C++, developers must understand several key concepts:

Thread: A thread is the smallest unit of processing that can be scheduled by an operating system. It contains its own stack and local variables, allowing it to execute code independently of other threads.

Concurrency vs. Parallelism:

- **Concurrency** refers to the ability of a system to manage multiple tasks simultaneously, allowing for interleaved execution. It doesn't necessarily imply that tasks are being executed at the same time.

- **Parallelism** involves executing multiple tasks at the exact same time, utilizing multiple cores or processors. While all parallel tasks are concurrent, not all concurrent tasks are parallel.

Synchronization: When multiple threads access shared resources, synchronization is crucial to avoid data corruption and ensure consistent state. Common synchronization techniques include mutexes, locks, and semaphores.

Thread Safety: A thread-safe function or data structure can be safely invoked or accessed by multiple threads concurrently without causing race conditions or inconsistencies.

Race Conditions: Occur when two or more threads access shared data simultaneously, and at least one thread modifies the data. This can lead to unpredictable results and hard-to-track bugs.

Multithreading in C++: The Standard Library

C++11 introduced a robust threading library as part of the standard library, providing developers with powerful tools to manage threads and synchronization. The key components include:

std::thread: The primary class for creating and managing threads. A thread is instantiated by passing a callable object (function, lambda, or functor) to its constructor.

```cpp
#include <iostream>
#include <thread>

void myFunction() {
    std::cout << "Hello from thread!" << std::endl;
}

int main() {
    std::thread myThread(myFunction);
    myThread.join();  // Wait for the thread to finish
    return 0;
}
```

std::mutex: A mutual exclusion object used to protect shared data from being accessed simultaneously by multiple threads. Mutexes prevent race conditions.

```cpp
#include <iostream>
#include <thread>
#include <mutex>

std::mutex mtx;  // Mutex for critical section

void printMessage(int threadID) {
    mtx.lock();  // Lock the mutex
    std::cout << "Message from thread " << threadID << std::endl;
    mtx.unlock();  // Unlock the mutex
}

int main() {
    std::thread threads[5];
    for (int i = 0; i < 5; ++i) {
        threads[i] = std::thread(printMessage, i);
    }
    for (auto& th : threads) {
        th.join();  // Wait for all threads to finish
    }
    return 0;
}
```

std::lock_guard: A convenient RAII-style mechanism that automatically locks a mutex upon creation and unlocks it when the guard goes out of scope, reducing the risk of forgetting to unlock a mutex.

```cpp
void printMessage(int threadID) {
    std::lock_guard<std::mutex> lock(mtx);  // Lock mutex
    automatically
    std::cout << "Message from thread " << threadID << std::endl;
}
```

std::condition_variable: Used for synchronization between threads. It allows one thread to notify others that a certain condition has occurred.

```cpp
std::condition_variable cv;
bool ready = false;

void worker() {
    std::unique_lock<std::mutex> lck(mtx);
    cv.wait(lck, [] { return ready; });   // Wait until ready is
    true
    std::cout << "Worker thread proceeding" << std::endl;
}

void go() {
    std::unique_lock<std::mutex> lck(mtx);
    ready = true;   // Set the condition
    cv.notify_all();   // Notify all waiting threads
}
```

Practical Considerations for Multithreading in Game Development

1. **Design Patterns**: Implement design patterns such as the Producer-Consumer pattern and the Thread Pool pattern to efficiently manage multiple threads and tasks.
2. **Avoid Over-Threading**: While multithreading can boost performance, overusing threads can lead to context-switching overhead and complexity. Balance the number of threads based on the tasks' nature and the hardware capabilities.
3. **Profiling and Debugging**: Use profiling tools to monitor thread performance and detect bottlenecks. Debugging multithreaded applications can be challenging; tools such as Valgrind, ThreadSanitizer, and built-in IDE debuggers can help identify issues.
4. **Thread Affinity**: Consider thread affinity when dealing with performance-sensitive applications. Binding threads to specific cores can reduce context-switching overhead and cache misses.

5. **Graceful Shutdown**: Implement mechanisms to ensure that all threads complete their execution properly during application shutdown, avoiding potential data corruption.

Multithreading is a powerful technique in game development that enables developers to build more efficient and responsive games. By understanding the fundamentals of multithreading, the C++ standard library's threading capabilities, and best practices for implementation, developers can harness the power of concurrent execution to create rich gaming experiences. As the gaming industry continues to evolve, proficiency in multithreading will remain an essential skill for developers aiming to push the boundaries of performance and interactivity.

Game Loops and Job Systems for Concurrent Processing

In game development, the game loop is a fundamental concept that drives the execution of the game. It ensures that the game runs smoothly, processing updates, rendering graphics, and handling user input in a continuous cycle. As games grow more complex, managing the workload becomes increasingly challenging. This is where concurrent processing through job systems comes into play, allowing developers to efficiently utilize multi-core processors and improve overall performance. This section explores the intricacies of game loops and job systems, highlighting how they can be implemented for optimal concurrency in game programming.

Understanding the Game Loop

The game loop is the core mechanism that keeps a game running. It repeatedly executes the same series of operations: processing input, updating game state, and rendering graphics. The structure of a basic game loop can be broken down into several key components:

1. **Initialization**: Setting up resources, loading assets, and initializing variables.

2. **Game State Update**: Processing user input, updating game entities, and handling game logic.
3. **Rendering**: Drawing the game state to the screen, displaying graphics and UI elements.
4. **Timing Control**: Ensuring that each iteration of the loop occurs at a consistent rate to maintain smooth performance.

A simple pseudocode representation of a game loop might look like this:

cpp

```
while (isRunning) {
    processInput();         // Handle user input
    updateGameState();      // Update game logic
    render();               // Render the current frame
    controlFrameRate();     // Control the timing
}
```

Timing Control

Maintaining a consistent frame rate is crucial for smooth gameplay. Developers often implement a timing control mechanism within the game loop to ensure that updates and rendering occur at a specific frequency, commonly referred to as **frames per second (FPS)**. Techniques such as delta time calculation allow for time-based movement and animations, making gameplay independent of the frame rate:

cpp

```
float deltaTime = currentTime - lastTime;
lastTime = currentTime;

// Update game state based on deltaTime
updateGameEntities(deltaTime);
```

Job Systems for Efficient Workload Distribution

As games become more resource-intensive, managing the workload efficiently is essential. Job systems provide a structured approach to offloading tasks from the main thread and distributing them across multiple threads. This enhances performance by leveraging the capabilities of multi-core processors.

Key Concepts of Job Systems

1. **Jobs**: In a job system, tasks are encapsulated as jobs. Each job represents a discrete unit of work that can be executed independently. Jobs can vary in complexity, from simple calculations to more extensive operations like loading assets.

2. **Job Queue**: A job queue manages the scheduling and execution of jobs. When the main thread generates jobs, they are pushed onto the queue, where worker threads can pull them off for processing. This decouples job creation from execution, allowing for greater flexibility and efficiency.

3. **Worker Threads**: These are threads dedicated to processing jobs from the queue. A fixed number of worker threads can be created, allowing them to run concurrently and process multiple jobs simultaneously.

4. **Synchronization**: Managing access to shared resources is crucial in a job system. Synchronization mechanisms such as mutexes, locks, and atomic operations are essential to prevent race conditions when multiple threads access the same data.

Implementing a Basic Job System

Here's a simplified implementation of a job system in C++:

cpp

```
#include <iostream>
#include <thread>
#include <queue>
#include <mutex>
#include <condition_variable>
#include <functional>
```

```cpp
#include <vector>

class JobSystem {
public:
    JobSystem(size_t numThreads) {
        for (size_t i = 0; i < numThreads; ++i) {
            workers.emplace_back(&JobSystem::workerThread, this);
        }
    }

    ~JobSystem() {
        {
            std::unique_lock<std::mutex> lock(queueMutex);
            isRunning = false; // Stop accepting jobs
        }
        condition.notify_all(); // Wake all worker threads to exit
        for (std::thread &worker : workers) {
            worker.join(); // Wait for all threads to finish
        }
    }

    void enqueueJob(std::function<void()> job) {
        {
            std::unique_lock<std::mutex> lock(queueMutex);
            jobs.push(job); // Add job to the queue
        }
        condition.notify_one(); // Notify one worker thread
    }

private:
    void workerThread() {
        while (true) {
            std::function<void()> job;
            {
                std::unique_lock<std::mutex> lock(queueMutex);
                condition.wait(lock, [this] { return !jobs.empty()
                || !isRunning; });
                if (!isRunning && jobs.empty()) return; // Exit if
                not running and queue is empty
                job = std::move(jobs.front()); // Get the job from
```

```
            the queue
            jobs.pop(); // Remove it from the queue
        }
        job(); // Execute the job
    }
}

    std::vector<std::thread> workers;
    std::queue<std::function<void()>> jobs;
    std::mutex queueMutex;
    std::condition_variable condition;
    bool isRunning = true;
};
```

In this example:

- The JobSystem class manages a thread pool and a job queue.
- Jobs can be enqueued using the enqueueJob method, which adds a job to the queue and notifies a worker thread.
- Each worker thread continuously checks for available jobs and executes them until the job system is stopped.

Combining Game Loops with Job Systems

Integrating a job system with the game loop allows for efficient processing of game logic and rendering. Developers can distribute various tasks, such as physics calculations, AI processing, and resource loading, across multiple threads, freeing up the main thread to focus on rendering and user input.

Example Integration

Here's a conceptual outline of how a game loop can interact with a job system:

cpp

```
JobSystem jobSystem(4); // Create a job system with 4 worker
threads
```

```
while (isRunning) {
    processInput(); // Handle user input

    // Enqueue jobs for concurrent processing
    jobSystem.enqueueJob([] { updatePhysics(); });
    jobSystem.enqueueJob([] { updateAI(); });
    jobSystem.enqueueJob([] { loadResources(); });

    // Perform rendering on the main thread
    render();

    controlFrameRate(); // Control the timing
}
```

In this implementation, tasks such as physics updates and AI processing are offloaded to the job system, allowing the main thread to concentrate on rendering and input handling, thus maintaining a responsive gameplay experience.

Game loops and job systems are essential components of concurrent processing in game development. By understanding and implementing these concepts, developers can create efficient, high-performance games that leverage modern multi-core processors. The combination of a well-structured game loop and a robust job system allows for effective workload distribution, improving overall game performance and providing players with a seamless and engaging experience. As the demand for more complex and immersive games continues to grow, mastering these techniques will be crucial for any game developer striving to push the boundaries of what is possible in the gaming industry.

Using C++ Threading Libraries and Async Functions

In modern game development, utilizing concurrency effectively is paramount for enhancing performance and responsiveness. C++ provides

228

several threading libraries and asynchronous programming features that allow developers to implement multi-threading capabilities in their games. This section explores the various threading libraries available in C++, focusing on how to leverage them effectively for game development, including the C++ Standard Library, the Boost library, and additional asynchronous functions.

The C++ Standard Library: Threads and Futures

The C++ Standard Library offers a robust set of features for multi-threading, making it easier for developers to work with threads, locks, and asynchronous operations.

Key Components

std::thread: This class represents a single thread of execution. You can create a thread by passing a callable (function or lambda) to its constructor.

cpp

```
#include <thread>

void doWork() {
    // Code to perform in a separate thread
}

std::thread worker(doWork); // Create a new thread
worker.join(); // Wait for the thread to finish
```

std::mutex: Used to protect shared data from concurrent access. A mutex ensures that only one thread can access a resource at a time, preventing data races.

cpp

```
#include <mutex>

std::mutex mtx;
```

```
void threadSafeFunction() {
    std::lock_guard<std::mutex> lock(mtx); // Automatically locks
    the mutex
    // Code to access shared resource
}
```

std::future and std::async: These classes facilitate asynchronous programming. The std::async function allows you to execute a function asynchronously and retrieve its result via a std::future.

```cpp
#include <future>

int calculate() {
    // Some time-consuming calculation
    return 42;
}

std::future<int> result = std::async(std::launch::async,
calculate); // Execute asynchronously
int value = result.get(); // Wait for the result
```

Benefits of Using Standard Library Features

- **Simplicity**: The standard library provides a straightforward interface for creating and managing threads.
- **Portability**: Code written using the C++ Standard Library is portable across different platforms and compilers.
- **Integration**: Standard features integrate well with other C++ features, such as exceptions and smart pointers.

Boost Library: Advanced Threading Capabilities

While the C++ Standard Library provides essential threading capabilities, the Boost library enhances these features with additional functionality and flexibility. Boost is a well-established collection of libraries that extend C++'s capabilities and can be especially beneficial in game development.

Key Features

Boost.Thread: This module offers a comprehensive threading library with advanced synchronization primitives, thread management, and thread-safe data structures.

cpp

```
#include <boost/thread.hpp>

void workerFunction() {
    // Thread work
}

boost::thread worker(workerFunction); // Start a new thread
worker.join(); // Wait for the thread to finish
```

Boost.Asio: A library for asynchronous I/O, Boost.Asio provides support for network programming and managing asynchronous operations. It's particularly useful for multiplayer games or any application needing non-blocking I/O.

cpp

```
#include <boost/asio.hpp>

void handleRequest(const boost::system::error_code& error) {
    // Handle network request
}

boost::asio::io_service ioService;
boost::asio::deadline_timer timer(ioService,
boost::posix_time::seconds(5));
timer.async_wait(handleRequest); // Asynchronous wait for the timer
ioService.run(); // Start processing events
```

Boost.Lambda: This library allows the creation of inline, anonymous functions (lambdas) which can simplify the syntax and improve readability when dealing with threading.

Asynchronous Programming in C++11 and Beyond

C++11 introduced several enhancements that make asynchronous programming more accessible and effective. Besides std::async, additional features have been included in the subsequent C++ standards.

Promises and Futures

In addition to std::future, C++ also provides std::promise, which allows you to set a value to be retrieved later by a std::future. This is particularly useful when a thread needs to communicate its result back to the main thread or another part of the application.

```cpp
#include <future>
#include <iostream>

void compute(std::promise<int> &&promise) {
    // Perform computation
    promise.set_value(42); // Set the result
}

int main() {
    std::promise<int> promise;
    std::future<int> future = promise.get_future(); // Get
    associated future
    std::thread t(compute, std::move(promise)); // Pass promise to
    thread

    // Wait for the result
    std::cout << "The answer is: " << future.get() << std::endl;
    t.join(); // Ensure thread completion
}
```

Lambda Expressions

With the introduction of lambda expressions in C++11, developers can easily create inline functions, making code involving threads more concise and expressive.

```cpp
#include <iostream>
#include <thread>

int main() {
    std::thread t([] {
        std::cout << "Hello from a thread!" << std::endl; //
        Lambda function
    });
    t.join(); // Wait for the thread to finish
}
```

Best Practices for Using C++ Threading

1. **Minimize Shared State**: Reduce the amount of shared data among threads to avoid complex synchronization issues. When shared data is necessary, use appropriate synchronization mechanisms.
2. **Use Lock-Free Structures**: Consider using lock-free data structures where possible, as they can reduce the overhead of locks and improve performance.
3. **Profile and Optimize**: Always profile your code to identify bottlenecks. Multi-threading can introduce overhead, so ensure that it genuinely improves performance.
4. **Avoid Premature Optimization**: Focus on clear and maintainable code first. Optimize only when profiling indicates performance issues.
5. **Thread Lifetime Management**: Ensure that threads are properly joined or detached to prevent resource leaks or undefined behavior.

Utilizing C++ threading libraries and asynchronous functions significantly enhances a game's performance by allowing for concurrent processing and efficient resource management. The C++ Standard Library and Boost library provide robust tools for managing threads, synchronizing data, and handling asynchronous tasks, while the introduction of modern features in C++11 and beyond makes concurrent programming more accessible. By understanding and applying these concepts effectively, game developers can create highly responsive and performant games that can take full advantage of multi-core architectures.

Synchronizing Game Entities with Lock-Free Data Structures

In game development, maintaining performance and responsiveness while managing the interactions between multiple entities is crucial. Traditional synchronization mechanisms, such as mutexes, can introduce overhead and potential bottlenecks, especially in scenarios where high-frequency updates are necessary. Lock-free data structures offer a compelling alternative by allowing multiple threads to access shared data without the need for locks, significantly reducing the risk of contention and improving overall performance.

Understanding Lock-Free Data Structures

Lock-free data structures enable concurrent access by ensuring that at least one thread can complete its operation without being blocked by others. This is achieved through atomic operations and carefully designed algorithms that prevent deadlock and minimize the time threads spend waiting for access to shared resources.

Key Characteristics

1. **Atomic Operations**: Lock-free data structures rely on atomic operations to read and write data safely from multiple threads. These operations guarantee that the changes made by one thread are visible to others immediately, ensuring data consistency.

2. **Non-blocking Algorithms**: Lock-free structures use non-blocking algorithms, meaning that no thread can be forced to wait indefinitely for

a resource. This is particularly important in game development, where maintaining a responsive experience is essential.

3. **Higher Throughput**: By eliminating locks, lock-free data structures can handle higher throughput under concurrent workloads, which is beneficial for game scenarios with frequent state changes or entity updates.

Implementing Lock-Free Data Structures

There are several common types of lock-free data structures used in game development:

Lock-Free Queues: Useful for message passing between game entities or for task scheduling. They allow multiple producers and consumers to operate simultaneously without locking.

Example implementation of a simple lock-free queue using C++11 atomic operations:

```cpp
cpp

#include <atomic>
#include <memory>

template<typename T>
class LockFreeQueue {
public:
    LockFreeQueue() : head(new Node()), tail(head.load()) {}

    void enqueue(T value) {
        Node* newNode = new Node(value);
        Node* oldTail = tail.exchange(newNode);
        oldTail->next.store(newNode); // Link the old tail to the
        new node
    }

    bool dequeue(T& result) {
        Node* oldHead = head.load();
        Node* newHead = oldHead->next.load();
```

```cpp
        if (!newHead) return false; // Queue is empty

        result = newHead->value;
        head.store(newHead); // Move head forward
        delete oldHead; // Free memory
        return true;
    }

private:
    struct Node {
        T value;
        std::atomic<Node*> next;

        Node() : next(nullptr) {}
        Node(T val) : value(val), next(nullptr) {}
    };

    std::atomic<Node*> head;
    std::atomic<Node*> tail;
};
```

Lock-Free Stacks: Effective for managing temporary storage or for implementing undo functionality. A lock-free stack allows entities to push and pop elements without blocking other threads.

Example of a lock-free stack implementation:

```cpp
cpp

#include <atomic>

template<typename T>
class LockFreeStack {
public:
    LockFreeStack() : head(nullptr) {}

    void push(T value) {
        Node* newNode = new Node(value);
        newNode->next = head.load();
        while (!head.compare_exchange_weak(newNode->next,
```

```
        newNode)); // Atomically set head
    }

    bool pop(T& result) {
        Node* oldHead = head.load();
        while (oldHead && !head.compare_exchange_weak(oldHead,
        oldHead->next)); // Attempt to pop
        if (!oldHead) return false; // Stack is empty

        result = oldHead->value;
        delete oldHead; // Free memory
        return true;
    }

private:
    struct Node {
        T value;
        Node* next;

        Node(T val) : value(val), next(nullptr) {}
    };

    std::atomic<Node*> head;
};
```

Lock-Free Sets and Maps: These structures provide efficient ways to manage collections of game entities, allowing for fast additions, deletions, and lookups without locks.

Benefits of Lock-Free Data Structures in Games

- **Reduced Latency**: Lock-free structures minimize waiting time for threads, leading to lower latency in gameplay experiences.
- **Improved Scalability**: As the number of threads increases, the performance gains from lock-free data structures become more pronounced, allowing games to scale effectively on multi-core systems.
- **Enhanced Responsiveness**: Game loops and entity updates can run smoothly, even under heavy load, because threads are not stalled by lock

contention.

Use Cases in Game Development

1. **Real-Time Multiplayer Games**: Lock-free data structures are ideal for handling player actions and updates in real-time environments, where performance is critical, and any delay can lead to a poor player experience.
2. **Physics Simulations**: Lock-free queues can manage the communication between physics engines and game logic, allowing for rapid state updates without introducing delays due to locking mechanisms.
3. **Event Handling Systems**: Implementing event queues with lock-free data structures can facilitate efficient message passing between game entities, enhancing the responsiveness of the game.

Challenges and Considerations

While lock-free data structures provide significant advantages, they also come with challenges:

- **Complexity**: Designing lock-free algorithms requires a deep understanding of concurrency and memory models. Debugging such code can be more challenging than traditional locking mechanisms.
- **Memory Management**: Careful management of memory allocation and deallocation is necessary to prevent memory leaks or corruption, particularly since lock-free structures often allocate memory dynamically.
- **Performance Overhead**: Although lock-free structures reduce contention, the overhead of atomic operations can still impact performance in scenarios with low concurrency. Profiling and testing are essential to determine the right balance.

Lock-free data structures are a powerful tool for game developers looking to synchronize game entities efficiently and effectively. By eliminating the need for locks, these structures enhance performance, reduce latency, and improve responsiveness, making them particularly suitable for real-time applications. While they introduce complexities and require careful design considerations, the benefits often outweigh the drawbacks, especially in high-performance gaming environments. Understanding and implementing lock-free data structures can significantly contribute to the development of modern, responsive, and scalable games.

Optimizing for Real-Time Performance in Multiplayer Games

Multiplayer games present unique challenges in achieving real-time performance, as they require seamless interaction among multiple players over potentially varying network conditions. To deliver a smooth gaming experience, developers must optimize both the game architecture and the networking code. This section explores key strategies to enhance real-time performance in multiplayer games.

1. Network Architecture Optimization

The architecture of the networking layer is critical for minimizing latency and ensuring smooth gameplay. Choosing the right model for your multiplayer game is the first step:

- **Client-Server Model**: In this architecture, the server maintains the authoritative game state, while clients send input and receive updates from the server. This approach simplifies synchronization and security but can introduce latency if not optimized.
- **Peer-to-Peer Model**: Each client communicates directly with other clients, reducing the reliance on a central server. While this can minimize latency, it can complicate state synchronization and increase the potential for cheating.

Optimizing the Network Model:

- **Use of Interpolation and Extrapolation**: To smooth out movement and actions in the game, use interpolation to predict the position of objects based on previous updates. Extrapolation can be applied to estimate the future state of entities when updates are delayed.
- **Network Tick Rate**: Adjust the frequency of updates sent between the server and clients. A higher tick rate provides more frequent updates but can increase bandwidth usage. Balance this with the acceptable latency for your game type.

2. Data Serialization and Compression

Efficient data serialization and compression techniques can significantly reduce the amount of data transmitted over the network, leading to improved performance.

- **Binary Serialization**: Use binary formats instead of text formats (like JSON or XML) to serialize game state and player input. This reduces the size of the messages sent and can speed up processing time.
- **Delta Compression**: Instead of sending the entire game state, send only the changes (deltas) that have occurred since the last update. This can greatly reduce the amount of data being transmitted, especially in games with many entities.
- **Data Compression Algorithms**: Implement lightweight compression algorithms, such as zlib, to reduce the size of network packets further. Care should be taken to balance compression time and decompression overhead.

3. Bandwidth Management

Managing bandwidth effectively is crucial for maintaining a stable connection in multiplayer games. Here are some strategies:

- **Client-side Prediction**: Allow clients to predict their own actions (e.g., character movements) while waiting for server confirmation. This can mask latency and provide immediate feedback to the player.

- **Prioritize Critical Updates**: Classify updates based on their importance. For instance, player movements and interactions should be prioritized over less critical updates, such as environmental changes. Implement a priority queue for sending network messages.
- **Network Rate Limiting**: Control the amount of data sent over the network by applying rate limiting. This prevents bandwidth saturation, particularly on slower connections, and ensures that the game remains responsive.

4. Optimizing Game Logic and State Management

The efficiency of game logic directly impacts the performance of multiplayer games. Here are some methods to optimize it:

- **State Synchronization Strategies**: Use techniques like snapshot synchronization, where the server sends periodic full state updates, or event-based synchronization, where only changes are communicated.
- **Culling and Level of Detail (LOD)**: Implement spatial partitioning techniques to reduce the number of entities processed for each player. For instance, players should only be aware of nearby objects, which can reduce the computational load.
- **Server-Side Authority**: Maintain authority on the server for critical game state changes. This prevents cheating and ensures that all clients are synchronized to the same game state.

5. Load Balancing and Scalability

As your multiplayer game grows in popularity, maintaining performance across a large player base is crucial. Consider these strategies for load balancing:

- **Dynamic Server Allocation**: Use cloud-based solutions to dynamically allocate servers based on player load. This allows the game to scale up during peak times and scale down when the demand decreases.

- **Region-Based Server Allocation**: Host servers in different geographical locations to reduce latency for players. Automatically assign players to the nearest server based on their location.
- **Matchmaking Optimization**: Use efficient algorithms for matchmaking to minimize wait times and ensure that players are paired based on skill levels, which can lead to more enjoyable games and reduced server load.

6. Profiling and Performance Monitoring

Regular profiling and monitoring are essential for identifying performance bottlenecks and optimizing the game further:

- **Use Profiling Tools**: Utilize profiling tools such as Valgrind, gprof, or built-in profiling features of your game engine to analyze CPU and memory usage during multiplayer sessions.
- **Network Performance Monitoring**: Implement logging and monitoring tools to track network performance metrics, such as latency, packet loss, and jitter. This data can inform adjustments to network configurations.
- **Benchmarking**: Conduct benchmarks with various configurations to find the optimal settings for your game. Compare performance across different hardware to ensure that your game performs well on a variety of systems.

Optimizing for real-time performance in multiplayer games involves a multifaceted approach that includes network architecture, data serialization, bandwidth management, efficient game logic, load balancing, and continuous profiling. By implementing these strategies, developers can create responsive and enjoyable multiplayer experiences that cater to a wide audience while minimizing latency and maximizing performance. Balancing the complexities of real-time interactions with effective optimizations is key to the success of any multiplayer game.

4o mini

Entity-Component-System (ECS) Architecture

U nderstanding ECS and Its Benefits in Game Design
The Entity-Component-System (ECS) architecture has become a cornerstone of modern game design, favored for its flexibility, performance, and scalability. ECS shifts away from traditional object-oriented models, enabling developers to create and manage complex game worlds in a modular, highly efficient manner. In ECS, game objects are constructed as entities, with specific behaviors and properties attached via components, and processed through systems.

This chapter delves into the core concepts of ECS architecture, examining how it optimizes game design, promotes code reusability, and supports scalability for increasingly complex game projects.

1. Core Concepts of ECS Architecture

ECS architecture consists of three main components—Entities, Components, and Systems—which work together to manage game objects and their behavior.

- **Entities**: In ECS, entities are the unique identifiers representing each game object. Entities themselves are devoid of data or behavior; they serve as containers for components that define their attributes. This allows entities to be flexible, representing any game object by attaching the necessary components.

- **Components**: Components are data containers that hold the attributes or characteristics of an entity. Each component is designed to store a specific piece of data, such as position, velocity, health, or texture. For example, a "Position" component could hold x, y, and z coordinates, while a "Health" component might store hit points. By breaking down attributes into individual components, ECS promotes a modular design that allows entities to be dynamically modified by adding or removing components.
- **Systems**: Systems are responsible for processing entities that possess specific components, implementing game logic based on the component data. Each system operates on a set of components that match its criteria; for example, a "Physics" system would update all entities that have position and velocity components. Systems separate behavior from data storage, promoting a clean and decoupled approach to managing game logic.

This modular separation of entities, components, and systems results in a highly flexible and reusable architecture, as components can be mixed and matched to create unique entities, and systems can be updated independently of component structures.

2. Benefits of ECS Architecture

The ECS model brings several notable advantages to game design, from improved performance to enhanced maintainability and flexibility.

- **Data-Oriented Design and Performance**: ECS is inherently data-oriented, focusing on efficient data storage and access. By storing components in contiguous memory and processing them in bulk, ECS minimizes cache misses and maximizes CPU efficiency. This approach contrasts with object-oriented designs that often lead to scattered memory access patterns. As a result, ECS can handle large numbers of entities and components without sacrificing performance, making it ideal for games with complex worlds and many active objects.

- **Enhanced Modularity and Code Reusability**: ECS promotes a modular design, as each component represents a single piece of data, and each system a discrete behavior. This modularity makes it easy to reuse components and systems across different entities. For example, a "Render" system can be reused for entities with visual components, regardless of their other properties. This separation reduces code duplication and allows developers to build complex behaviors by combining simple, reusable modules.

- **Scalability for Large and Complex Games**: ECS architecture is highly scalable, capable of managing thousands of entities without significant performance degradation. As games grow in complexity, the ECS approach allows developers to add new components and systems without overhauling existing code. For instance, adding a "Sound" system requires only a corresponding component and does not impact other systems. This modularity is particularly beneficial for games with evolving features or expansions.

- **Flexible Game Object Composition**: In ECS, game objects can be composed dynamically by attaching or detaching components as needed. For instance, if a character enters a "stealth" state, a "Stealth" component can be temporarily added, and removed once the state ends. This allows for dynamic object behavior without complex inheritance structures, making ECS well-suited for games that require runtime flexibility.

- **Ease of Maintenance and Debugging**: Since ECS decouples data (components) from behavior (systems), it is easier to isolate and fix issues in each part of the architecture. Bugs related to a particular behavior can often be traced to a single system, while data-related issues can be identified within specific components. This separation of concerns simplifies debugging and makes the codebase easier to maintain over time.

3. ECS in Practice: Building Flexible Game Objects

ECS allows developers to construct game objects flexibly by combining different components. For example:

- **Player Character**: A player character entity could be composed of components like "Position," "Health," "Inventory," "Input," and "Render." The associated systems—movement, health management, rendering, etc.—would each process this entity based on its components.
- **Non-Player Characters (NPCs)**: NPCs might use similar components (e.g., "Position" and "Render") but also include components unique to AI behavior, such as "Aggression" or "Pathfinding." The AI system would update only entities with these AI-related components, leaving other systems unaffected.
- **Projectiles**: A projectile might consist of "Position," "Velocity," and "Damage" components. When launched, a "ProjectileSystem" processes all entities with these components to move them and check for collisions, applying the "Damage" component data as necessary.

This approach allows entities to share common characteristics (like "Position" or "Render") while remaining distinct based on other components. Game developers can create diverse objects with minimal code duplication by combining reusable components.

4. Designing Systems for Efficient Data Processing

Efficient system design is central to maximizing ECS performance, as systems process all matching entities every frame. Here are some best practices:

- **Selective Component Processing**: Systems should operate only on entities with the required component combinations. For example, a "Physics" system might only process entities with both "Position" and "Velocity," avoiding unnecessary computations.
- **Minimizing Dependencies Between Systems**: Avoid dependencies between systems by designing each system to work independently on its data. For instance, a "Render" system should operate on visual components without relying on physics data. If dependencies are necessary, consider implementing a communication mechanism between

systems rather than directly linking them.

- **Batch Processing and Cache Optimization**: To leverage CPU cache efficiency, store similar components contiguously in memory and process them in batches. For instance, if a system requires both "Position" and "Velocity" components, arrange them in memory so they can be accessed sequentially, reducing cache misses and improving performance.
- **Parallelizing Systems**: ECS architecture is well-suited for parallel processing. Independent systems, such as physics and rendering, can run in parallel to optimize CPU utilization. By leveraging multithreading, ECS-based games can achieve better performance on modern multi-core processors.

5. Challenges and Considerations in ECS

While ECS offers numerous benefits, it also introduces challenges that developers should consider:

- **Initial Complexity**: Implementing ECS requires a shift in mindset from traditional object-oriented programming. Structuring data as components and separating logic into systems can be challenging for developers new to data-oriented programming.
- **Component Granularity**: Finding the right level of granularity for components is crucial. Too few components can reduce flexibility, while too many can complicate system design and degrade performance. Striking a balance is essential to harness ECS's modularity and efficiency.
- **System Coordination**: Although systems should operate independently, certain systems, such as physics and collision detection, may require coordination. Implementing communication between systems without creating dependencies can be complex and may require additional architectural planning.

The Entity-Component-System architecture is a transformative approach to game design, enabling efficient data management, high scalability, and flexible object composition. By separating data, behavior, and entity structure, ECS promotes a modular, maintainable codebase that can adapt to the evolving needs of complex games. Embracing ECS requires a shift to data-oriented design principles but yields significant performance and flexibility benefits, especially for games with dynamic, interactive worlds. For developers aiming to create robust, scalable games, ECS provides an ideal framework that supports efficient and reusable code, empowering teams to deliver rich, immersive experiences to players.

Implementing ECS in C++: Data-Driven Game Design

Implementing an Entity-Component-System (ECS) in C++ introduces data-driven design principles, promoting performance optimization and modularity essential for complex games. In ECS, game objects are structured as data (components) and logic (systems), allowing developers to manage and update entities efficiently. C++ offers a powerful set of tools and constructs that enable high-performance ECS design, leveraging its memory management capabilities, templates, and type safety to create a robust ECS framework.

This section provides a guide to implementing ECS in C++, focusing on structuring entities, components, and systems to facilitate data-driven game design.

1. Setting Up Entities: Structuring Game Objects

Entities in ECS are identifiers (often integers or pointers) representing game objects without inherent data or behavior. Instead, components added to each entity define their properties and states.

Example: Defining Entity IDs

A simple way to represent entities in C++ is to use an EntityID, typically an integer:

```cpp
using EntityID = std::uint32_t;
```

Entities can be created, stored in a container, and managed by an EntityManager that tracks available entity IDs and handles recycling when entities are destroyed.

Entity Management Class Example

An EntityManager is typically responsible for creating, removing, and reusing entity IDs:

```cpp
class EntityManager {
public:
    EntityID createEntity() {
        if (!availableIDs.empty()) {
            EntityID id = availableIDs.back();
            availableIDs.pop_back();
            return id;
        }
        return nextID++;
    }

    void destroyEntity(EntityID id) {
        availableIDs.push_back(id);
    }

private:
    std::vector<EntityID> availableIDs;
    EntityID nextID = 1;
};
```

This basic EntityManager allocates unique IDs and manages the reuse of IDs to avoid memory leaks and ensure efficient entity handling.

2. Defining Components: Structuring Entity Data

Components in ECS are simple data structures containing only fields relevant to a specific attribute of an entity, like Position, Velocity, or Health. C++'s struct or class is ideal for defining components.

Example: Creating Components in C++

For example, a Position component might store x and y coordinates, while a Velocity component holds speed and direction:

cpp

```
struct Position {
    float x, y;
};

struct Velocity {
    float dx, dy;
};
```

Components are typically stored in a contiguous memory array, enhancing cache performance. An std::unordered_map with an EntityID key and a component array can store components effectively, allowing fast lookups and updates.

3. Associating Components with Entities

In ECS, components are assigned to entities, allowing them to be uniquely defined by their component composition. Associating components with entities can be done using a ComponentManager to maintain a collection of components for each entity.

Component Manager Example

The ComponentManager can track components and enable efficient data access:

cpp

```cpp
template <typename T>
class ComponentManager {
public:
    void addComponent(EntityID entity, T component) {
        components[entity] = component;
    }

    void removeComponent(EntityID entity) {
        components.erase(entity);
    }

    T* getComponent(EntityID entity) {
        auto it = components.find(entity);
        return (it != components.end()) ? &it->second : nullptr;
    }

private:
    std::unordered_map<EntityID, T> components;
};
```

Using this design, each ComponentManager is responsible for a specific component type (e.g., PositionManager for Position), enabling efficient retrieval and update of individual components.

4. Implementing Systems: Game Logic Processing

Systems in ECS are responsible for processing entities with relevant components. A System iterates over entities with required components and performs operations based on their data.

Example: Movement System for Position and Velocity Components

Consider a MovementSystem that updates each entity's Position based on its Velocity:

cpp

```cpp
class MovementSystem {
public:
```

```cpp
void update(EntityManager& entityManager,
ComponentManager<Position>& positionManager,
ComponentManager<Velocity>& velocityManager, float deltaTime) {
    for (EntityID entity : entityManager.getActiveEntities()) {
        Position* pos = positionManager.getComponent(entity);
        Velocity* vel = velocityManager.getComponent(entity);

        if (pos && vel) {
            pos->x += vel->dx * deltaTime;
            pos->y += vel->dy * deltaTime;
        }
    }
}
};
```

This update function retrieves Position and Velocity components for each entity, applying the velocity data to move the entity. By decoupling data and behavior, systems remain flexible, independent of changes to other components or systems.

5. Efficient Data Access with Bitsets and Entity Signatures

For efficiency, systems often use bitsets to match entities with specific components. A bitset, or "entity signature," tracks which components an entity possesses. For instance, if an entity has both Position and Velocity components, its signature will have bits set for both components.

Example: Using Bitsets for Efficient Component Matching

cpp

```cpp
using ComponentType = std::uint8_t;
constexpr ComponentType PositionComponent = 0;
constexpr ComponentType VelocityComponent = 1;

std::bitset<32> entitySignature;
entitySignature.set(PositionComponent);
entitySignature.set(VelocityComponent);
```

A System can then filter entities based on their bitset signature, ensuring only relevant entities are processed. This approach reduces the overhead of iterating through unnecessary components, enhancing runtime performance.

6. Leveraging C++ Templates and Polymorphism

In C++, templates enable a flexible and type-safe ECS implementation, allowing the ComponentManager to handle different component types. For example, a generic System base class can be extended with templates, facilitating a more modular ECS design.

Template-Based System Example

```cpp
template <typename... Components>
class System {
public:
    virtual void update(EntityManager& entityManager,
    ComponentManager<Components>&... managers, float deltaTime) =
    0;
};
```

By utilizing templates, C++ ECS implementations avoid costly runtime type checks, maximizing compile-time safety and performance.

7. Optimizing for Cache and Memory Performance

Efficient ECS systems store components in contiguous memory to optimize cache usage. Consider using std::vector for dense component storage, ensuring sequential memory access, which is cache-friendly. Additionally, pre-allocating memory for entities and components can reduce fragmentation and enhance performance, especially in games with high entity counts.

Optimized Component Storage Example

```cpp
```

```
std::vector<Position> positionComponents;
std::vector<Velocity> velocityComponents;
```

Using arrays like std::vector for component storage minimizes cache misses, significantly improving performance in real-time applications.

8. Challenges in ECS Implementation

Implementing ECS in C++ offers efficiency but comes with specific challenges:

- **Memory Management**: ECS relies on careful memory allocation, especially when entities are frequently created and destroyed. Custom allocators and memory pools can address fragmentation, but they add complexity.
- **Component Dependencies**: Some systems may depend on others (e.g., a CollisionSystem depending on PhysicsSystem), which can introduce complexity in system ordering and data dependency handling.
- **Debugging Complexity**: Decoupling behavior and data increases debugging difficulty, as data inconsistencies may stem from multiple systems or entities. Logging and visual debugging tools can mitigate this but require additional setup.

Implementing ECS in C++ offers a high-performance, modular architecture well-suited for complex, data-driven games. By managing data as components, behavior as systems, and objects as flexible entities, ECS empowers developers to build scalable games while optimizing for CPU cache efficiency and multithreading. Despite initial setup complexity, C++'s templates, bitsets, and memory management capabilities make it ideal for a robust ECS design, leading to flexible, reusable, and highly performant game code.

Building an ECS Framework: Systems, Components, and Entities

Creating a complete Entity-Component-System (ECS) framework in C++ requires structuring entities, components, and systems to function cohesively. This section focuses on establishing a robust architecture for managing components and entities, coordinating systems, and integrating each part into an efficient ECS model. By modularizing game object behaviors, the ECS design enhances performance, memory management, and flexibility in game development.

1. Establishing the Core Entity Structure

In ECS, entities are merely identifiers, typically represented by simple types like integers or structs. Entities don't hold data directly; instead, they acquire properties through components. Here's a foundational setup:

Example: Defining Basic Entities

```cpp
cpp

using EntityID = std::uint32_t;

class EntityManager {
public:
    EntityID createEntity() {
        if (!availableIDs.empty()) {
            EntityID id = availableIDs.back();
            availableIDs.pop_back();
            return id;
        }
        return nextID++;
    }

    void destroyEntity(EntityID id) {
        availableIDs.push_back(id);
    }

private:
    std::vector<EntityID> availableIDs;
    EntityID nextID = 1;
};
```

In this EntityManager class, createEntity and destroyEntity methods manage entity IDs, allowing them to be recycled and reducing fragmentation. The simple ID-based structure allows efficient lookup and avoids excess memory use.

2. Designing Components: Defining and Managing Game Data

Components encapsulate properties or attributes of an entity (e.g., Position, Velocity, Health). Components are often implemented as plain structs, ensuring minimal overhead and easy access.

Example: Defining Components

```cpp
struct Position {
    float x, y;
};

struct Velocity {
    float dx, dy;
};

struct Health {
    int hitPoints;
};
```

To manage components efficiently, each component type has a dedicated ComponentManager. This allows for organizing, accessing, and modifying components without direct linkage to entities, maintaining loose coupling between data and behavior.

Component Management Class

```cpp
template <typename T>
class ComponentManager {
public:
```

```cpp
    void addComponent(EntityID entity, T component) {
        components[entity] = component;
    }

    void removeComponent(EntityID entity) {
        components.erase(entity);
    }

    T* getComponent(EntityID entity) {
        auto it = components.find(entity);
        return (it != components.end()) ? &it->second : nullptr;
    }

private:
    std::unordered_map<EntityID, T> components;
};
```

The ComponentManager stores components in a map, where each entity has its corresponding component data. This approach enables O(1) access to components and allows for efficient management and retrieval.

3. Implementing Systems: Processing Entity Data

Systems in ECS apply logic to entities based on their components. Each system operates independently, iterating through relevant entities to update or query data.

System Example: Movement System

The MovementSystem applies a Velocity component to modify an entity's Position, demonstrating a common ECS pattern of isolated data and behavior.

```cpp
cpp

class MovementSystem {
public:
    void update(EntityManager& entityManager,
    ComponentManager<Position>& positionManager,
    ComponentManager<Velocity>& velocityManager, float deltaTime) {
```

```
for (EntityID entity : entityManager.getActiveEntities()) {
    Position* pos = positionManager.getComponent(entity);
    Velocity* vel = velocityManager.getComponent(entity);

    if (pos && vel) {
        pos->x += vel->dx * deltaTime;
        pos->y += vel->dy * deltaTime;
    }
}
}
};
```

The update function runs every frame, adjusting Position based on Velocity for each relevant entity. This modularity allows MovementSystem to operate independently, only interacting with required components.

4. Building an Entity Signature System with Bitsets

A bitset-based signature system improves the efficiency of entity-component matching by defining which components an entity has. This approach allows systems to quickly determine if an entity contains the necessary components for processing.

Example: Bitset Signatures for Component Matching

cpp

```
using ComponentType = std::uint8_t;
constexpr ComponentType PositionComponent = 0;
constexpr ComponentType VelocityComponent = 1;

std::bitset<32> entitySignature;
entitySignature.set(PositionComponent);
entitySignature.set(VelocityComponent);
```

Using a std::bitset as a signature for each entity enables systems to match required components via bitwise operations, significantly reducing iteration times over irrelevant entities.

5. Structuring a Framework: Integrating Entities, Components, and Systems

With the core pieces defined, the ECS framework needs integration to work as a cohesive whole. This includes tying together the EntityManager, ComponentManagers, and systems to operate seamlessly.

Framework Integration Example

```cpp
class ECSFramework {
public:
    EntityID createEntity() { return entityManager.createEntity();
    }
    void destroyEntity(EntityID entity) {
    entityManager.destroyEntity(entity); }

    template <typename T>
    void addComponent(EntityID entity, T component) {
        getComponentManager<T>().addComponent(entity, component);
    }

    template <typename T>
    T* getComponent(EntityID entity) {
        return getComponentManager<T>().getComponent(entity);
    }

    void updateSystems(float deltaTime) {
        movementSystem.update(entityManager, positionManager,
        velocityManager, deltaTime);
    }

private:
    EntityManager entityManager;
    ComponentManager<Position> positionManager;
    ComponentManager<Velocity> velocityManager;
    MovementSystem movementSystem;

    template <typename T>
    ComponentManager<T>& getComponentManager();
```

```
};
```

In this ECSFramework class, the createEntity and destroyEntity methods provide a simple interface for managing entities. Components are added or retrieved through templated functions, and the updateSystems function calls each system's update method, enabling a unified game loop.

6. Optimizing and Extending the ECS Framework

After setting up the ECS framework, various optimizations can enhance performance:

- **Memory Optimization**: Store frequently accessed components in contiguous memory to improve cache locality.
- **Multithreading**: Divide system updates across multiple threads, handling concurrency with care.
- **Event Messaging**: Use an event queue to facilitate communication between systems, reducing dependencies and synchronizing actions like collision handling or AI state transitions.

Example: Event Messaging System

An event system allows systems to publish or subscribe to events without tight coupling:

```cpp
cpp

enum class EventType { Collision, Damage };

struct Event {
    EventType type;
    EntityID entity;
    int damage;
};

class EventManager {
public:
    void publish(Event event) {
```

```
        eventQueue.push(event);
    }

    void processEvents() {
        while (!eventQueue.empty()) {
            Event event = eventQueue.front();
            eventQueue.pop();
            // Process event
        }
    }

private:
    std::queue<Event> eventQueue;
};
```

Event-driven updates provide flexibility and decouple systems, ensuring that actions like damage responses or score updates trigger independently of entity state.

Building an ECS framework in C++ with entities, components, and systems results in a highly efficient and extensible architecture for game development. By separating data, logic, and behavior, ECS promotes modularity, reusability, and performance optimization. The final architecture provides a powerful foundation, allowing developers to build complex, data-driven games while leveraging C++'s memory management and type safety.

Optimizing ECS for Large-Scale Games

For large-scale games, especially those with many entities and complex interactions, a standard Entity-Component-System (ECS) architecture requires specific optimizations to maintain performance and scalability. Efficient memory usage, cache optimization, and multithreading can all enhance ECS performance, allowing the architecture to scale for extensive game worlds, large simulations, and intricate gameplay mechanics.

1. Memory Layout Optimization for Cache Efficiency

In ECS, each component type is often stored in contiguous memory blocks. This design improves cache locality, making it faster to access data for entities with multiple components. By organizing components this way, data access times are minimized, improving system performance across the board.

- **Contiguous Memory Allocation**: Store each component type in a separate, contiguous array rather than a hash map or linked list. This approach reduces cache misses and allows components to be accessed in sequence.
- **Struct of Arrays (SoA)**: Use SoA instead of Array of Structs (AoS). SoA separates each field of a component into its own array, improving cache usage during sequential operations.

Example: Struct of Arrays for Position and Velocity

```cpp
Copy code
struct PositionComponent {
    std::vector<float> x, y;
};

struct VelocityComponent {
    std::vector<float> dx, dy;
};
```

By using SoA, PositionComponent stores all x values and all y values in separate arrays, allowing the CPU to access multiple values in one cache line and speeding up operations like rendering or physics calculations.

2. Implementing Spatial Partitioning

For large-scale games, especially open-world environments, spatial partitioning helps reduce the number of entities that need to be processed. Common methods include grids, quadtrees, and octrees, depending on the dimensionality and complexity of the game world.

- **Grid Partitioning**: Suitable for games with relatively flat or uniform

263

maps, where entities can be divided into cells. This reduces the need to check interactions across all entities.

- **Quadtrees and Octrees**: Effective for managing 2D and 3D spaces, respectively. These data structures dynamically split space based on entity density, allowing systems like collision detection to work only on relevant sectors.

Example: Quadtree for Spatial Partitioning

```cpp
Copy code
class Quadtree {
public:
    void insert(EntityID entity, const Position& position);
    std::vector<EntityID> retrieve(const Position& area);

private:
    std::vector<EntityID> entities;
    Quadtree* children[4];
};
```

With a quadtree, only entities within the vicinity of a given area are checked, vastly reducing processing time for collision detection, rendering, and AI calculations in large environments.

3. Multithreading and Job Systems

Multithreading in ECS can leverage multiple CPU cores, distributing tasks like physics calculations, AI, and rendering preparation across threads. A job system, or task-based threading, splits work into small, independent jobs, which can then be processed concurrently. This approach requires careful synchronization to avoid race conditions and data corruption.

- **Job Systems**: Split tasks into jobs (e.g., each AI agent as a separate job) and process them in parallel, allowing multiple systems to update simultaneously.

- **Task Pools and Workers**: Utilize a pool of worker threads to dynamically assign jobs, improving load balancing and maximizing CPU utilization.

Example: Task-Based Multithreading

```cpp
Copy code
class Task {
public:
    virtual void execute() = 0;
};

class TaskManager {
public:
    void submit(Task* task);
    void runAll();

private:
    std::vector<Task*> taskQueue;
    std::mutex queueMutex;
};
```

In this setup, tasks are dynamically queued and processed by available worker threads. Systems like rendering, physics, and AI can be delegated to the job system, improving ECS scalability and responsiveness.

4. Batch Processing and Grouping Entities

Batch processing optimizes ECS performance by processing groups of entities with the same components simultaneously. By grouping entities based on their component signatures, ECS systems can iterate over relevant entities efficiently, avoiding unnecessary checks.

- **Entity Grouping**: Pre-group entities with specific component combinations, so each system processes only the entities relevant to it. This avoids repeated component-checking overhead.

- **Batch Execution**: Apply updates to all entities in a group before moving on to the next system. This is especially beneficial in large games where entities often share similar component structures.

Example: Grouping Entities by Component Signature

```cpp
Copy code
std::unordered_map<ComponentSignature, std::vector<EntityID>>
entityGroups;

void registerEntityToGroup(EntityID entity, ComponentSignature
signature) {
    entityGroups[signature].push_back(entity);
}
```

By grouping entities in this way, each system can process a single group without filtering irrelevant entities, thus reducing processing time.

5. Efficient Event Messaging and Dependency Management

Large-scale games with many systems and entities benefit from a decoupled event-driven architecture, which helps prevent systems from needing to know about each other. However, a high frequency of events can lead to bottlenecks.

- **Event Buffering**: Collect and process events in batches to minimize the overhead associated with handling each event individually. For real-time systems, prioritize latency-sensitive events, and defer non-urgent events.
- **Dependency Resolution**: Minimize dependencies between systems. Where dependencies are necessary, organize system updates to maintain order and prevent lock contention in multithreaded scenarios.

Example: Buffered Event Handling

```cpp
Copy code
std::vector<Event> eventBuffer;

void queueEvent(Event event) {
    eventBuffer.push_back(event);
}

void processEvents() {
    for (const auto& event : eventBuffer) {
        // Dispatch or handle the event
    }
    eventBuffer.clear();
}
```

Buffered event handling ensures that events are processed in batches, improving performance when numerous events are generated by AI, physics, or other systems in large games.

6. Memory Pools and Object Recycling

Memory pools allocate a fixed-size block of memory, reducing fragmentation and improving cache efficiency. In ECS, frequently created and destroyed components (e.g., bullets or temporary objects) benefit from memory pooling and recycling.

- **Memory Pools**: Allocate fixed-size memory chunks for each component type. This avoids constant allocation/deallocation overhead and improves locality for frequently used components.
- **Object Recycling**: For transient entities (e.g., projectiles), reuse memory by cycling through allocated memory instead of deallocating and reallocating.

Example: Memory Pool Implementation

```cpp
Copy code
template <typename T>
class MemoryPool {
public:
    T* allocate() { /* Allocate from pool */ }
    void deallocate(T* object) { /* Return to pool */ }

private:
    std::vector<T> pool;
};
```

Memory pools enhance performance by reducing dynamic allocation, while object recycling minimizes memory fragmentation, essential for real-time performance in large games.

Optimizing ECS for large-scale games involves a combination of data organization, memory management, multithreading, and efficient event processing. By tailoring ECS design to fit high-entity-count environments, these optimizations significantly improve runtime performance, reduce memory footprint, and ensure smooth gameplay. With these strategies, ECS frameworks can effectively handle the demands of expansive, interactive game worlds and real-time simulation requirements.

Case Study: Applying ECS to a 2D Platformer

In this case study, we will apply the Entity-Component-System (ECS) architecture to build a simple yet effective 2D platformer. The platformer will feature a player character with movement and jumping abilities, a set of platforms, and collectible items. This will demonstrate how to effectively manage entities, components, and systems in a game setting.

1. Setting Up Core Entities

For our 2D platformer, the core entities will include:

- **Player**: Controlled by the user, capable of jumping and moving.
- **Platform**: Static entities that the player can stand or jump on.
- **Collectibles**: Items the player can collect, such as coins or power-ups.

Each entity is created by the EntityManager and assigned specific components based on its type and behavior.

```cpp
Copy code
EntityID player = entityManager.createEntity();
EntityID platform = entityManager.createEntity();
EntityID collectible = entityManager.createEntity();
```

2. Defining Key Components

Each entity type requires specific attributes to function within the platformer's rules. Here are the essential components:

- **Position**: Used by all entities to define their location in the world.
- **Velocity**: Used for entities that move, such as the player.
- **Collider**: Defines the collision boundaries of entities like platforms and collectibles.
- **PlayerControl**: Allows the player entity to respond to input events.

Example Component Definitions

```cpp
Copy code
struct Position {
    float x, y;
};

struct Velocity {
    float dx = 0.0f, dy = 0.0f;
};
```

```cpp
struct Collider {
    float width, height;
};

struct PlayerControl {
    bool isJumping = false;
    bool isGrounded = false;
};
```

Each component holds data only, without methods or logic, keeping the design purely data-driven and aligned with ECS principles.

3. Implementing Systems for Platformer Mechanics

To create a functioning game loop and responsive gameplay, several systems will be implemented:

1. **Movement System**: Updates entity positions based on velocity.
2. **Collision System**: Manages collisions between entities (e.g., player and platform).
3. **Input System**: Processes player input to control movement.
4. **Collectible System**: Manages collection events between player and items.

Movement System: Handling Position Updates

The movement system reads the Position and Velocity components of each entity to update their positions, considering gravity for a platformer environment.

```cpp
cpp
Copy code
class MovementSystem {
public:
    void update(ComponentManager<Position>& positionManager,
    ComponentManager<Velocity>& velocityManager, float deltaTime) {
```

```cpp
    for (auto& [entity, pos] :
    positionManager.getComponents()) {
        if (auto* vel = velocityManager.getComponent(entity)) {
            pos.x += vel->dx * deltaTime;
            pos.y += vel->dy * deltaTime;
            // Simulate gravity
            vel->dy += 9.8f * deltaTime;  // Gravity effect
        }
    }
  }
};
```

The movement system iterates over entities with both Position and Velocity components, applying gravity by adjusting the dy (y-velocity).

Collision System: Detecting and Resolving Collisions

In platformers, precise collision detection is critical to ensure realistic physics and player interaction with platforms. The collision system uses the Collider component to detect intersections between entities, managing responses like stopping player movement when grounded.

```cpp
cpp
Copy code
class CollisionSystem {
public:
    void update(EntityManager& entityManager,
    ComponentManager<Position>& positionManager,
    ComponentManager<Collider>& colliderManager) {
        for (auto& [entity, pos] :
        positionManager.getComponents()) {
            if (auto* collider =
            colliderManager.getComponent(entity)) {
                // Check for platform collisions and resolve
                if (isCollidingWithPlatform(pos, *collider)) {
                    resolveCollision(pos, *collider);
                }
            }
```

```
        }
    }

    bool isCollidingWithPlatform(const Position& pos, const
    Collider& collider) {
        // Collision detection logic here
    }

    void resolveCollision(Position& pos, const Collider& collider)
    {
        // Adjust position to simulate grounded player
    }
};
```

The resolveCollision function handles adjustments, such as positioning the player on top of a platform when a collision is detected.

Input System: Processing Player Input

The input system captures keyboard or controller input, modifying the player's Velocity to move left, right, or jump.

```cpp
Copy code
class InputSystem {
public:
    void update(ComponentManager<PlayerControl>& controlManager,
    ComponentManager<Velocity>& velocityManager) {
        for (auto& [entity, control] :
        controlManager.getComponents()) {
            if (auto* velocity =
            velocityManager.getComponent(entity)) {
                // Move left or right
                if (isKeyPressed(KEY_LEFT)) velocity->dx = -5.0f;
                if (isKeyPressed(KEY_RIGHT)) velocity->dx = 5.0f;

                // Jump
                if (isKeyPressed(KEY_JUMP) && control.isGrounded) {
```

```cpp
                velocity->dy = -10.0f;   // Jump force
                control.isJumping = true;
                control.isGrounded = false;
            }
        }
    }
  }
};
```

This system ensures that player movements are smooth and responsive, using control flags to limit jumps while in the air.

Collectible System: Managing Collection Events

The collectible system checks for collisions between the player and collectible items, triggering collection events.

```cpp
cpp
Copy code
class CollectibleSystem {
public:
    void update(ComponentManager<Position>& positionManager,
    ComponentManager<Collider>& colliderManager, EntityID
    playerEntity) {
        auto* playerPos =
        positionManager.getComponent(playerEntity);
        auto* playerCollider =
        colliderManager.getComponent(playerEntity);

        for (auto& [entity, pos] :
        positionManager.getComponents()) {
            if (entity != playerEntity) {
                if (isColliding(*playerPos, *playerCollider, pos,
                *colliderManager.getComponent(entity))) {
                    collectItem(entity);
                }
            }
        }
    }
```

```cpp
    }

    void collectItem(EntityID entity) {
        // Handle item collection (e.g., increase score)
    }

    bool isColliding(const Position& playerPos, const Collider&
    playerCollider, const Position& itemPos, const Collider&
    itemCollider) {
        // Implement collision detection between player and item
    }
};
```

This system is responsible for scoring and inventory updates, ensuring collected items are handled effectively without mixing these mechanics with other systems.

4. Integrating Systems into a Game Loop

The ECS architecture allows for easy integration of all systems within a centralized game loop. Each system performs its tasks sequentially, ensuring smooth gameplay and effective resource management.

```cpp
cpp
Copy code
void gameLoop() {
    while (isGameRunning()) {
        float deltaTime = calculateDeltaTime();

        inputSystem.update(controlManager, velocityManager);
        movementSystem.update(positionManager, velocityManager,
        deltaTime);
        collisionSystem.update(entityManager, positionManager,
        colliderManager);
        collectibleSystem.update(positionManager, colliderManager,
        playerEntity);

        render();
```

```
    }
}
```

In this loop:

- **inputSystem.update** captures player commands.
- **movementSystem.update** adjusts positions and applies gravity.
- **collisionSystem.update** checks and resolves collisions.
- **collectibleSystem.update** handles item collections.
- **render** displays updated entity states to the screen.

Each system remains decoupled, keeping the code modular and flexible for future expansions or changes.

Applying ECS to a 2D platformer showcases the benefits of modular, data-driven design in game development. Each system operates independently, updating only the components it needs to function, which enhances efficiency and simplifies debugging. This case study exemplifies how ECS enables scalable and maintainable game code, providing a flexible foundation for building and extending game mechanics.

Advanced Game Development Patterns and Techniques

G ame Design Patterns: Singleton, Factory, and Observer
Game development frequently involves complex architectures and extensive interactions between game objects. Design patterns offer reusable solutions to recurring problems in this context, improving code organization, flexibility, and scalability. In this section, we will explore three foundational design patterns: Singleton, Factory, and Observer. These patterns are highly beneficial in game development, enabling efficient management of resources, creation of game objects, and communication between components.

1. Singleton Pattern: Managing Unique Instances

The Singleton pattern ensures that a class has only one instance and provides a global point of access to it. In game development, this is particularly useful for managing resources that should be globally accessible but only have one instance, such as the game engine, audio manager, or input manager.

Use Cases in Game Development:

- **Audio Manager**: Ensures only one audio manager is controlling sounds and music across the game.
- **Game Configuration**: Provides global access to configuration settings without multiple copies in memory.
- **Resource Management**: Manages assets like textures and sounds to

prevent redundant loading.

Implementation of Singleton Pattern in C++

```cpp
Copy code
class AudioManager {
public:
    // Public accessor for the single instance
    static AudioManager& getInstance() {
        static AudioManager instance; // Guaranteed to be created
        only once
        return instance;
    }

    void playSound(const std::string& soundID) {
        // Code to play sound
    }

    void stopSound(const std::string& soundID) {
        // Code to stop sound
    }

private:
    // Constructor, copy constructor, and assignment operator are
    private
    AudioManager() {} // Private constructor
    AudioManager(const AudioManager&) = delete;
    AudioManager& operator=(const AudioManager&) = delete;
};
```

In this example, the getInstance function provides access to a single AudioManager instance. The private constructor prevents external instantiation, while the delete directives for the copy constructor and assignment operator enforce the Singleton's unique instance requirement.

2. Factory Pattern: Flexible Object Creation

The Factory pattern is a creational design pattern that delegates the instantiation of classes to specialized creator methods. This is particularly valuable in games where different types of objects share a common interface or base class but have unique behaviors or properties, such as enemies, power-ups, or NPCs.

Use Cases in Game Development:

- **Enemy Spawner**: Generates various enemy types based on difficulty or level requirements.
- **Item Factory**: Creates different collectible items with varying effects, such as health boosts or speed increases.
- **Weapon Factory**: Instantiates different weapon types based on player choice or character class.

Implementation of Factory Pattern in C++

Consider a game where enemies are of different types, such as Zombie, Alien, and Robot. These enemies inherit from a base Enemy class, and a EnemyFactory class handles their creation.

```cpp
Copy code
class Enemy {
public:
    virtual void attack() = 0;
    virtual ~Enemy() = default;
};

class Zombie : public Enemy {
public:
    void attack() override {
        // Zombie-specific attack code
    }
};

class Alien : public Enemy {
public:
    void attack() override {
```

```
        // Alien-specific attack code
    }
};

class EnemyFactory {
public:
    static std::unique_ptr<Enemy> createEnemy(const std::string&
    type) {
        if (type == "Zombie") {
            return std::make_unique<Zombie>();
        } else if (type == "Alien") {
            return std::make_unique<Alien>();
        }
        return nullptr;
    }
};
```

Using this factory method, the EnemyFactory can dynamically create enemies based on a string input. This approach simplifies the code and allows new enemy types to be added with minimal changes to the core game logic.

3. Observer Pattern: Efficient Event Handling

The Observer pattern allows an object, known as the subject, to maintain a list of dependents, known as observers, and notify them of state changes. In games, this is useful for decoupling objects that need to react to specific events without direct dependencies, enabling flexible, event-driven architectures.

Use Cases in Game Development:

- **Event System**: Allows multiple game components (e.g., UI, audio, animations) to react to events like "player scored," "enemy defeated," or "level completed."
- **Health System**: Updates various UI elements and triggers effects when the player's health changes.
- **Quest System**: Notifies the quest log, UI, and other game elements when objectives are completed.

Implementation of Observer Pattern in C++

In a game where we want different systems to respond to changes in the player's health, the Player class can act as the subject, while various observers respond to health changes.

Subject Interface

```cpp
Copy code
class IObserver {
public:
    virtual void update(int health) = 0;
    virtual ~IObserver() = default;
};

class Player {
    int health;
    std::vector<IObserver*> observers;

public:
    void addObserver(IObserver* observer) {
        observers.push_back(observer);
    }

    void removeObserver(IObserver* observer) {
        observers.erase(std::remove(observers.begin(),
        observers.end(), observer), observers.end());
    }

    void takeDamage(int damage) {
        health -= damage;
        notifyObservers();
    }

private:
    void notifyObservers() {
        for (auto* observer : observers) {
            observer->update(health);
        }
    }
}
```

```
};
```

Observer Implementation

We can now create various classes that observe the player's health, such as HealthDisplay for the UI and AudioManager for triggering sounds when the player takes damage.

```cpp
Copy code
class HealthDisplay : public IObserver {
public:
    void update(int health) override {
        // Update the health display on screen
    }
};

class AudioManager : public IObserver {
public:
    void update(int health) override {
        if (health < 50) {
            // Play low health warning sound
        }
    }
};
```

Connecting Observers to the Subject

To use the Observer pattern, instantiate HealthDisplay and AudioManager objects and register them with the Player instance. They will then receive updates whenever the player's health changes.

```cpp
Copy code
Player player;
HealthDisplay healthDisplay;
AudioManager audioManager;
```

```
player.addObserver(&healthDisplay);
player.addObserver(&audioManager);

player.takeDamage(20);  // Observers will be notified of health
change
```

The Singleton, Factory, and Observer patterns provide a robust foundation for organizing game code, making it more modular and adaptable. Each pattern addresses specific needs in game development:

- **Singleton** controls unique resources.
- **Factory** allows for flexible object creation.
- **Observer** enables efficient event management.

These patterns not only streamline the development process but also improve maintainability, allowing complex systems to be expanded with minimal disruption. By mastering these design patterns, developers can create efficient and scalable code architectures essential for high-quality game development.

Real-Time Optimization Techniques for Game Engines

Efficiently managing computational resources is essential for smooth and responsive gameplay, especially for real-time and performance-intensive games. Optimization techniques allow game engines to handle graphics rendering, physics calculations, AI, and other intensive processes without compromising on frame rates or visual quality. This section delves into core optimization techniques tailored for game engines, focusing on real-time performance improvements through code optimization, asset management, memory handling, and rendering strategies.

1. Code Optimization: Profiling and Reducing Bottlenecks

Profiling is the first step in identifying performance bottlenecks. Tools like **Visual Studio Profiler, Valgrind**, and **gProfiler** help track CPU and memory usage, showing which functions or sections of code are the most resource-intensive. Once identified, optimization techniques can target these areas:

- **Inlining Functions**: Reduces the overhead of function calls by embedding function code directly into the caller's code, especially for small, frequently called functions.
- **Reducing Expensive Operations**: Replacing costly floating-point operations or complex mathematical calculations with approximations, particularly in physics or AI calculations, can boost performance.
- **Loop Unrolling and Reducing Iterations**: For loops that perform the same operation repeatedly, reducing the iteration count or unrolling loops (i.e., performing multiple operations per iteration) can improve cache efficiency and speed.

2. Memory Optimization: Efficient Allocation and Access Patterns

Memory management is critical in game engines due to the sheer volume of assets and dynamic object creation. Efficient memory allocation, access, and reuse prevent unnecessary fragmentation and improve data locality, which is crucial for high-performance games.

- **Object Pooling**: Reuse frequently created and destroyed objects, such as bullets or enemies, by storing them in pools. This reduces the cost of repetitive memory allocation and deallocation.
- **Cache-Friendly Data Structures**: Structure data to take advantage of CPU caching, ensuring that frequently accessed data is stored contiguously. For example, storing game entities in **structs of arrays (SoA)** rather than arrays of structs (AoS) can improve cache performance.
- **Memory Alignment**: Ensure data is properly aligned in memory to prevent performance penalties. Aligning data to cache line boundaries allows the CPU to retrieve it in fewer cycles.
- **Smart Pointers for Resource Management**: Utilize C++ smart point-

ers, such as std::unique_ptr and std::shared_ptr, to manage object lifetimes and prevent memory leaks.

3. Rendering Optimization: Reducing Draw Calls and Batch Processing

Rendering is often the most performance-intensive task in game engines. Optimizing the rendering pipeline can significantly impact frame rates and visual performance, especially in high-resolution or high-complexity scenes.

- **Reducing Draw Calls**: Each draw call incurs a performance cost as it interacts with the GPU. Combining multiple objects into a single draw call, such as by **batching** (merging meshes or textures), reduces the number of GPU interactions.
- **Level of Detail (LOD)**: Use different models or textures depending on the object's distance from the camera. Low-detail models for distant objects and high-detail models for close-ups reduce the load on the GPU.
- **Frustum Culling**: Skip rendering objects outside the camera's view frustum (the visible area of the game world). This technique prevents unnecessary rendering and frees resources for objects in view.
- **Occlusion Culling**: Avoid rendering objects blocked by other objects. For example, if a wall blocks a character, the engine can skip rendering the character, saving GPU cycles.

4. Physics Optimization: Reducing Collision Calculations

Physics simulations are essential for realism but can be computationally demanding. Optimizing physics calculations, particularly collision detection and resolution, is crucial for real-time performance.

- **Spatial Partitioning**: Divide the game world into smaller sections to limit the number of objects checked for collision. Techniques like **quadtrees, octrees**, and **grid-based partitioning** only check nearby objects, reducing collision checks.
- **Broad-Phase and Narrow-Phase Collision Detection**: In a broad phase, quickly exclude objects that cannot possibly collide (e.g., using

bounding boxes). The narrow phase then performs precise collision checks only on objects identified in the broad phase.

- **Continuous Collision Detection (CCD)**: For fast-moving objects, CCD prevents objects from "tunneling" through each other by accounting for movement between frames. Use it selectively to avoid the high computational cost for all objects.

5. AI Optimization: Managing CPU Load for Game AI

AI is crucial for dynamic and interactive gameplay, yet it is often CPU-intensive. Optimizing AI routines ensures that complex behaviors do not degrade performance.

- **Behavior Trees and Finite State Machines (FSMs)**: These models structure AI behaviors efficiently, only processing one state or decision at a time. This minimizes the computation needed for decision-making, especially for simple AI behaviors.
- **Pathfinding Optimization**: Precompute paths or simplify pathfinding with techniques like *A pruning** or **hierarchical pathfinding** for large maps. You can also cache paths for common routes to save recalculating them.
- **Multi-Threaded AI Calculations**: Offload complex AI routines to separate threads, allowing concurrent processing without affecting the main game loop's performance.

6. Audio Optimization: Streamlining Sound Processing

Audio, while less resource-intensive than graphics or physics, still requires optimization to prevent stuttering and ensure real-time playback, especially for 3D positional audio.

- **Audio Pooling**: Similar to object pooling, reusing audio sources for common sounds (such as footsteps or gunfire) reduces resource usage.
- **Preload Common Audio Assets**: Preloading frequently used sounds, such as background music or ambient noise, can prevent delays caused

by loading sounds during gameplay.

- **Dynamic Audio Loading**: For large games with extensive soundscapes, load audio assets dynamically based on player location or context, rather than preloading everything.

7. Multithreading and Parallel Processing

Real-time performance in modern games often depends on multithreading to allow multiple operations, such as physics, rendering, and AI, to run concurrently. By separating tasks across threads, game engines can utilize CPU cores more effectively.

- **Job Systems**: Break down game tasks into smaller, manageable jobs that can be processed in parallel, allowing the engine to balance the CPU workload dynamically.
- **Thread Pools**: Use a fixed number of threads to execute game engine tasks. Thread pools prevent the overhead of creating and destroying threads, as they keep a set number of threads running and ready to process jobs.
- **Asynchronous Loading**: Load assets and data asynchronously to prevent loading screens or stutters during gameplay. This can enhance the experience, particularly in open-world games.

Implementing real-time optimization techniques across all aspects of a game engine can greatly enhance both performance and player experience. By focusing on code efficiency, memory management, rendering strategies, and the strategic use of multithreading, developers can ensure that games run smoothly even in demanding scenarios. These optimizations create a strong foundation for handling high-performance requirements, providing a seamless, immersive gaming experience.

Implementing Save/Load Systems with Serialization

In game development, save/load functionality allows players to store their progress, settings, and game states, which can be resumed later. Implementing robust save/load systems requires serializing the game state—converting in-memory data into a format that can be stored in a file or database, and then deserializing it to reload the saved state. This process involves managing data consistency, optimizing storage, and ensuring security.

1. Serialization Basics

Serialization is the process of converting complex game data, such as player stats, level data, or inventory, into a linear format that can be saved to disk or transferred over networks. Key aspects of serialization include:

- **Data Encoding**: Serialized data is typically encoded in formats like JSON, XML, or binary. Text formats like JSON and XML are human-readable and easy to debug, while binary serialization is more compact and faster for processing.
- **Data Integrity**: Ensuring serialized data accurately represents the current game state is essential. Avoid partial serialization (incomplete saves) by serializing all relevant data or batching it in stages.
- **Data Consistency**: Handle inconsistencies by storing version information with each save file, allowing the game to detect and manage updates to data structures or game logic between versions.

2. Structuring Game Data for Serialization

Efficient serialization requires organizing game data so that only essential components are saved. This includes selecting relevant objects and structuring the data logically:

- **Selective Serialization**: Only save objects necessary to recreate the game state. For instance, avoid saving temporary or dynamically generated objects, like transient effects or procedural decorations.
- **Hierarchical Data**: Organize data hierarchically (e.g., Game > Player > Inventory > Items), reflecting game relationships to simplify serialization. Each level in the hierarchy can serialize its child objects, simplifying the

deserialization process.

- **Minimal Data Representation**: Save only data that is unique to the game state. For example, store only inventory items the player holds, rather than a full list of all items, as these can be reconstructed from templates in memory.

3. Implementing Serialization with C++ Libraries

In C++, there are several libraries available for serialization. Common choices include **Boost.Serialization** for binary serialization, **cereal** for flexibility across JSON, XML, and binary formats, and **RapidJSON** for high-performance JSON serialization.

- **Boost.Serialization**: This library supports binary, text, and XML formats and offers efficient serialization with minimal boilerplate code.

```cpp
Copy code
std::ofstream ofs("savegame.dat");
boost::archive::text_oarchive oa(ofs);
oa << playerState;
```

- **cereal**: Known for its versatility and ease of use, cereal supports serialization across multiple formats with minimal overhead.

```cpp
Copy code
std::ofstream os("savegame.json");
cereal::JSONOutputArchive archive(os);
archive(CEREAL_NVP(playerState));
```

Choose a library that aligns with your game's needs and data size requirements.

288

4. Saving Game State: Structuring and Storing Data

A typical save system involves the following steps:

- **Gather Data**: Identify and collect data from objects and systems that reflect the game state, including player stats, world state, and quest progress.
- **Serialize**: Convert the gathered data to a serialized format. For binary serialization, save data as compactly as possible to optimize loading speed and storage requirements.
- **Store**: Write serialized data to a file. Save files can be versioned or split by save slots to allow multiple save points.

Example structure for saving a game in C++:

```cpp
Copy code
GameState gameState; // Struct with all game data
std::ofstream outFile("savefile.dat", std::ios::binary);
cereal::BinaryOutputArchive archive(outFile);
archive(gameState);
```

5. Loading Game State: Deserializing and Restoring Data

Loading game state involves deserializing the saved file and reconstructing objects in memory. This is typically done as follows:

- **Read and Parse File**: Read the save file and deserialize data. Using a format like binary reduces file size and increases load speed but requires versioning if the structure changes.
- **Rebuild Game Objects**: Using the deserialized data, recreate in-game objects. This may involve reconstructing player stats, position, and progress data, along with loading assets (textures, models) as needed.
- **Error Handling**: Include checks to validate the integrity of deserialized data, handling corrupted or incomplete files gracefully.

Example of loading a save file in C++:

```cpp
Copy code
GameState gameState;
std::ifstream inFile("savefile.dat", std::ios::binary);
cereal::BinaryInputArchive archive(inFile);
archive(gameState);
```

6. Managing Version Compatibility

When game data structures change due to updates or patches, compatibility with older save files can become an issue. To manage this:

- **Include Version Numbers**: Save a version identifier with each file. During deserialization, check the version and, if necessary, convert data from older formats.
- **Backward Compatibility**: Implement logic to handle different versions within deserialization code. Libraries like Boost.Serialization allow versioning of individual classes, which can simplify this process.
- **Migrators for Data Upgrades**: When making significant changes to save data structure, use migrators that detect and update older data files to match the new structure, maintaining compatibility across updates.

7. Data Security and File Integrity

Protecting save files from corruption or tampering is crucial, especially in multiplayer games where progression and inventory integrity are important:

- **Checksums**: Add a checksum or hash to the save file to verify its integrity upon loading. If the file's checksum doesn't match, the game can prompt the player or attempt to recover.
- **Encryption**: For sensitive data, such as player credentials or high-stakes multiplayer games, encrypt save files to prevent tampering.
- **Auto-Saving and Backup Files**: Implement automatic backup saves to reduce the risk of data loss. Store multiple versions or use auto-saving

periodically.

8. Advanced Serialization Techniques

For complex game worlds, additional serialization techniques can improve performance and user experience:

- **Lazy Loading**: Only load necessary data initially and deserialize additional information as needed. Useful in large worlds or with extensive inventories.
- **Incremental Saving**: Instead of full saves, only serialize changes since the last save, reducing save times in large games. This approach requires a robust change-tracking mechanism.
- **Cloud Saving**: Enable cloud saves to allow players to transfer progress across devices or recover from data loss. For this, data should be stored in a lightweight, cross-device-compatible format like JSON.

Implementing a robust save/load system with serialization is essential for ensuring players' progress is reliably stored and easily loaded. Through structured data management, selective serialization, and careful handling of compatibility, developers can create efficient, secure, and user-friendly save systems that enhance the gaming experience.

Networking Basics: Creating Multiplayer Components

Creating multiplayer components in games involves implementing systems that enable players to interact in real-time over a network. Key areas in multiplayer development include understanding network protocols, handling latency, managing data synchronization, and building a robust server-client architecture. By mastering these aspects, game developers can design multiplayer systems that are smooth, reliable, and secure.

1. Client-Server vs. Peer-to-Peer Architectures

The two primary architectures for multiplayer games are client-server and peer-to-peer. Each has distinct advantages and challenges based on the game's requirements:

- **Client-Server Architecture**: In this model, a centralized server controls the game state, while clients (players) communicate with the server to receive updates and send actions. This approach provides better security and easier control over game logic, making it ideal for competitive and large-scale games. However, it requires a reliable server infrastructure and can incur higher latency.
- **Peer-to-Peer (P2P) Architecture**: Here, each client communicates directly with others, distributing the game logic and reducing server reliance. This approach reduces server costs and latency but introduces challenges in security, such as cheating prevention, and is harder to synchronize effectively, especially with multiple players.

2. Network Protocols: TCP vs. UDP

Choosing the right transport protocol is crucial for multiplayer games, where data speed and reliability are essential:

- **UDP (User Datagram Protocol)**: UDP is fast and efficient for real-time data transmission, such as player position updates. Although it does not guarantee packet delivery, it is ideal for situations where losing occasional packets is acceptable, such as player movements in action games.
- **TCP (Transmission Control Protocol)**: TCP ensures data integrity and delivery, making it suitable for reliable data, like player login information, chat messages, or inventory updates. However, TCP's acknowledgment system can introduce latency, making it less suitable for real-time gameplay updates.

For most real-time games, UDP is used for gameplay data, while TCP may be employed for less time-sensitive data.

3. Implementing Sockets for Communication

In C++, networking libraries like **Boost.Asio** and **Enet** provide convenient abstractions for implementing sockets and managing network connections.

- **Sockets**: Sockets act as endpoints for sending and receiving data. A basic socket setup requires initializing a socket, binding it to a port, and defining handlers for incoming and outgoing data.
- **Asynchronous Communication**: For performance, asynchronous sockets allow non-blocking operations, which is especially important in multiplayer games where lag can impact gameplay.

Example of using UDP sockets with Boost.Asio:

```cpp
Copy code
boost::asio::io_service ioService;
boost::asio::ip::udp::socket socket(ioService,
boost::asio::ip::udp::endpoint(boost::asio::ip::udp::v4(), 12345));
// Prepare and send data
std::string message = "PlayerMove";
socket.send_to(boost::asio::buffer(message), endpoint);
```

4. Data Synchronization and Latency Management

Network latency can disrupt gameplay, especially in fast-paced multiplayer games. Key strategies for managing latency include:

- **Prediction and Interpolation**: To reduce visible lag, use client-side prediction where the game client simulates actions before receiving confirmation from the server. Interpolation helps smooth out sudden position changes when the server's updates arrive.
- **Time Stamping**: Add timestamps to packets to allow clients to apply updates at the correct time, reducing discrepancies in entity positions across clients.
- **Lag Compensation**: Use server-side lag compensation to ensure fair hit detection by accounting for the delay between a player's action and the server's reception of that action.

5. Game State Replication and Authority

Multiplayer games require precise state synchronization to ensure all players have a consistent view of the game world:

- **Server Authority**: In a client-server model, the server maintains the "authoritative" game state. The server validates player actions to prevent cheating and periodically sends state updates to clients.
- **Entity Interpolation and Snapshot Updates**: The server can send "snapshots" of the game state at intervals. Clients interpolate between these snapshots to smooth gameplay and reduce visible lag.
- **Dead Reckoning**: Predictive algorithms like dead reckoning can estimate an object's future position, reducing the impact of packet loss and smoothing object movements across clients.

6. Implementing Matchmaking and Lobby Systems

Matchmaking allows players to join or create games with minimal effort, enhancing the multiplayer experience. Core elements include:

- **Lobby Management**: A lobby provides a waiting area where players can set up teams, choose maps, or adjust settings before starting a match. Implement a lobby that displays player information, chat, and options.
- **Matchmaking Algorithms**: Use ranking systems or ELO algorithms to match players of similar skill levels, providing a balanced experience. For large games, regional matchmaking servers can reduce latency by connecting players in close geographic proximity.

7. Security Considerations: Preventing Cheating and Ensuring Fair Play

Security is crucial in multiplayer games, where cheating or hacking can ruin the experience. Common security measures include:

- **Anti-Cheat Systems**: Implement server-side validation for critical actions, such as movement and combat interactions. Consider integrating anti-cheat software to detect unauthorized modifications.

- **Encrypted Data Transmission**: Use SSL/TLS encryption for sensitive data like login credentials. Encrypt gameplay data if cheating prevention is essential.
- **Obfuscation**: Obfuscate game protocol data to make it more difficult for hackers to interpret or modify packets. While this doesn't prevent hacking, it adds an extra layer of difficulty.

8. Testing and Debugging Multiplayer Components

Testing multiplayer systems requires careful planning and reliable debugging tools:

- **Simulate Network Conditions**: Use network simulation tools to test performance under various conditions, such as high latency or packet loss. Tools like **Clumsy** allow simulation of network faults to see how the game handles adverse conditions.
- **Log Network Traffic**: Maintain logs of network activity to trace issues in player actions, data synchronization, or latency spikes. Logging allows developers to review past connections and optimize server load.
- **Stress Testing**: Perform stress tests to determine the maximum number of players the server can handle. Measure server performance metrics, such as CPU and memory usage, and optimize as needed.

9. Optimizing Server Performance for Scalability

To handle more players and scale efficiently, consider server optimizations:

- **Instance Management**: Use cloud services or virtual machines to create new server instances dynamically, balancing player load across servers and maintaining performance.
- **Load Balancing**: For large multiplayer games, load balancers distribute player connections across multiple servers, preventing any single server from becoming overloaded.
- **Connection Pooling**: Minimize the cost of establishing and tearing

down connections by reusing open connections where possible.

Building multiplayer components requires a comprehensive understanding of networking, synchronization, and security. By implementing efficient network protocols, data synchronization techniques, and security measures, developers can create smooth, reliable, and engaging multiplayer experiences.

Integrating Third-Party Libraries and Middleware

Integrating third-party libraries and middleware in game development can streamline the creation of complex systems and reduce development time. Middleware provides pre-built solutions for graphics, physics, audio, networking, and AI, allowing developers to focus on game design and unique features rather than reinventing foundational components.

1. Benefits of Using Third-Party Libraries

Incorporating third-party tools can offer several advantages:
- **Accelerated Development**: Ready-made libraries speed up development by providing essential functionality out of the box.
- **Improved Performance**: Many libraries are highly optimized and battle-tested, often performing better than custom-built solutions.
- **Cross-Platform Support**: Well-established libraries often come with cross-platform compatibility, allowing for easier deployment on multiple platforms.
- **Community Support and Documentation**: Popular libraries have strong communities, extensive documentation, and consistent updates, making it easier to troubleshoot and expand functionality.

2. Selecting the Right Libraries

Choosing libraries that align with the game's technical requirements and design goals is critical. Factors to consider include:

- **Compatibility**: Ensure the library is compatible with the programming language, game engine, and platforms the game will target.
- **Licensing**: Review the library's licensing terms to understand any commercial restrictions, attribution requirements, or costs associated with using it in a commercial game.
- **Performance**: Evaluate the library's performance under conditions that match the game's needs. Some libraries may perform better in certain types of games than others.
- **Documentation and Support**: A well-documented library with active community support is essential for ease of use and debugging.

Examples of popular libraries and middleware include **FMOD** for audio, **Box2D** for physics, and **RakNet** for networking.

3. Integrating Libraries: Linking and Building

Integrating third-party libraries into a C++ project typically involves linking the library files, importing headers, and configuring the build environment:

- **Static vs. Dynamic Linking**: Choose between static libraries (compiled into the game's executable) and dynamic libraries (separate files loaded at runtime). Static libraries increase the file size of the executable but simplify deployment, while dynamic libraries reduce executable size and allow for runtime updates.
- **Build Configuration**: Modify the project's build settings to include the library's directories and ensure compatibility with compilers. Most C++ libraries provide guidance for integrating with popular build systems like CMake or Make.
- **Error Handling**: Check return codes or exception handling mechanisms provided by the library to manage errors gracefully and prevent crashes.

Example with CMake for adding an external library:

```cmake
cmake
Copy code
# Include path to the library
include_directories(${PROJECT_SOURCE_DIR}/external/library/include)

# Link to the library
target_link_libraries(MyGameProject PUBLIC library_name)
```

4. Middleware for Specific Game Systems

Middleware solutions provide robust, specialized systems that enhance various gameplay aspects:

- **Physics Middleware**: Tools like **Havok** and **PhysX** simplify physics simulation for collisions, rigid bodies, and fluid dynamics. These libraries are highly optimized for performance and offer realistic physics simulations for games.
- **AI Middleware**: Libraries such as **Xaitment** and **Kythera** provide advanced AI functionality, including pathfinding, behavior trees, and crowd simulation. These tools save time when building complex AI systems for characters and non-player entities.
- **Audio Middleware**: **FMOD** and **Wwise** are powerful tools for managing in-game audio, including sound effects, dynamic music, and 3D positional audio. Both libraries allow designers to modify audio settings in real time, offering more flexibility than basic audio libraries.

5. Example: Integrating OpenAL for Audio

OpenAL is a cross-platform audio library that enables developers to add 3D sound effects to games. Here's a step-by-step outline for integrating OpenAL in a C++ game project:

- **Install and Link OpenAL**: Download the OpenAL SDK, link the OpenAL library to the project, and add the necessary include directories.
- **Initialize OpenAL**: Set up the audio context and initialize OpenAL, which prepares the system for audio playback.

- **Load and Play Sounds**: Load audio files into buffers, then associate them with OpenAL sources to play sound effects. OpenAL supports 3D positioning, allowing for immersive soundscapes.

Example initialization and playback with OpenAL:

```cpp
Copy code
// Initialize OpenAL
ALCdevice *device = alcOpenDevice(nullptr);
ALCcontext *context = alcCreateContext(device, nullptr);
alcMakeContextCurrent(context);

// Load sound into buffer and set up source
ALuint buffer, source;
alGenBuffers(1, &buffer);
alGenSources(1, &source);
alSourcei(source, AL_BUFFER, buffer);
alSourcePlay(source);
```

6. Performance and Optimization with Middleware

When integrating middleware, it's essential to monitor performance, as external libraries can introduce overhead. Strategies include:

- **Efficient Use of Resources**: Avoid excessive instantiation of objects provided by middleware. For instance, use object pooling for reusable objects like audio sources.
- **Profiling**: Profile middleware functions to identify bottlenecks. Many libraries offer built-in profiling or debugging tools to optimize specific areas.
- **Batch Processing**: Where possible, process data in batches to reduce the number of calls to the middleware, which can improve efficiency and minimize CPU load.

7. Keeping Libraries Updated

Middleware providers often release updates that include bug fixes, performance improvements, and new features. Regularly update libraries to ensure compatibility with other tools and take advantage of the latest optimizations.

- **Version Control**: Use a version control system to manage updates, as updates can occasionally introduce breaking changes. Tagging versions of the code when updating a library helps in rolling back if issues arise.
- **Changelogs and Documentation**: Review changelogs and updated documentation before upgrading. It helps in identifying potential compatibility issues and new features that could benefit the game.

Integrating third-party libraries and middleware in game development offers significant advantages, reducing development time and enhancing game functionality. Careful selection, configuration, and management of these tools enable developers to leverage powerful features while maintaining control over performance and compatibility. By understanding the integration process and effectively managing middleware, developers can build richer, more efficient games.

Hands-On Game Projects

Project 1: Classic Arcade Shooter (2D) – Concepts and Implementation

Developing a 2D arcade shooter game offers a strong introduction to game mechanics and programming concepts fundamental to game development. This hands-on project will cover the essential stages in creating a simple yet engaging shooter, focusing on design principles, game loops, collision detection, player controls, scoring, and basic AI for enemy behavior. We'll use C++ with SDL or SFML, both of which are suitable for 2D game development and provide robust tools for graphics, input handling, and audio.

1. Game Concept and Design Overview

In a classic 2D arcade shooter, the player controls a spaceship that can move along a fixed axis and shoot projectiles at waves of incoming enemies. The goal is to survive for as long as possible while racking up points by destroying enemies.

- **Game Mechanics**: The player's spaceship can shoot projectiles, dodge enemies, and collect power-ups. Enemies spawn in waves and follow basic AI patterns, such as moving toward the player's position or randomly dropping projectiles.
- **Game Loop**: The game loop will control frame timing, player input, game state updates, and rendering.
- **Scoring and Lives**: Implement a basic scoring system where each enemy destroyed adds points. The player has a limited number of lives, with the

game ending upon depletion.

- **User Interface (UI)**: Display the score, remaining lives, and game over screen upon failure.

2. Setting Up the Project: Frameworks and Assets

Choosing the Framework: SDL or SFML

For this project, SDL or SFML can both serve as suitable choices. SDL is highly portable and widely used, while SFML is known for ease of use and simplicity in handling graphics and audio. Install the library, configure your development environment, and link the necessary dependencies.

Setting Up Game Assets

Gather essential assets, including:

- **Sprites**: Player spaceship, enemy ships, projectiles, and explosions.
- **Audio**: Background music, shooting sounds, and explosion effects.
- **Fonts**: Text display for score and UI elements.

Both SDL and SFML support common asset formats (PNG, WAV, etc.). Organize assets in directories for easy access and load them upon game initialization.

3. Implementing Core Game Components

Player and Enemy Classes

Define classes to represent the player and enemies, encapsulating properties like position, speed, and health. Implement movement functions to update these entities in each game loop.

```cpp
Copy code
class Player {
public:
    float x, y;         // Position
    float speed;        // Speed of movement
```

```cpp
    int health;            // Player health

    void moveLeft();
    void moveRight();
    void shoot();
};

class Enemy {
public:
    float x, y;            // Position
    float speed;           // Speed
    bool isDestroyed;      // Status for collision

    void move();
};
```

Each class should manage its own behavior and have methods for movement, shooting, and destruction. The **Player** class handles user input for left/right movement and shooting. The **Enemy** class manages automated movement and interaction with the player.

Projectiles and Collision Detection

Create a Projectile class to handle bullet positions, velocities, and lifetimes. Use a vector to store active projectiles and update their positions each frame. Implement a basic bounding box collision detection between the player's projectiles and enemies.

```cpp
cpp
Copy code
bool checkCollision(Entity* a, Entity* b) {
    // Basic AABB (Axis-Aligned Bounding Box) collision detection
    return (a->x < b->x + b->width &&
            a->x + a->width > b->x &&
            a->y < b->y + b->height &&
            a->y + a->height > b->y);
}
```

Upon collision, mark the enemy or projectile as destroyed, increment the score, and trigger an explosion sound.

4. Game Loop Implementation

The game loop drives the entire game, handling frame updates, input, physics, and rendering.

```cpp
Copy code
void gameLoop() {
    while (isRunning) {
        handleInput();          // Capture player input
        updateGameObjects();    // Move player, enemies, and
        projectiles
        checkCollisions();      // Check for collisions and update
        scores
        render();               // Draw everything on the screen
        delay();                // Ensure consistent frame rate
    }
}
```

- **Input Handling**: Capture user inputs to control the player's spaceship and trigger shooting actions.
- **Updating Game Objects**: Move all game objects and remove any destroyed entities.
- **Collision Checking**: Detect collisions between projectiles and enemies.
- **Rendering**: Render the background, player, enemies, projectiles, and UI elements.
- **Frame Timing**: Control frame rate to ensure smooth gameplay using SDL_Delay or SFML's sf::sleep.

5. Implementing the UI and Scoring System

Create a scoring mechanism to display points on the screen and update them when an enemy is destroyed. Use text rendering functions provided by SDL_ttf or SFML's font capabilities.

```cpp
Copy code
int score = 0;

void renderScore() {
    // Convert score to string and render
    std::string scoreText = "Score: " + std::to_string(score);
    drawText(scoreText, positionX, positionY); // Example
    pseudocode
}
```

Display remaining lives, the player's health, and the game-over screen when health reaches zero.

6. Adding Basic Enemy AI

To add challenge, introduce simple enemy AI. For instance, create patterns where enemies either:

- Move downwards in waves.
- Track the player's position horizontally, or
- Shoot projectiles at intervals.

Each enemy AI type can be controlled by a simple state machine.

```cpp
Copy code
enum EnemyState { PATROL, ATTACK };

class Enemy {
    EnemyState state;

    void update() {
        switch (state) {
            case PATROL:
                // Move downward
```

```
            break;
        case ATTACK:
            // Shoot toward player
            break;
    }
  }
};
```

Adjust enemy behavior by changing states and parameters to create variety.

7. Adding Sound Effects and Background Music

Integrate audio using SDL_Mixer or SFML Audio. Load sound effects and background music, setting them to play under specific in-game events (e.g., shooting, enemy destruction).

```cpp
Copy code
Mix_Chunk* shootSound = Mix_LoadWAV("shoot.wav");
Mix_PlayChannel(-1, shootSound, 0);  // Play sound on shooting
```

Configure background music to loop and add sound effects for gameplay events to enhance the experience.

8. Polishing and Final Testing

After implementing core features, polish the game by testing and refining it for consistency:

- **Debugging**: Ensure collision detection, scoring, and enemy behaviors work as expected.
- **Performance Optimization**: Optimize memory usage and rendering to maintain a smooth frame rate.
- **Balancing Difficulty**: Adjust enemy spawn rates, movement speeds, and player health for an engaging difficulty curve.
- **Testing Across Platforms**: If deploying to multiple platforms, test the game on each to ensure compatibility.

This project provides a foundational understanding of implementing an arcade shooter, covering essential elements such as input handling, collision detection, AI behavior, and UI management. Completing this game offers valuable experience in structuring and managing game code, making it a versatile template for expanding into more complex game designs.

Project 2: Tile-Based RPG Game – Map Design, AI, and Combat Systems

Creating a tile-based RPG game introduces several core game development concepts, including map design, tile rendering, pathfinding, character AI, and combat mechanics. This project will focus on implementing these elements to create a fully functional and engaging RPG experience. The RPG will feature a player character navigating a world of tile-based maps, interacting with NPCs, engaging in turn-based combat, and progressing through quests or objectives.

1. Game Concept and Design Overview

In a tile-based RPG, players control a character navigating a grid-based world. The player explores various environments, encounters enemies, interacts with NPCs, and gains experience or items to progress. The game structure is modular, with separate maps that load dynamically and an interface for combat and inventory management.

- **Game Mechanics**: Movement on a grid-based map, dialogue with NPCs, turn-based combat, and item collection.
- **Map and Level Design**: A tile-based map system allows easy creation of diverse levels, with tiles representing different terrains, obstacles, and interactive elements.
- **Combat System**: A simple turn-based combat system with attack, defense, and item options, engaging players in tactical decision-making.
- **User Interface (UI)**: A HUD displaying health, experience, inventory, and dialogue, along with screens for quests, inventory, and combat.

2. Setting Up the Project: Frameworks and Assets

Framework Selection

Choose a framework like SDL or SFML, which are well-suited for 2D games and provide the tools for graphics, input, audio, and text rendering. Ensure the environment is set up with the necessary libraries and dependencies linked.

Asset Preparation

Gather assets for tiles, character sprites, enemies, items, and UI elements:

- **Tiles**: Represent different terrain types (e.g., grass, water, walls) and interactive objects (doors, chests).
- **Character and Enemy Sprites**: Sprites for the player and NPCs with basic animations (walking, attacking).
- **Audio**: Background music for exploration and combat, along with sound effects for actions.
- **Fonts**: Display character dialogues, stats, and other interface elements.

Organize assets in appropriate directories and load them upon game initialization to make development modular and efficient.

3. Implementing the Tile-Based Map System

Tilemap Structure

Represent the game world as a 2D array, where each cell corresponds to a specific tile type. Each tile type has associated properties, such as passability, terrain type, and interaction.

```cpp
Copy code
enum TileType { GRASS, WALL, WATER, DOOR, CHEST };

class Tile {
public:
    TileType type;
    bool isPassable;   // Whether the player can walk on this tile
```

```cpp
    Tile(TileType type, bool isPassable) : type(type),
    isPassable(isPassable) {}
};
```

Loading and Rendering the Map

Use a tilemap file (e.g., a simple text file or JSON) that defines the map layout. Load this data at runtime and render the tiles based on their positions in the 2D array.

```cpp
cpp
Copy code
void loadMap(const std::string& fileName) {
    // Parse map file and load tiles into 2D array
}

void renderMap() {
    for (int y = 0; y < mapHeight; ++y) {
        for (int x = 0; x < mapWidth; ++x) {
            drawTile(map[y][x].type, x, y);
        }
    }
}
```

Tiles are rendered in a loop, creating a grid-based world. The map layout is modular, allowing for easy adjustments and expansions.

4. Player Movement and Interaction

Implement movement controls to navigate the grid. Check for tile passability before moving and add functions to handle interactions (e.g., opening doors or chests).

```cpp
cpp
Copy code
void movePlayer(Direction dir) {
    int newX = player.x + directionOffsets[dir].x;
```

```
    int newY = player.y + directionOffsets[dir].y;

    if (map[newY][newX].isPassable) {
        player.x = newX;
        player.y = newY;
    }
}
```

Add interaction options when the player is adjacent to interactive objects. For example, if the player faces a door tile, pressing a specific key opens the door.

5. Implementing AI and Pathfinding

Basic AI for NPCs and Enemies

Define behaviors for NPCs and enemies using finite state machines (FSMs) with states such as IDLE, PATROL, ATTACK, and CHASE.

```cpp
cpp
Copy code
enum AIState { IDLE, PATROL, CHASE, ATTACK };

class NPC {
    AIState state;

    void update() {
        switch (state) {
            case PATROL:
                // Random or fixed path movement
                break;
            case CHASE:
                // Move toward player
                break;
            case ATTACK:
                // Engage in combat
                break;
        }
    }
}
```

```
};
```

Pathfinding with A* Algorithm

Use the A* algorithm for pathfinding, allowing NPCs to navigate around obstacles toward a target. This is especially useful for enemy AI that follows the player on the grid.

```cpp
Copy code
std::vector<Tile> findPath(Tile start, Tile goal) {
    // Implement A* search here
    return path;
}
```

This algorithm calculates the most efficient path by balancing travel cost and distance to the goal, making it suitable for dynamic gameplay.

6. Combat System: Turn-Based Mechanics

Turn-Based Combat Design

Create a combat system where the player and enemies take turns to act. Each turn, the player can attack, defend, use an item, or flee.

```cpp
Copy code
enum ActionType { ATTACK, DEFEND, USE_ITEM, FLEE };

class CombatSystem {
    void playerAction(ActionType action) {
        switch (action) {
            case ATTACK:
                // Calculate damage to enemy
                break;
            case DEFEND:
                // Increase player defense
                break;
            case USE_ITEM:
```

```
                    // Apply item effect
                    break;
              case FLEE:
                    // Attempt to escape
                    break;
          }
      }
};
```

Health, Damage, and Experience

Each character has health and stats that affect combat outcomes. Define formulas for damage calculation, including critical hits, misses, and stat-based influences. Track experience points (XP) and level up the player based on accrued XP.

```cpp
Copy code
void calculateDamage(Character& attacker, Character& defender) {
    int damage = (attacker.attack - defender.defense);
    defender.health -= std::max(damage, 0);
}
```

After each combat, award XP to the player, increasing stats on level-up to signify progression.

7. Dialogue and Quest System

Dialogue System

Define a dialogue system that allows NPCs to display text when the player interacts with them. Use a simple data structure to store conversations, triggered by player actions.

```cpp
Copy code
class Dialogue {
    std::vector<std::string> lines;
```

```cpp
    int currentLine;

    void displayNextLine() {
        if (currentLine < lines.size()) {
            renderText(lines[currentLine]);
            ++currentLine;
        }
    }
};
```

Quest Management

Implement a basic quest system to guide players through objectives, rewarding them with items, experience, or story progression upon completion.

```cpp
cpp
Copy code
class Quest {
    std::string description;
    bool isCompleted;
    Reward reward;

    void completeQuest() {
        isCompleted = true;
        applyReward();
    }
};
```

Quests can be triggered by talking to specific NPCs or interacting with objects in the world, giving players objectives and a sense of progression.

8. User Interface (UI) and HUD Design

Displaying Player Stats and Inventory

Create a HUD to show the player's health, inventory, and quest progress. Use text overlays to present these elements clearly.

```cpp
Copy code
void renderHUD() {
    drawText("Health: " + std::to_string(player.health), hudX,
    hudY);
    drawText("Inventory: " + formatInventory(), hudX, hudY +
    offset);
}
```

Add a simple menu for inventory and quest tracking, allowing players to navigate using the keyboard or mouse.

9. Polishing and Testing

Debugging and Balancing

Test AI behavior, pathfinding, and combat systems to ensure balanced gameplay. Adjust NPC health, enemy strength, and quest requirements based on testing feedback.

Performance Optimization

Optimize pathfinding and rendering to ensure smooth gameplay. Consider using spatial partitioning for large maps or limiting NPCs in memory to reduce processing load.

Cross-Platform Testing

If the game is to be deployed on multiple platforms, test it on each one to ensure consistent performance and functionality.

Building a tile-based RPG introduces foundational elements of game design, including map navigation, AI-driven NPCs, turn-based combat, and a quest-driven narrative. This project serves as a template for complex RPG mechanics, laying the groundwork for more extensive role-playing games.

Project 3: Physics-Based Platformer – Realistic Jump Mechanics and Collisions

Developing a physics-based platformer requires attention to realistic motion, collision detection, and response systems to ensure smooth and engaging gameplay. This project focuses on implementing realistic jump mechanics, gravity, and collision detection that accurately reflects player interactions with the game world. Additionally, it includes handling platform-specific challenges, such as slopes, moving platforms, and environmental hazards.

1. Concept and Design Overview

In a physics-based platformer, players navigate a character through levels by jumping, avoiding obstacles, and interacting with platforms. The gameplay emphasizes tight, responsive control, with mechanics that include:

- **Jump Mechanics**: Realistic jump arcs influenced by gravity, momentum, and environmental conditions.
- **Collision Detection**: Handling player interactions with platforms, walls, and obstacles.
- **Physics Elements**: Implementation of gravity, friction, and momentum for realistic motion.
- **Environmental Elements**: Platforms, slopes, moving objects, and dynamic obstacles that challenge player timing and skill.

2. Setting Up the Project Environment

Framework and Library Choice

For a 2D platformer, SDL or SFML can provide rendering and input handling, while Box2D or Chipmunk may be used for physics simulation. This allows the flexibility to add physics-based interactions without extensive custom calculations.

Asset Preparation

- **Sprite Sheets**: For player animations, platforms, obstacles, and environment objects.
- **Tile Sets**: For background elements, floors, walls, and environmental hazards.

315

- **Audio Files**: Jump sounds, collision effects, and background music for a more immersive experience.

Organize assets in distinct folders, and load them at the game's start to streamline level design and asset management.

3. Implementing Jump Mechanics and Gravity

Jump Calculation

Jumping in a physics-based platformer is generally implemented as an initial upward velocity, followed by a gradual reduction due to gravity. The jump height is influenced by initial force, player speed, and gravity strength.

```cpp
Copy code
const float GRAVITY = 9.8f;
const float JUMP_FORCE = 15.0f;
float verticalVelocity = 0.0f;
bool isJumping = false;

void startJump() {
    if (!isJumping) {
        verticalVelocity = -JUMP_FORCE;  // Negative value to go up
        isJumping = true;
    }
}

void applyGravity(float deltaTime) {
    if (isJumping) {
        verticalVelocity += GRAVITY * deltaTime;
        player.y += verticalVelocity * deltaTime;
    }
}
```

Variable Jump Heights

Allow players to control jump height based on how long they press the jump button. Release of the button dampens the upward force, providing a more precise control over jumps.

```cpp
Copy code
if (!isJumpKeyHeld && verticalVelocity < 0) {
    verticalVelocity /= 2;   // Reduces upward force for lower jumps
}
```

This makes jump mechanics feel dynamic and responsive, essential for a platformer.

4. Handling Collision Detection and Response

Basic Collision Detection

Use a bounding-box approach for detecting collisions between the player and the environment. Each platform, wall, or obstacle is represented by a rectangular hitbox, and a collision is detected when the player's bounding box intersects with any object's hitbox.

```cpp
Copy code
bool checkCollision(const Rectangle& player, const Rectangle&
object) {
    return (player.x < object.x + object.width &&
            player.x + player.width > object.x &&
            player.y < object.y + object.height &&
            player.y + player.height > object.y);
}
```

Collision Response

Adjust the player's position upon collision. If the collision is from below, reset the jump and set the player's vertical velocity to zero, effectively "grounding" the player.

```cpp
Copy code
```

317

```cpp
void resolveCollision(Player& player, const Platform& platform) {
    if (verticalVelocity > 0 && player.y + player.height >=
    platform.y) {
        player.y = platform.y - player.height;  // Position above
        platform
        verticalVelocity = 0;  // Stop downward movement
        isJumping = false;  // Reset jump
    }
}
```

Slope Handling

To allow movement on slopes, calculate the player's position along the incline. This requires adjusting the collision response to consider the slope angle and modify the player's y-position based on x-movement.

5. Implementing Moving Platforms and Dynamic Obstacles

Moving Platform Logic

Create moving platforms that move along a set path or oscillate between two points. Update the platform's position each frame, and adjust the player's position relative to the platform when they're standing on it.

```cpp
cpp
Copy code
void updateMovingPlatform(Platform& platform, float deltaTime) {
    platform.x += platform.speed * deltaTime;
    // Reverse direction if platform reaches endpoints
    if (platform.x < platform.minX || platform.x > platform.maxX) {
        platform.speed = -platform.speed;
    }
}
```

When the player is on a moving platform, add the platform's velocity to the player's movement to ensure they stay aligned with the platform.

Hazardous Obstacles

Define areas that act as hazards, such as spikes or lava pools. When a player collides with a hazard, apply effects like health reduction or respawn.

6. Enhancing Jump Mechanics with Wall Jumping and Double Jumps

Wall Jumping

Allow players to "stick" to walls for a brief period when colliding with a vertical surface. While attached, they can jump away from the wall, providing a powerful tool for platforming.

```cpp
Copy code
bool canWallJump = false;

if (checkCollision(player, wall)) {
    canWallJump = true;
    if (jumpKeyPressed) {
        verticalVelocity = -JUMP_FORCE;
        player.x += wallJumpPushBack;  // Push away from wall
    }
}
```

Double Jumping

Implement a double jump mechanic by tracking the jump count. Reset the jump count upon landing, allowing a second jump in mid-air.

```cpp
Copy code
int jumpCount = 0;

void startJump() {
    if (jumpCount < 2) {
        verticalVelocity = -JUMP_FORCE;
        jumpCount++;
    }
}

void resetJump() {
    if (isOnGround()) {
        jumpCount = 0;
    }
}
```

```
}
```

7. Physics Optimization and Real-Time Collision Handling

Fixed-Time Step Physics

To ensure consistency across devices, implement a fixed time step for physics calculations, decoupling them from the frame rate and smoothing gameplay.

```cpp
Copy code
const float fixedTimeStep = 1.0f / 60.0f;   // 60 updates per second
float accumulator = 0.0f;

void gameLoop(float deltaTime) {
    accumulator += deltaTime;
    while (accumulator >= fixedTimeStep) {
        updatePhysics(fixedTimeStep);
        accumulator -= fixedTimeStep;
    }
    render();
}
```

Efficient Collision Checks

Optimize collision detection by partitioning the game world (e.g., using a quadtree) to only check collisions between nearby objects, improving performance in larger or more complex levels.

8. Adding User Interface Elements for Platforming

HUD Display

Display elements such as player health, score, and level progression on the screen. For a more immersive experience, consider adding particle effects when the player jumps or collides with obstacles.

```cpp
Copy code
```

```
void renderHUD() {
    drawText("Health: " + std::to_string(player.health), hudX,
    hudY);
    drawText("Score: " + std::to_string(score), hudX, hudY +
    offset);
}
```

Level Transitions and Checkpoints

Create checkpoints within each level to save player progress, especially in more challenging sections. If the player falls or fails, they respawn at the latest checkpoint.

A physics-based platformer like this introduces players to advanced mechanics, including realistic jumps, responsive collision handling, and physics-based interactions. With customizable movement, diverse platform types, and engaging obstacles, this project showcases the essentials of physics-driven gameplay and provides the foundation for building more complex platformers in the future.

Project 4: Simple 3D Shooter – Graphics, AI, and Physics Integration

Creating a 3D shooter involves multiple elements that come together to deliver immersive gameplay: 3D graphics, enemy AI, and realistic physics. This project will focus on building a basic 3D shooter game that includes player movement and shooting mechanics, AI for enemy entities, and integration of physics for realistic interactions.

1. Concept and Design Overview

In a 3D shooter, the player navigates a 3D environment to target and eliminate AI-controlled enemies. Core mechanics include:

- **Player Controls**: Movement, aiming, shooting, and health management.
- **Enemy AI**: Pathfinding, target acquisition, and attack patterns.
- **Physics**: Bullet trajectories, collision detection, and environmental

interactions.

- **Graphics**: 3D rendering, lighting, and shaders for immersive visuals.

2. Setting Up the 3D Environment

Choosing a 3D Engine and Libraries

Engines like **Unreal Engine** or **Unity** offer extensive tools, but for custom development in C++, **OpenGL** or **DirectX** may be preferred for direct rendering. For physics, **Bullet Physics** can handle collisions, and **OpenAL** may provide 3D sound capabilities.

Asset Preparation

- **Models**: 3D models for player, enemies, and environmental objects.
- **Textures**: For walls, ground, enemies, and other objects.
- **Animations**: For enemy movement, attack, and player interactions.
- **Audio Files**: For gunfire, enemy sounds, and environmental effects.

3. Implementing Player Controls and Shooting Mechanics

Player Movement and Camera Control

Implement WASD for movement with mouse input for camera orientation, giving the player full control over movement and aiming in the 3D environment.

```cpp
Copy code
void handlePlayerInput(float deltaTime) {
    if (isKeyPressed(W_KEY)) player.position += player.forward *
    speed * deltaTime;
    if (isKeyPressed(S_KEY)) player.position -= player.forward *
    speed * deltaTime;
    // Similarly handle A and D for strafing
}

void updateCamera() {
    camera.position = player.position;
    camera.lookAt(player.position + player.forward);
```

```
}
```

Shooting Mechanics

For shooting, create projectiles that move forward from the player's position along the aiming direction. Each projectile has a lifespan and despawns when it collides with an object.

```cpp
Copy code
struct Bullet {
    Vector3 position;
    Vector3 direction;
    float speed;
    float lifespan;
};

void shootBullet() {
    Bullet bullet;
    bullet.position = player.position;
    bullet.direction = player.forward;
    bullet.speed = bulletSpeed;
    bullets.push_back(bullet);
}
```

Update each bullet's position every frame, and check for collisions to determine if it hits an enemy.

4. Enemy AI: Pathfinding, Targeting, and Attacking

Basic Enemy Pathfinding and Movement

Implement basic pathfinding using **A*** or grid-based navigation to allow enemies to move toward the player. Enemies should identify obstacles and navigate around them.

```cpp
Copy code
```

```cpp
void updateEnemyAI(Enemy& enemy, const Vector3& playerPosition) {
    if (canSeePlayer(enemy, playerPosition)) {
        enemy.moveTo(playerPosition);  // Direct path if player is
        visible
    } else {
        enemy.followPath(AStar(enemy.position, playerPosition));
    }
}
```

Target Acquisition and Attack Patterns

Enemies should detect the player within a specified radius and switch to an attack state. Basic attack patterns could include:

- **Melee Attack**: Close-range enemies directly approach and attempt to deal damage.
- **Ranged Attack**: Enemies shoot projectiles toward the player from a distance, requiring aim adjustments based on player movement.

5. Integrating Physics: Bullet Collision and Environmental Interactions

Bullet Collision Detection

Each bullet checks for intersections with enemy hitboxes or environmental objects. Using a bounding-box or raycasting method can improve detection accuracy and performance.

```cpp
cpp
Copy code
void checkBulletCollisions() {
    for (auto& bullet : bullets) {
        for (auto& enemy : enemies) {
            if (checkCollision(bullet.position,
            enemy.boundingBox)) {
                enemy.takeDamage(bulletDamage);
                bullet.active = false;
            }
```

```
        }
    }
}
```

Physics-Based Environmental Interactions

Use a physics engine to add dynamic interactions, like explosive barrels that impact nearby enemies when hit, or obstacles that block bullets.

6. Advanced Graphics: Lighting, Shading, and Effects

Realistic Lighting and Shadows

Implement point lights for muzzle flashes and spotlights for player vision, and add shadow mapping for realistic shadows. Lighting can be handled via **Phong shading** or **Blinn-Phong** for realistic effects.

```glsl
Copy code
// Fragment Shader
vec3 phongLighting(vec3 normal, vec3 viewDir, vec3 lightDir, vec3
lightColor) {
    float diff = max(dot(normal, lightDir), 0.0);
    vec3 diffuse = diff * lightColor;

    vec3 reflectDir = reflect(-lightDir, normal);
    float spec = pow(max(dot(viewDir, reflectDir), 0.0),
    shininess);
    vec3 specular = spec * lightColor;

    return (ambient + diffuse + specular);
}
```

Post-Processing Effects

Apply post-processing for a polished look. Effects like motion blur, depth of field, and bloom can enhance visual immersion.

- **Bloom**: Enhances light from explosions and gunfire.
- **Motion Blur**: Adds realism during rapid player or enemy movement.

7. Adding 3D Audio for Immersive Sound Design

Using 3D sound libraries like **OpenAL**, place sounds based on in-game events and entity positions for spatial audio effects. For example, footsteps and gunfire should change in volume and direction relative to the player's location.

8. Implementing a Heads-Up Display (HUD)

Health, Ammo, and Score Display

Create a HUD to show essential information, such as the player's health, remaining ammo, and score. Position HUD elements at fixed screen coordinates for easy visibility.

```cpp
Copy code
void renderHUD() {
    drawText("Health: " + std::to_string(player.health), hudX,
    hudY);
    drawText("Ammo: " + std::to_string(player.ammo), hudX, hudY +
    offset);
}
```

Mini-Map for Enemy and Objective Tracking

Add a mini-map that highlights enemy positions and objectives. A simplified overhead view aids in spatial awareness and tactical planning.

9. Level Design and Wave Management

Designing Engaging Levels

Create varied levels with obstacles, cover, and elevated platforms. Design layouts that encourage strategic movement and add replayability.

Enemy Waves and Difficulty Scaling

Implement wave management where new enemy waves spawn after a timer or after the player clears a level. Increase difficulty progressively by introducing stronger enemies or reducing resources.

```cpp
Copy code
void spawnEnemyWave(int waveNumber) {
    for (int i = 0; i < waveNumber * baseEnemyCount; ++i) {
        spawnEnemy(enemySpawnPoints[i % enemySpawnPoints.size()]);
    }
}
```

This 3D shooter project combines graphics, AI, physics, and audio to build a cohesive gameplay experience. By implementing core shooting mechanics, enemy AI, and physics-based interactions, this project provides a foundation for more complex 3D game development. The addition of immersive graphics, spatial audio, and a well-designed HUD elevates the player's experience, making this a compelling and interactive game.

Project 5: Real-Time Strategy Game Prototype – Pathfinding, AI, and Resource Management

Creating a Real-Time Strategy (RTS) game prototype involves multiple complex systems, including unit management, resource gathering, and intelligent enemy behaviors. This project will outline the development of a simple RTS game, focusing on essential mechanics such as pathfinding, artificial intelligence for unit behavior, and resource management.

1. Concept and Design Overview

In this RTS prototype, players will control units to gather resources, construct buildings, and engage in combat with enemy units. The game will feature:

- **Unit Controls**: Selecting and directing multiple units.
- **Resource Gathering**: Collecting resources for building and upgrades.
- **Building Mechanisms**: Constructing structures for unit production and upgrades.

- **AI Opponents**: Enemies that exhibit strategic behavior and react to player actions.

2. Setting Up the RTS Environment

Choosing a Game Engine and Tools

Select an appropriate game engine like **Unity** or **Godot**, which provides built-in support for 2D/3D graphics, physics, and networking. For custom development, C++ with **SFML** or **SDL** is viable.

Asset Preparation

Prepare the following assets:

- **Unit Models**: 3D or 2D sprites for different unit types (workers, soldiers, etc.).
- **Building Models**: Structures for production and defenses.
- **Resources**: Models for resources such as gold, wood, or food.
- **Audio Effects**: Sounds for gathering, attacking, and unit movements.

3. Implementing Unit Controls and Selection

Unit Selection Mechanism

Implement a unit selection system that allows players to select multiple units using box selection or individual clicks. Highlight selected units with visual cues (e.g., borders or color changes).

```cpp
Copy code
void selectUnits(Vector2 clickPosition) {
    for (Unit& unit : units) {
        if (unit.contains(clickPosition)) {
            unit.selected = true;
            selectedUnits.push_back(unit);
        }
    }
}
```

Movement Commands

Implement a command system for directing selected units to move to a specified location. This involves calculating a path using the A* algorithm to avoid obstacles.

```cpp
Copy code
void moveSelectedUnits(Vector2 targetPosition) {
    for (Unit& unit : selectedUnits) {
        unit.path = AStar(unit.position, targetPosition);
        unit.currentWaypoint = 0;
    }
}
```

4. Pathfinding with A* Algorithm

Implementing A* Pathfinding

The A* algorithm will enable units to navigate the game world efficiently. Nodes will represent positions on a grid, and the algorithm will calculate the shortest path from the unit's current location to its target.

```cpp
Copy code
std::vector<Node> AStar(Vector2 start, Vector2 goal) {
    // Initialize open and closed lists
    std::vector<Node> openList, closedList;
    openList.push_back(startNode);

    while (!openList.empty()) {
        Node currentNode = getLowestCostNode(openList);

        if (currentNode == goal) {
            return reconstructPath(currentNode);
        }

        openList.remove(currentNode);
        closedList.push_back(currentNode);

        for (Node& neighbor : getNeighbors(currentNode)) {
            if (std::find(closedList.begin(), closedList.end(),
```

```
    neighbor) != closedList.end()) {
        continue; // Ignore already evaluated nodes
    }

    float tentativeG = currentNode.g +
    distance(currentNode, neighbor);
    if (tentativeG < neighbor.g) {
        neighbor.parent = currentNode;
        neighbor.g = tentativeG;
        neighbor.f = neighbor.g + heuristic(neighbor,
        goal);

        if (std::find(openList.begin(), openList.end(),
        neighbor) == openList.end()) {
            openList.push_back(neighbor);
        }
    }
    }
}
    return std::vector<Node>(); // Return empty if no path found
}
```

5. Resource Management System

Implementing Resource Gathering

Units should gather resources from specific locations (e.g., trees, mines) and deposit them at a base or storage facility. Set up resource points that can be harvested by worker units.

```cpp
Copy code
void gatherResource(Unit& worker, Resource& resource) {
    if (worker.isInRange(resource)) {
        worker.currentResource = resource.type;
        resource.amount -= worker.gatherSpeed;
        worker.carrying = true;
    }
}
```

Resource Management and Economy

Create a resource management system that tracks resources collected and spent. Implement UI elements to display current resource counts and allow players to build units or structures based on available resources.

```cpp
Copy code
void updateResourceCounts() {
    for (Unit& unit : units) {
        if (unit.carrying) {
            resourceCounts[unit.currentResource] +=
            unit.gatherAmount;
        }
    }
}
```

6. Building Mechanisms

Implementing Construction and Unit Production

Create buildings where players can produce units or gather resources. Implement a system that allows players to place buildings within certain areas and manage construction time.

```cpp
Copy code
void constructBuilding(BuildingType type, Vector2 position) {
    if (resourceCounts["wood"] >= buildingCost[type].wood &&
        resourceCounts["gold"] >= buildingCost[type].gold) {
        Building newBuilding(type, position);
        buildings.push_back(newBuilding);
        resourceCounts["wood"] -= buildingCost[type].wood;
        resourceCounts["gold"] -= buildingCost[type].gold;
    }
}
```

7. AI for Enemy Units

Basic AI Behavior

Implement AI for enemy units to manage resources, attack the player, and defend their territory. Use a simple finite state machine (FSM) to control behaviors.

```cpp
Copy code
enum class AIState { Idle, Gathering, Attacking };

void updateAI(Enemy& enemy, Player& player) {
    switch (enemy.state) {
        case AIState::Idle:
            if (enemy.canSeePlayer(player.position)) {
                enemy.state = AIState::Attacking;
            }
            break;
        case AIState::Gathering:
            gatherResource(enemy, resource);
            break;
        case AIState::Attacking:
            attackPlayer(enemy, player);
            break;
    }
}
```

Targeting and Attack Strategies

AI should prioritize targets based on certain criteria (e.g., weak units or buildings). Implement basic attack logic that allows enemies to engage when within range.

```cpp
Copy code
void attackPlayer(Enemy& enemy, Player& player) {
    if (distance(enemy.position, player.position) <
    enemy.attackRange) {
        player.health -= enemy.attackDamage;
    }
}
```

8. User Interface and Feedback

Implementing a User Interface (UI)

Design a UI to provide feedback on selected units, resources, and build options. Use an overlay to show health bars, resource counts, and commands available.

```cpp
Copy code
void renderUI() {
    drawText("Wood: " + std::to_string(resourceCounts["wood"]),
    10, 10);
    drawText("Gold: " + std::to_string(resourceCounts["gold"]),
    10, 30);
    for (Unit& unit : selectedUnits) {
        drawHealthBar(unit.position, unit.health);
    }
}
```

9. Game Flow and Mechanics

Implementing Game Flow

Define how the game progresses, including victory and defeat conditions, such as eliminating all enemy units or capturing key locations.

Difficulty Scaling and Dynamic Events

Consider incorporating dynamic difficulty adjustments based on player performance or in-game events, like enemy reinforcements or natural disasters.

This Real-Time Strategy game prototype serves as a foundational framework that incorporates unit control, pathfinding, AI behavior, and resource management. By combining these systems, developers can create engaging gameplay that challenges players to think strategically and respond to dynamic scenarios. The prototype can be expanded upon with additional features such as multiplayer capabilities, advanced AI strategies, and more complex resource management systems, ultimately leading to a rich gaming experience.

Profiling, Debugging, and Performance Tuning

U sing Profiling Tools: Visual Studio Profiler, gprof, Valgrind
Effective profiling and debugging are critical components in game development, as they help identify performance bottlenecks, memory leaks, and other inefficiencies in code. In this chapter, we will explore three prominent profiling tools: **Visual Studio Profiler**, **gprof**, and **Valgrind**. Each tool has its unique features and strengths, making them suitable for different profiling scenarios in C++ game development.

1. Visual Studio Profiler
Overview
Visual Studio Profiler is integrated into the Visual Studio IDE, offering powerful profiling capabilities for C++ applications, including games. It provides developers with insights into CPU usage, memory allocation, and call stack analysis, allowing for targeted optimizations.

Key Features

- **CPU Usage Analysis**: Visualizes the CPU time spent on different functions, helping developers identify performance-critical areas.
- **Memory Usage Tracking**: Monitors memory allocations, helping detect leaks and excessive memory consumption.
- **Call Tree**: Displays a hierarchical view of function calls, making it easier to understand the flow of execution and identify costly operations.

- **Instrumentation**: Offers both sampling and instrumentation-based profiling, enabling fine-grained analysis of code performance.

Using Visual Studio Profiler
Setting Up the Profiler:

- Open your project in Visual Studio.
- Navigate to Debug > Performance Profiler or use the shortcut Alt + F2.
- Select the profiling tools you wish to use, such as **CPU Usage** or **Memory Usage**.

Running the Profiler:

- Click on Start, then interact with your game to capture profiling data.
- Once finished, stop the profiling session to generate a report.

Analyzing Results:

- Review the CPU Usage report, focusing on hot paths and function calls that consume significant resources.
- Use the Memory Usage report to identify memory leaks and track down unnecessary allocations.

Optimizing Code:

- Based on the profiling data, refactor or optimize code segments that are identified as performance bottlenecks.
- Rerun the profiler after making changes to assess the impact of your optimizations.

Best Practices

- Use the profiler during various stages of development, not just at the end.

- Focus on one performance metric at a time for clarity.
- Prioritize optimization efforts based on profiling results rather than assumptions.

2. gprof

Overview

gprof is a profiling tool for Unix-like systems, part of the GNU Binutils package. It uses a sampling approach to collect call graph data, which is particularly useful for identifying performance hotspots in C++ applications.

Key Features

- **Call Graph Generation**: Provides a visual representation of function calls and their relationships, helping identify which functions consume the most time.
- **Flat Profile**: Displays a list of functions and the amount of time spent in each, allowing for quick identification of slow functions.
- **Ease of Use**: Integrated with the GCC compiler, making it straightforward to use in a development workflow.

Using gprof

Compiling with Profiling Support:

- Compile your application with the -pg flag:

```bash
Copy code
g++ -pg -o mygame mygame.cpp
```

Running the Application:

- Execute your compiled game. This will generate a file named gmon.out, which contains profiling data.

```bash
Copy code
./mygame
```

Generating the Report:

- Run gprof to process the profiling data:

```bash
Copy code
gprof mygame gmon.out > profile_report.txt
```

Analyzing the Report:

- Open profile_report.txt to review the flat profile and call graph. Focus on functions with high execution times and deep call stacks.

Best Practices

- Regularly profile your application during development to catch performance issues early.
- Combine gprof results with other profiling tools for a more comprehensive view.

3. Valgrind

Overview

Valgrind is a powerful suite of tools for debugging and profiling applications on Linux and macOS. It is primarily known for its memory analysis capabilities but also offers profiling functionalities through tools like callgrind.

Key Features

- **Memory Leak Detection**: Identifies memory leaks and memory-related errors, which are common issues in C++ applications.
- **Cache Grading**: Analyzes cache usage patterns to help optimize memory access.
- **Callgrind**: A Valgrind tool that generates detailed call graphs and function profiling data.

Using Valgrind
Installing Valgrind:

- Ensure Valgrind is installed on your system:

```bash
Copy code
sudo apt-get install valgrind
```

Running Valgrind:

- Use Valgrind to run your application with memory leak detection:

```bash
Copy code
valgrind --leak-check=full ./mygame
```

Using Callgrind for Profiling:

- Enable Callgrind to analyze function call patterns:

```bash
Copy code
valgrind --tool=callgrind ./mygame
```

Analyzing Results:

- Use the callgrind_annotate tool to interpret the data:

```bash
Copy code
callgrind_annotate callgrind.out.<pid>
```

Visualizing Callgrind Data:

- For better visualization, use KCachegrind or QCachegrind:

```bash
Copy code
kcachegrind callgrind.out.<pid>
```

Best Practices

- Use Valgrind in conjunction with your regular debugging workflow.
- Regularly check for memory leaks and optimize memory usage.
- Pay attention to cache utilization patterns to enhance performance.

Profiling tools are essential for developing high-performance games. **Visual Studio Profiler** offers deep integration for Windows-based development, while **gprof** provides a straightforward sampling approach on Unix-like systems. **Valgrind** excels in memory analysis and profiling. By leveraging these tools effectively, developers can identify performance bottlenecks, optimize resource usage, and create efficient game applications that provide a better user experience. Regular profiling and performance tuning will ensure that games run smoothly, maximizing player enjoyment and engagement.

Identifying and Fixing Performance Bottlenecks

In game development, performance bottlenecks can significantly degrade the player experience, leading to frame drops, latency issues, and an overall unresponsive game. This section will outline the systematic approach to identifying and fixing performance bottlenecks using profiling tools, performance metrics, and optimization techniques.

1. Understanding Performance Bottlenecks

A performance bottleneck occurs when a particular component of a game application limits the overall performance of the system. Common areas where bottlenecks occur include:

- **CPU**: High computational demand in physics calculations, AI processing, or game logic.
- **GPU**: Excessive draw calls, complex shaders, or large texture sizes causing rendering delays.
- **Memory**: Inefficient memory usage leading to fragmentation, cache misses, or excessive allocations.
- **Disk I/O**: Slow loading times due to large asset files or inefficient loading strategies.

Recognizing the signs of bottlenecks, such as frame rate drops or stuttering during gameplay, is the first step toward resolution.

2. Using Profiling Tools to Identify Bottlenecks

Profiling tools provide valuable insights into application performance. The following methods can help pinpoint bottlenecks effectively:

a. Frame Rate Analysis

- **Frame Time Metrics**: Monitor the time taken to render each frame using tools like Visual Studio Profiler or built-in engine profilers (e.g., Unity Profiler). A consistent frame time above a target (e.g., 16.67 ms for 60 FPS) indicates a potential bottleneck.

b. CPU Profiling

- **Call Graphs and Flat Profiles**: Use gprof or Visual Studio Profiler to analyze CPU usage. Look for functions that consume a disproportionate amount of CPU time, particularly in the game loop.

c. Memory Profiling

- **Memory Usage Reports**: Utilize Valgrind to track memory allocations and deallocations. High memory usage or frequent allocations can indicate areas to optimize.

d. GPU Profiling

- **Graphics Profiling**: Use tools like NVIDIA Nsight or AMD Radeon GPU Profiler to analyze rendering performance. Identify costly draw calls, shader executions, and resource management issues.

3. Fixing Identified Bottlenecks

Once bottlenecks have been identified, the following strategies can be employed to address them:

a. Optimizing CPU Performance
Algorithm Optimization:

- Replace inefficient algorithms with more efficient ones. For example, if using a nested loop to check for collisions, consider spatial partitioning techniques to reduce the number of checks.

Reducing Work in the Main Loop:

- Minimize the amount of processing done in the game loop by pre-calculating values or deferring less critical operations to background threads.

Batch Processing:

- Implement batch processing techniques for tasks like rendering and physics calculations to reduce overhead and improve efficiency.

b. Enhancing GPU Performance
Reduce Draw Calls:

- Combine meshes and use texture atlases to reduce the number of draw calls, improving rendering performance.

Optimize Shaders:

- Simplify shaders by reducing complexity, eliminating unused features, or using simpler techniques (e.g., flat shading instead of complex lighting models).

Level of Detail (LOD):

- Implement LOD techniques to reduce the rendering load for distant objects by using lower-resolution models.

c. Managing Memory Usage
Implement Object Pooling:

- Use object pooling to manage frequently created and destroyed objects, minimizing the overhead of dynamic memory allocation.

Optimize Asset Loading:

- Use asynchronous loading techniques and compress assets to reduce memory footprint and improve load times.

Monitor Memory Leaks:

- Regularly use tools like Valgrind to detect and fix memory leaks, ensuring efficient memory usage throughout the application.

d. Improving Disk I/O Performance
Asynchronous Asset Loading:

- Load assets asynchronously to prevent blocking the game loop during resource loading. This can be achieved using background threads or task-based systems.

Data Compression:

- Utilize data compression for assets to reduce load times, particularly for large texture and sound files.

4. Continuous Monitoring and Iteration
Performance optimization is an ongoing process. Following initial fixes, developers should:

- **Continuously Profile**: Regularly use profiling tools throughout development to monitor performance after making changes.
- **Establish Benchmarks**: Set performance benchmarks and regularly test against them to ensure that optimizations are effective.
- **Iterate and Refine**: Optimize iteratively based on feedback and profiling results, maintaining a balance between performance and game quality.

Identifying and fixing performance bottlenecks is a crucial aspect of game development that directly impacts user experience. By systematically profiling the application and applying targeted optimization strategies, developers can ensure their games run smoothly, enhancing player satisfaction and engagement. As game development progresses, maintaining an ongoing focus on performance will help create polished, high-quality games capable of standing out in a competitive market.

Debugging Techniques for Complex Game Systems

Debugging is an essential part of the game development process, especially when working with complex systems where numerous interacting components can introduce bugs and performance issues. This section outlines effective debugging techniques tailored for complex game systems, covering best practices, tools, and strategies to identify and resolve issues efficiently.

1. Understanding the Debugging Process

Debugging is the systematic process of identifying, isolating, and fixing issues within a game. It often involves the following steps:

- **Reproducing the Bug**: Clearly understand how to recreate the problem.
- **Identifying the Source**: Use various techniques to pinpoint where the issue originates.
- **Implementing a Fix**: Apply a solution and ensure it resolves the problem without introducing new issues.
- **Testing**: Rigorously test the game to verify that the fix works and that no other parts of the game have been adversely affected.

2. Effective Debugging Techniques
a. Logging and Monitoring
Implement Extensive Logging:

- Use logging libraries to track events, function calls, and variable states throughout the game. This can help trace the flow of execution and identify where things go wrong.
- Example: Log the entry and exit of functions, as well as critical variable values at different stages of processing.

Use Conditional Logging:

- Implement conditional logging that activates only under certain conditions (e.g., when a specific variable exceeds a threshold). This reduces performance overhead during regular gameplay while still capturing crucial data when needed.

Performance Monitoring:
Incorporate performance metrics that log frame rates, memory usage, and CPU/GPU loads. This can highlight performance issues during gameplay, such as slowdowns due to specific events.

b. Breakpoints and Step-Through Debugging
Utilize Breakpoints:

- Set breakpoints in the code to pause execution at specific points, allowing for inspection of the program state. This is especially useful for checking variable values and control flow at critical junctures.

Step-Through Execution:

- Use the step-through debugging feature to execute the game line-by-line, observing the state of variables and objects as they change. This can help identify unexpected behavior and logical errors.

Watch Variables:

- Monitor specific variables in real-time as you step through the code to observe how their values change, making it easier to spot anomalies.

c. Visual Debugging Tools
Use Visual Debuggers:

- Many IDEs (like Visual Studio or JetBrains Rider) come with integrated visual debugging tools that provide graphical representations of data structures and object hierarchies. This can be invaluable for understanding complex interactions between game entities.

Utilize Debug Draw Functions:

- Implement debug draw functions to visually represent physics bodies, collision boxes, and AI paths. This can help understand how different components interact in the game world and where issues might arise.

In-Game Debugging Overlays:

- Create overlays that show real-time game data such as FPS, memory usage, and entity states. This information can help identify performance bottlenecks and bugs during gameplay.

d. Unit Testing and Automated Testing
Implement Unit Tests:

- Develop unit tests for individual components to verify that each part behaves as expected. This can catch bugs early in the development process and ensure that changes do not break existing functionality.

Automated Testing Frameworks:

- Use automated testing frameworks to run tests regularly, especially after making changes to the codebase. This can help catch regressions and ensure the game remains stable.

Behavioral Testing for AI:

- Implement behavioral tests for AI components to ensure they behave as expected under various conditions. This can help identify issues with decision-making and pathfinding.

e. Profiling and Performance Analysis
Use Profilers:

- Regularly use profiling tools (e.g., Visual Studio Profiler, gprof, Valgrind) to analyze performance and identify slow-running functions or memory leaks. This helps ensure that performance bottlenecks are addressed proactively.

Analyze Call Stacks:

- Examine call stacks in profilers to trace the origin of performance issues, identifying which functions consume the most resources and why.

3. Strategies for Debugging Complex Interactions
a. Divide and Conquer

- **Isolate Components**:
- Break down complex systems into smaller, manageable components. Test and debug each component independently before integrating them back into the larger system.
- **Component Testing**:
- Focus on specific features or systems one at a time to simplify debugging. For example, isolate the AI system from the rendering engine and test each independently.

b. Use Version Control Wisely

- **Branching for Debugging**:
- Create branches in your version control system for debugging purposes. This allows you to experiment with potential fixes without affecting the main development branch.
- **Track Changes**:
- Use commit messages to track changes that may introduce bugs, making it easier to identify when and where a problem was introduced.

4. Collaborating and Getting Help
a. Peer Reviews

- **Code Reviews**:
- Conduct regular code reviews with peers to catch potential issues early and share insights on debugging strategies.

b. Community and Forums

- **Seek Help from Developer Communities**:
- Utilize online forums, such as Stack Overflow or game development-specific communities, to seek advice and solutions from experienced developers who may have encountered similar issues.

Debugging complex game systems requires a strategic approach, combining various techniques and tools. By implementing robust logging, using visual debugging tools, and isolating components, developers can effectively identify and fix issues, ensuring a smoother and more enjoyable player experience. As development progresses, maintaining a strong debugging practice will facilitate the creation of high-quality games that stand up to rigorous testing and scrutiny.

Balancing Performance and Visual Quality

Balancing performance with visual quality is a critical aspect of game development, particularly as high-quality graphics can significantly impact both player engagement and system performance. This section covers strategies for achieving a visually rich experience while ensuring that games run smoothly across a range of devices, from high-end PCs to mobile platforms.

1. Understanding the Balance Between Graphics and Performance

In modern game development, graphical fidelity often comes at the cost of performance, requiring careful planning and optimization. Key considerations include:

- **Frame Rate Consistency**: High-quality graphics must not compromise stable frame rates, as smooth gameplay is essential for an enjoyable user experience.
- **Platform-Specific Constraints**: Hardware capabilities vary widely, so balancing visual quality and performance may require tailoring graphics for different platforms.
- **Optimizing Resource Usage**: Efficient use of CPU, GPU, and memory resources allows for visually stunning graphics without overwhelming the hardware.

2. Techniques for Optimizing Visual Quality
a. Level of Detail (LOD)
Dynamic LOD Scaling:

- Implement LOD techniques to reduce the complexity of models as they move farther from the camera. This helps maintain visual quality close-up without overtaxing the system as objects recede.

Distance-Based Rendering:

- Adjust texture resolution and model detail based on the player's distance to an object. For example, distant objects can use lower-resolution textures and simplified meshes, reducing the load on the GPU.

b. Texture Optimization
Efficient Texture Compression:

- Use texture compression formats (e.g., DXT, ETC, or ASTC) that reduce memory usage without sacrificing too much visual fidelity. Compressed textures load faster and consume less GPU memory, improving performance.

Mipmapping:

- Implement mipmaps, which are pre-calculated, smaller versions of a texture that display based on an object's size on screen. Mipmapping improves performance by reducing the texture sampling load, especially on objects that appear smaller or farther away.

Texture Atlases:

- Combine multiple smaller textures into a single atlas, reducing the number of draw calls and texture switches, which can significantly improve rendering efficiency.

c. Shading Optimization
Simplified Shading for Background Elements:

- Use basic shading models or ambient-only lighting for background elements. High-quality shading should be reserved for prominent objects, while simpler shading suffices for less noticeable elements.

Screen Space Reflections (SSR):

- For reflections, consider using screen space reflections for objects in the foreground rather than physically accurate reflections. SSR can approximate reflections without the high computational cost of ray tracing.

Deferred Rendering Pipeline:

- For scenes with many dynamic lights, a deferred rendering pipeline can process lighting effects more efficiently by decoupling geometry rendering from lighting calculations. This approach optimizes lighting performance in scenes with complex light interactions.

d. Anti-Aliasing Techniques
Temporal Anti-Aliasing (TAA):

- Temporal anti-aliasing combines data from previous frames to smooth edges in the current frame, reducing shimmering and jagged edges without significantly impacting performance.

Screen-Space Anti-Aliasing (SSAA):

- Options like FXAA or MSAA are effective for maintaining quality at a lower performance cost. For mobile platforms, FXAA is typically more efficient and less demanding on resources.

3. Techniques for Improving Performance Without Sacrificing Visual Quality
a. Culling and Occlusion
Frustum Culling:

- Implement frustum culling to exclude objects outside the camera's view, reducing the number of draw calls and GPU load. This approach ensures that only visible objects are processed and rendered.

Occlusion Culling:

- Use occlusion culling to avoid rendering objects blocked by other geometry. This technique is especially useful in complex scenes with numerous objects where some may be entirely hidden from view.

Distance-Based Culling:

- Objects that are far enough from the camera can be culled to minimize rendering demands. This technique is effective in open-world games with expansive landscapes where distant details are unnecessary.

b. Particle System Optimization
GPU-Based Particle Systems:

- Offload particle system calculations to the GPU, allowing for a large number of particles without overloading the CPU. GPU-based systems are effective for effects like smoke, fire, and explosions.

Use LOD on Particle Systems:

- Implement LOD for particle effects, reducing particle count and complexity based on camera distance. This preserves visual fidelity up close while enhancing performance in distant scenes.

Billboarding for Particles:

- Use billboards (flat images that always face the camera) for particle effects instead of fully modeled objects, especially for small particles such as sparks or smoke.

c. Lighting Optimization
Light Baking for Static Objects:

- Bake lighting for static objects and environments where shadows and lighting don't change. This approach reduces real-time lighting calculations, allowing for high-quality lighting with minimal performance impact.

Dynamic and Static Light Mixing:

- Use a combination of baked static lighting and dynamic lighting. Dynamic lighting can be limited to key areas where lighting changes are essential, reducing the overall lighting load.

Shadow Cascading and Resolution Adjustment:

- Implement shadow cascading and dynamic resolution adjustment for shadows, where the resolution decreases as the shadow's distance from the camera increases. This technique preserves high-quality shadows close to the camera while minimizing impact from distant shadows.

d. Memory and Resource Management
Efficient Asset Streaming:

- Stream assets like textures, audio, and animations only as needed, reducing memory overhead. For large, open-world games, streaming assets can prevent memory overload by loading assets in and out as the player moves through the environment.

Texture and Mesh Instancing:

- Use instancing for repeating assets (e.g., trees, rocks) to reduce memory usage and draw calls. Instanced meshes share the same geometry data, significantly improving rendering efficiency.

Asynchronous Loading:

- Load heavy assets asynchronously to prevent gameplay interruptions. This method is especially useful for complex textures, animations, and sounds, allowing assets to load in the background without disrupting gameplay.

4. Balancing Visual Quality with Cross-Platform Optimization

Creating a visually rich game requires an adaptable approach for different hardware capabilities. Consider these strategies:

- **Scalable Graphics Settings**:
- Offer adjustable graphics settings such as texture resolution, shadow quality, and anti-aliasing to allow players to tailor visual quality to their hardware.
- **Resolution Scaling and Dynamic Resolution**:
- Implement resolution scaling to adjust the game's render resolution based on performance. This allows the game to dynamically scale down in demanding scenes and scale up in less demanding moments, maintaining a consistent frame rate.
- **Shader Model Optimization**:
- For mobile platforms, use shaders optimized for lower power consumption and efficiency. Prioritize simpler shading techniques that still convey quality while maintaining battery efficiency.

Balancing performance and visual quality is a dynamic process that combines effective resource management, intelligent asset handling, and platform-specific optimizations. By using advanced culling techniques, level-of-detail adjustments, optimized lighting, and efficient particle handling, developers can achieve visually compelling graphics without sacrificing smooth gameplay. This balance is essential for delivering a visually captivating game that performs well across a range of hardware configurations, ultimately enhancing the player experience.

Case Study: Optimizing a Real-Time Game with Profiling Insights

In this case study, we'll examine the process of optimizing a real-time game by leveraging profiling tools to identify bottlenecks, analyze performance metrics, and apply targeted improvements. Through each optimization phase, profiling insights help guide decisions, making the process efficient and measurable.

1. Setting the Stage: Initial Game State and Profiling Goals

Our starting point is a 3D action game with high-resolution textures, particle effects, complex AI, and a real-time physics engine. While the game performs well on high-end PCs, it struggles with frame rate drops on mid-range and low-end devices. The goal is to optimize the game's performance for smooth, consistent frame rates on a broader range of hardware, focusing on reducing CPU and GPU load.

2. Phase 1: Initial Profiling and Baseline Metrics

To establish a performance baseline, we profile the game using tools like Visual Studio Profiler, NVIDIA Nsight, and gprof. Key metrics are gathered in a demanding scene with multiple AI entities, dynamic lighting, and particle effects.

- **CPU and GPU Usage**: CPU usage peaks at around 90%, and GPU usage is at 95%, indicating high load.
- **Frame Rate**: The frame rate hovers around 40 FPS, dropping significantly in complex scenes.
- **Memory Usage**: Memory consumption is high, suggesting potential memory management issues.
- **Identified Bottlenecks**: The main performance culprits are high draw calls, extensive AI processing, and complex particle systems.

3. Phase 2: Optimization Techniques Based on Profiling Insights

Using insights from initial profiling, we focus on specific areas to enhance performance, applying optimization techniques and re-profiling after each phase to measure improvement.

a. Draw Call Optimization
Batch Rendering and Instancing:

- The initial profiling revealed excessive draw calls due to repeated models like trees, rocks, and barrels. Implementing instancing reduces draw calls by combining identical models into a single call.
- **Result**: Frame rate improves by around 5 FPS, and GPU load decreases by about 7%.

Using Texture Atlases:

- To minimize texture switching, texture atlases are introduced for small textures (e.g., UI elements and repeating textures).
- **Result**: GPU overhead drops, and the frame rate stabilizes during scenes with frequent texture changes.

b. AI Processing Optimization
Simplified AI Behavior for Background NPCs:

- AI profiling indicates that background NPCs consume a significant portion of CPU time due to complex behavior trees. We simplify AI behaviors for distant NPCs, using a basic Finite State Machine (FSM) that activates more complex behavior only within a defined radius of the player.
- **Result**: CPU usage drops by approximately 12%, and the frame rate improves by 3 FPS.

Asynchronous AI Processing:

- Non-critical AI functions are moved to separate threads, reducing their load on the main game loop. For example, pathfinding for background NPCs is run asynchronously.
- **Result**: Further reduces CPU load and improves frame rate consistency.

c. Particle System Optimization
GPU-Based Particle Systems:

- CPU profiling highlights that particle effects consume significant CPU resources due to real-time calculations. By shifting these calculations to the GPU, we offload the work and reduce the CPU's burden.
- **Result**: CPU usage drops by 8%, and the game achieves smoother frame rates, particularly during high-particle scenes.

Level of Detail (LOD) for Particles:

- We implement LOD on particle systems, reducing the particle count and complexity for distant particle effects. This allows intense scenes (e.g., explosions) to display fewer particles without compromising visual quality.
- **Result**: GPU usage decreases by 10% in particle-heavy scenes, and the frame rate becomes more stable.

4. Phase 3: Memory Management and Caching Optimization

Memory profiling reveals frequent memory allocation and deallocation, especially during rapid texture and asset loading in open-world areas. To address this, we implement optimized memory management techniques.

Object Pooling for Reusable Entities:

- Commonly used entities (e.g., projectiles, NPCs) are pooled, reducing memory allocation frequency and preventing memory fragmentation.
- **Result**: Memory usage stabilizes, and frame rates increase by 3 FPS due to reduced garbage collection.

Efficient Asset Streaming:

- Using streaming for assets like textures and sounds in open-world areas, we dynamically load and unload assets based on the player's location, decreasing memory load.

- **Result**: Improved memory usage during gameplay and smoother transitions between different game zones.

5. Phase 4: Real-Time Lighting and Shadow Optimization

Dynamic lighting and shadows consume a substantial portion of GPU resources, so we target these for optimization.

Baked Lighting for Static Objects:

- We pre-bake lighting for static objects, reducing real-time lighting calculations. Only moving characters and dynamic elements utilize real-time lighting.
- **Result**: Reduced GPU load by 10% and improved frame rate stability in scenes with complex lighting.

Shadow Cascading and Dynamic Resolution:

- Using shadow cascading, we adjust shadow quality based on the distance from the camera. Close-up shadows retain high detail, while distant shadows use a lower resolution.
- **Result**: GPU load decreases, and visual quality remains intact. Frame rates improve by 4 FPS in outdoor scenes.

6. Phase 5: Final Profiling and Results Analysis

After each optimization phase, profiling tools are used to gather updated metrics, with the final results showing substantial performance gains:

- **CPU and GPU Usage**: CPU usage drops to around 70%, and GPU usage stabilizes at 80%, providing headroom for complex scenes.
- **Frame Rate**: Frame rate now averages 60 FPS, even in demanding scenes, with fewer dips below this threshold.
- **Memory Usage**: Memory usage is optimized, with smoother loading and transitions between game zones.

7. Lessons Learned and Key Takeaways
Profiling as a Continuous Process:

- Regular profiling and optimization cycles allow for gradual performance gains, enabling developers to address bottlenecks without compromising game features.

Targeted Optimization:

- Focusing on high-impact areas such as draw calls, AI processing, and particle effects provided immediate performance benefits, showing the value of prioritized optimizations.

Importance of Memory Management:

- Proper memory management, including object pooling and efficient streaming, prevented fragmentation and minimized performance loss due to frequent memory operations.

Balancing Quality and Performance:

- Techniques like LOD, shadow cascading, and texture atlases maintained visual fidelity while optimizing performance, achieving an ideal balance between visuals and efficiency.

This case study illustrates how profiling and targeted optimizations can transform a resource-intensive game into a well-performing application, broadening its appeal and delivering a smooth experience across diverse hardware.

Packaging and Publishing Your Game

Preparing Game Builds for Different Platforms: Windows, Mac, Linux

Successfully preparing and distributing game builds across platforms requires knowledge of operating system-specific nuances, as well as tools that enable compatibility and optimization. Each platform comes with its own set of requirements, tools, and best practices for ensuring stable performance and ease of installation for end-users. This section covers the essentials of cross-platform preparation, including build configuration, testing, and packaging techniques for Windows, macOS, and Linux.

1. Setting Up a Cross-Platform Build Environment

Creating a unified build environment saves time and helps ensure consistency across all versions of the game. Utilizing a cross-platform game engine or framework like Unity, Unreal Engine, or a custom C++ game engine can simplify development. Here are key steps in setting up a cross-platform build environment:

- **Choose Compatible Libraries and APIs**: Opt for cross-platform libraries such as SDL2, OpenAL, and OpenGL to avoid dependency issues across operating systems.
- **Use Cross-Platform Build Tools**: Tools like CMake, which can generate platform-specific build files, and build managers like Ninja streamline the compilation process across multiple platforms.
- **Set Up a Version-Controlled Build Configuration**: Maintain separate

build configurations for each platform within your version control system, including custom settings for assets, paths, and platform-specific code.

2. Building for Windows

Building games for Windows involves targeting the most widely used OS versions and creating an installation package that ensures easy distribution.

a. **Windows Build Configuration**
Selecting the Target Architecture:

- Choose between x86, x64, and ARM64 architectures based on your audience. Most games target x64 for modern systems but providing x86 compatibility can reach more users on older hardware.

DirectX or OpenGL:

- While OpenGL works cross-platform, Windows offers additional support for DirectX, which can leverage hardware features. DirectX 12 is recommended for high-performance applications but requires extra coding for backward compatibility with older DirectX versions if needed.

b. **Packaging and Distribution**
Executable Creation and Packaging:

- Use tools like Inno Setup, NSIS (Nullsoft Scriptable Install System), or WiX Toolset to bundle executables, assets, and libraries into a single installer. These tools allow custom installation options and provide straightforward setup for end-users.

Ensuring Compatibility with Windows Defender and Antivirus Software:

- Digitally sign your game executable to prevent issues with Windows

Defender. An unsigned executable may be flagged as suspicious, so using a trusted code-signing certificate helps avoid unnecessary warnings.

Testing Across Windows Versions:

- Test your build on different Windows versions (Windows 10 and Windows 11) and with various graphics settings. Microsoft's Windows App Certification Kit can help ensure compatibility with Windows Store policies, should you wish to distribute via the Microsoft Store.

3. Building for macOS

Building for macOS involves using Apple's development tools, ensuring compatibility with the latest macOS versions, and following Apple's distribution guidelines.

a. **macOS Build Configuration**
Using Xcode:

- Set up your build environment in Xcode, Apple's development platform. Configure your game as a macOS target in Xcode, defining build settings that are compatible with macOS Catalina and later.

Metal vs. OpenGL:

- Although macOS supports OpenGL, it's deprecated in favor of Metal, Apple's graphics API optimized for macOS. Utilizing Metal ensures better performance and future compatibility, though it requires additional code adaptation.

b. **Packaging and Distribution**
Creating a Standalone App Bundle:

- macOS applications are distributed as .app bundles, which package all necessary files into a single directory. Create an Info.plist file to define the application's metadata, such as the app's name, version, and icon.

Code Signing and Notarization:

- Apple mandates that apps be code-signed and notarized. Use Xcode or command-line tools to code-sign your application, then submit it to Apple for notarization to avoid security warnings for users.

Testing for Compatibility and Performance:

- Test the build across multiple macOS versions (at least the last three) to confirm compatibility. Apple's Device Compatibility Checker can help identify potential issues with macOS and hardware configurations.

4. Building for Linux

Linux, while less standardized than Windows or macOS, provides powerful open-source tools and extensive user customization options. Given the diversity of Linux distributions, special care is needed to ensure compatibility across different setups.

a. **Linux Build Configuration**

Selecting Supported Distributions:

- Target popular distributions such as Ubuntu, Fedora, and Debian, focusing on compatibility with mainstream desktop environments like GNOME and KDE.

Configuring Dependencies:

- Package all required dependencies, such as SDL2, OpenAL, and OpenGL. Using static linking for essential libraries can improve compatibility but increases the executable size, while dynamic linking requires users to have the libraries installed.

Compiling with GCC:

- Most Linux games are built using GCC, which provides broad compatibility across distributions. Compile your game as a .AppImage, .deb, or .rpm package, depending on the target distributions.

b. **Packaging and Distribution**
Creating Distribution Packages:

- Consider packaging formats like .AppImage for a universal Linux build, .deb for Debian-based distributions, and .rpm for Red Hat-based systems. Flatpak and Snap are also viable options for providing sandboxed applications across distributions.

Open-Source Compliance:

- Linux users often expect open-source compliance, so ensure that any open-source libraries used adhere to their licensing requirements. If your game uses proprietary assets, clearly document them in your release notes to avoid conflicts with open-source principles.

Testing Across Distros:

- Linux has a fragmented environment, so testing on different distributions and desktop environments is critical. Tools like VirtualBox or Docker can simulate different Linux environments for thorough testing.

5. Cross-Platform Testing and Debugging
Cross-platform testing is essential to identify any platform-specific issues or bugs. Each platform has unique performance characteristics, API requirements, and user expectations, which necessitates thorough testing.
Automated Testing Pipelines:

- Set up automated CI/CD (Continuous Integration/Continuous Deployment) pipelines to compile and test your game on multiple platforms. Tools like GitHub Actions, GitLab CI, and Jenkins facilitate automated builds, helping ensure code stability and cross-platform compatibility.

Compatibility and Regression Testing:

- Test critical gameplay features and mechanics across platforms. Regression testing is particularly important if you update dependencies or modify core gameplay features, as even minor updates may produce unexpected behaviors on one or more platforms.

Handling Platform-Specific Bugs:

- Certain issues may only appear on specific platforms. Debugging tools like Visual Studio for Windows, Xcode for macOS, and gdb for Linux are essential for diagnosing and fixing these platform-specific issues efficiently.

6. Optimizing Performance for Each Platform

Each platform has unique hardware configurations and optimization requirements. Tailor your optimizations for the best possible performance on each target system.

Graphics Optimization:

- Optimize shaders and graphical assets for each platform, choosing the most appropriate API (DirectX, Metal, OpenGL) to ensure efficient rendering.

Input and Controller Mapping:

- Windows, macOS, and Linux handle input devices differently, so implement platform-specific input handling where needed. Tools like SDL2 support cross-platform input, but additional adjustments may be required to optimize response times and compatibility.

Resource Management:

- On Windows and macOS, resource management techniques like asset streaming, LOD (Level of Detail) models, and compressed textures optimize memory usage. On Linux, ensure efficient file handling and data loading, as Linux filesystems may differ significantly across distributions.

7. Distribution and Updating

Once the game builds are prepared and tested for all platforms, determine the best distribution channels for each OS.

Steam and Other Distribution Platforms:

- Steam supports Windows, macOS, and Linux and provides a unified platform for updating and distributing your game. Other platforms like GOG and the Epic Games Store also support multi-platform distribution.

Updating and Patching:

- Develop a version management and update strategy, as patching and versioning are critical for addressing platform-specific issues post-launch. Consider using platforms like Steam for automatic updates or developing custom updaters if distributing independently.

Platform-Specific Documentation:

- Include platform-specific installation instructions and known issues in your documentation, as this enhances user experience and minimizes support queries.

By tailoring builds for Windows, macOS, and Linux, you maximize your game's reach, ensure compatibility, and deliver a seamless experience to players on each platform. Platform-specific optimizations and thorough testing further enhance performance and reliability, setting the stage for a successful cross-platform launch.

Packaging with CMake and Cross-Platform Compatibility

CMake is a powerful build system generator that simplifies cross-platform packaging by allowing developers to define a single build configuration that works across different operating systems and compilers. Utilizing CMake's versatile configuration settings enables efficient build management and packaging, especially for games intended to run on multiple platforms. This section delves into using CMake to structure, build, and package games for Windows, macOS, and Linux, addressing the unique requirements for each platform.

1. Setting Up a CMake Project for Cross-Platform Builds

CMake simplifies the compilation process across platforms by generating build files compatible with native build systems like Visual Studio (Windows), Xcode (macOS), and Makefiles (Linux). Here are key steps to get started:

- **Define Project Structure in CMakeLists.txt**:
- Create a main CMakeLists.txt file at the root of your project directory, specifying the project name, version, and required CMake version.
- Organize source code and assets in folders, keeping platform-specific code separate if necessary.
- **Specify Cross-Platform Compatible Libraries**:
- Link against libraries that support cross-platform compatibility, like SDL2, OpenAL, and OpenGL. CMake can locate and link libraries differently depending on the operating system, making it essential to check for dependencies explicitly within your CMakeLists.txt.
- **Set Compiler Flags and Options**:
- Use CMake variables to set platform-specific compiler flags for optimization, warnings, and debugging. For example, you might use -O2 for

optimized builds on all platforms or -Wall for comprehensive warnings on GCC and Clang.

Example CMakeLists.txt Structure

```cmake
cmake
Copy code
cmake_minimum_required(VERSION 3.10)
project(MyGameProject VERSION 1.0 LANGUAGES CXX)

# Set C++ standard
set(CMAKE_CXX_STANDARD 17)
set(CMAKE_CXX_STANDARD_REQUIRED True)

# Define source files and target executable
file(GLOB_RECURSE SOURCES "src/*.cpp")
add_executable(MyGame ${SOURCES})

# Find and link libraries
find_package(SDL2 REQUIRED)
find_package(OpenGL REQUIRED)
target_link_libraries(MyGame SDL2::SDL2 OpenGL::GL)

# Platform-specific configurations
if (WIN32)
    # Windows specific settings
    target_compile_definitions(MyGame PRIVATE PLATFORM_WINDOWS)
elseif(APPLE)
    # macOS specific settings
    target_compile_definitions(MyGame PRIVATE PLATFORM_MACOS)
elseif(UNIX)
    # Linux specific settings
    target_compile_definitions(MyGame PRIVATE PLATFORM_LINUX)
endif()
```

2. Platform-Specific Packaging with CMake

Once you've set up CMake to build your project, packaging it for each platform requires different approaches due to variations in executable formats and distribution conventions.

a. **Windows**
Generate Visual Studio Project Files:

- Use CMake to generate Visual Studio project files (.sln) for easy debugging and packaging within the Visual Studio environment.
- Run cmake -G "Visual Studio 16 2019" .. to generate project files for Visual Studio, specifying the version as needed.

Creating an Installer:

- Use CMake's integration with third-party tools like NSIS or WiX to create a Windows installer. Include all necessary DLLs, game assets, and configuration files.
- In CMakeLists.txt, define a custom target for packaging with NSIS.

b. **macOS**
Generating Xcode Project Files:

- Run cmake -G "Xcode" .. to create an Xcode project, which integrates smoothly with the macOS build system and simplifies debugging.

Building an .app Bundle:

- macOS applications are typically packaged as .app bundles, containing the executable and resources within a single directory structure.
- CMake can assist in creating this structure by specifying MA-COSX_BUNDLE in add_executable and configuring Info.plist files for metadata.
- Example:

```cmake
cmake
Copy code
add_executable(MyGame MACOSX_BUNDLE ${SOURCES})
set_target_properties(MyGame PROPERTIES MACOSX_BUNDLE_INFO_PLIST
${CMAKE_SOURCE_DIR}/Info.plist)
```

Code-Signing and Notarization:

- Automate code-signing and notarization in Xcode or through command-line commands. This step is crucial for distributing macOS applications outside the App Store.

c. **Linux**

Building with Makefiles:

- Run cmake .. to generate Makefiles, and then use make to build the project on Linux systems.

Packaging as an .AppImage or .deb Package:

- CMake supports custom commands for packaging the game into Linux distribution formats. An .AppImage file provides a single executable that works across distributions, while .deb and .rpm packages cater to Debian and Red Hat-based systems, respectively.
- Use CMake's CPACK_GENERATOR variable to specify packaging formats:

```cmake
cmake
Copy code
set(CPACK_GENERATOR "DEB;RPM")
include(CPack)
```

Managing Dependencies:

- On Linux, it's common to dynamically link libraries and ensure they are either bundled with the game or readily available on the user's system. Use ldd to verify that all necessary libraries are accessible.

3. Cross-Platform Testing and Deployment with CMake

Testing builds across platforms helps identify platform-specific bugs and performance issues. CMake's support for automated testing and CI/CD integration is beneficial for ensuring consistency and stability.

Continuous Integration:

- Set up CI pipelines using tools like GitHub Actions, GitLab CI, or Jenkins to automatically build and test your game across Windows, macOS, and Linux. Use CMake commands to automate the build process within these CI environments.

CMake and CTest for Unit and Integration Testing:

- Incorporate unit tests and integration tests using CTest, which CMake natively supports. These tests ensure that individual components and the full game build function as expected on all platforms.
- Example:

```cmake
Copy code
enable_testing()
add_test(NAME MyTest COMMAND MyGameTestExecutable)
```

Deployment Automation:

- Define CMake targets to automate packaging and deployment, reducing manual work for each platform.
- Use CMake's scripting abilities to automate post-build tasks like zipping files, creating installers, or uploading binaries to distribution platforms.

4. Enhancing Cross-Platform Compatibility

Cross-platform compatibility goes beyond the technical aspects of building and packaging; it also involves testing for performance consistency and interface behavior across different platforms. Here are key techniques:

- **Conditional Compilation for Platform-Specific Code**:
- Use #ifdef preprocessor directives to conditionally compile code specific to each platform, maintaining clean and manageable code while addressing platform-specific requirements.
- **Unified Asset Management**:
- Ensure assets such as textures, models, and sounds load correctly across all platforms by standardizing paths and using CMake to define asset directories.
- **Platform-Specific User Input Handling**:
- Handle keyboard, mouse, and controller inputs differently on each platform where needed to provide a consistent experience.

By leveraging CMake's flexible configuration and scripting capabilities, you can streamline the packaging and distribution of game builds across platforms. With a consistent CMake setup, you'll reduce errors, save development time, and ensure your game runs optimally on Windows, macOS, and Linux. This approach also positions you well to expand to other platforms if needed, such as Android or iOS, using CMake's extended support for mobile platforms.

Advanced Packaging with CMake and Ensuring Cross-Platform Compatibility

Efficient packaging for various platforms is crucial for distributing games across Windows, macOS, and Linux. CMake simplifies the process by providing a unified setup for multiple operating systems, and by configuring specific files for each platform. This section covers advanced CMake packaging techniques and considerations for achieving the best cross-platform compatibility for your game.

1. Fine-Tuning CMakeLists for Platform-Dependent Libraries and Assets

To achieve smooth cross-platform compatibility, it's essential to handle platform-specific libraries and assets directly within CMakeLists.txt. This includes selecting the correct libraries, paths, and build configurations for each platform.

- **Dynamic vs. Static Linking**:
- Depending on the platform, you may need to switch between dynamic and static linking of libraries. Static linking ensures that dependencies are bundled with the executable, while dynamic linking relies on system libraries or DLLs.
- For Windows, bundling DLLs with the game executable is often preferable, whereas Linux and macOS may favor dynamic linking for easy compatibility with shared libraries.
- **Platform-Conditioned File Inclusion**:
- Organize platform-specific files in separate directories and use conditional statements in CMake to include them as needed. For example, DirectX might be used for Windows, while OpenGL works across macOS and Linux.

```cmake
Copy code
if (WIN32)
    set(PLATFORM_LIBS d3d9.lib d3dx9.lib)
    add_definitions(-DPLATFORM_WINDOWS)
elseif(APPLE)
    set(PLATFORM_LIBS "-framework OpenGL")
    add_definitions(-DPLATFORM_MACOS)
elseif(UNIX)
    find_package(OpenGL REQUIRED)
    set(PLATFORM_LIBS ${OPENGL_LIBRARIES})
    add_definitions(-DPLATFORM_LINUX)
endif()
```

```
target_link_libraries(MyGame ${PLATFORM_LIBS})
```

- **Asset Path Management**:
- Use CMake variables to standardize asset paths across platforms. This allows the game to correctly locate assets, regardless of OS-specific directory structures.

2. Using CPack with CMake for Simplified Distribution

CPack is an extension of CMake designed for generating installer packages, streamlining the process of creating platform-specific installers. Here's how to set up CPack to distribute your game on different platforms:

a. **Setting Up CPack Configuration**

Define CPack Variables:

- Configure project metadata, such as version numbers and package names, using CPack variables. This metadata ensures each package is correctly labeled and versioned across platforms.

```cmake
cmake
Copy code
set(CPACK_PACKAGE_NAME "MyGame")
set(CPACK_PACKAGE_VERSION "1.0")
set(CPACK_PACKAGE_CONTACT "support@mygame.com")
```

Specify Package Format:

- Use CPACK_GENERATOR to define package formats. For example, NSIS is suitable for Windows installers, DragNDrop for macOS, and DEB or RPM for Linux distributions.

```cmake
Copy code
if(WIN32)
    set(CPACK_GENERATOR "NSIS")
elseif(APPLE)
    set(CPACK_GENERATOR "DragNDrop")
elseif(UNIX)
    set(CPACK_GENERATOR "DEB;RPM")
endif()
include(CPack)
```

b. Generating Platform-Specific Installers
Windows with NSIS:

- CPack, in conjunction with NSIS, can generate Windows .exe installers, bundling DLLs and dependencies alongside the executable.
- Include a custom .nsi script if you need advanced control over the installation steps, such as registry entries or shortcuts.

macOS with DragNDrop:

- For macOS, DragNDrop packaging creates a disk image (.dmg) that users can open and drag into their Applications folder. To configure this, specify application icons and Info.plist files in your CMake project.

Linux Packages (DEB and RPM):

- DEB and RPM are common Linux package formats that enable seamless integration with Debian and Red Hat-based systems.
- Use CPack's DEB and RPM configurations to specify Linux-specific metadata, dependencies, and paths.

```
cmake
Copy code
set(CPACK_DEBIAN_PACKAGE_MAINTAINER "support@mygame.com")
set(CPACK_RPM_PACKAGE_LICENSE "MIT")
```

3. Cross-Platform Compatibility Testing and Build Validation

Testing the game across platforms ensures consistent performance, functionality, and visual quality. Here are best practices for validating your game builds on each operating system:

a. Automating Cross-Platform Builds with CI/CD Pipelines

Using CI/CD (Continuous Integration/Continuous Deployment) services like GitHub Actions, GitLab CI, or Jenkins allows you to automate builds and tests across Windows, macOS, and Linux. Configure CI/CD to:

- Run platform-specific CMake builds and unit tests.
- Deploy generated builds to a staging server or file-sharing service for team access and review.

b. Testing with CMake's CTest Integration

CTest, bundled with CMake, provides a powerful framework for running automated tests. Use it to run unit tests on game modules, verifying functionality and catching platform-specific issues early.

```
cmake
Copy code
enable_testing()
add_test(NAME GameTest COMMAND MyGameTestExecutable)
```

c. Verifying Asset Compatibility and Path Structures

Cross-platform compatibility includes ensuring assets load correctly and paths are handled consistently. Test builds on each OS to ensure that textures, models, and sounds load and display as expected.

4. Performance Optimization for Each Platform

Each platform has unique performance considerations. For example, DirectX may yield better performance on Windows, while OpenGL offers more cross-platform consistency. Fine-tune these aspects:

Windows:

- Use DirectX optimizations and ensure the game takes advantage of multi-core processing on Windows systems. Test on a variety of hardware configurations.

macOS:

- Optimize for Metal if targeting newer macOS versions, as Metal offers better performance than OpenGL on Apple hardware.
- Adjust memory usage to align with Apple's recommendations for system resource management.

Linux:

- Ensure compatibility with a range of distributions and hardware configurations by building with OpenGL and managing dependencies flexibly.

5. Deployment and Updating on Digital Platforms

If deploying to digital stores like Steam, Epic Games Store, or macOS App Store, integrate platform-specific build steps for compliance with store requirements. For example:

- **Steam**:
- Use Steamworks SDK with CMake to automate build and deployment processes, ensuring builds meet Steam's requirements for updates and multiplayer functionality.
- **macOS App Store**:
- Package your game with appropriate code-signing and notarization steps in CMake, automating App Store requirements directly into the build

process.

By optimizing packaging and compatibility, you'll ensure a seamless experience for players across all platforms. Combining CMake's configuration flexibility with rigorous cross-platform testing helps deliver a polished game that meets the demands of diverse operating systems and distribution platforms.

Game Testing and Quality Assurance (QA)

Quality assurance (QA) and testing are critical steps in game development to ensure that a game runs smoothly, is free from critical bugs, and provides an enjoyable user experience. Effective game testing spans multiple types of tests, covering gameplay, performance, compatibility, and compliance, ensuring the game meets high standards across different platforms and configurations. Below is a comprehensive breakdown of strategies, tools, and best practices to maintain a rigorous QA process for your game.

1. Types of Game Testing

Effective game testing requires different approaches to cover the breadth of scenarios players may encounter. Here are the primary types of tests used in game development:

a. **Functional Testing**

Functional testing ensures that each part of the game works as expected, verifying individual features like character controls, physics, and AI. It focuses on the core gameplay mechanics and involves detailed verification of specific functions.

- **Gameplay Mechanics**: Test character movement, inventory, combat, and physics-based interactions.
- **Menu and Interface**: Ensure the UI is accessible, responsive, and consistent.
- **Edge Cases**: Look for unexpected inputs or actions, such as boundary testing for controls or item interactions.

b. Performance Testing

This testing assesses how well the game performs under different conditions. Performance testing is crucial for maintaining a smooth frame rate, minimizing load times, and optimizing resource usage.

- **Frame Rate Stability**: Monitor FPS across different scenes and gameplay situations.
- **Memory Usage**: Track memory usage, looking for potential leaks or spikes during play.
- **Stress Tests**: Run the game with high numbers of assets, enemies, or complex scenes to evaluate resource handling.

c. Compatibility Testing

Compatibility testing ensures the game works across different platforms, operating systems, and hardware configurations. This is particularly important for cross-platform games on Windows, macOS, and Linux, and across various hardware setups.

- **Platform Testing**: Verify the game on different OS versions and configurations.
- **Hardware Variability**: Test on low-end, mid-range, and high-end hardware to identify bottlenecks.
- **Input Devices**: Check compatibility with controllers, keyboards, and any other supported devices.

d. Localization Testing

Localization testing is essential if the game is distributed internationally. This involves verifying that all text, audio, and cultural references are accurately adapted for different languages and regions.

- **Language Verification**: Ensure translated text displays correctly and doesn't break the UI.
- **Cultural Sensitivity**: Check that in-game references and symbols are

appropriate for various regions.

e. Regression Testing

Regression testing ensures that new features or bug fixes don't introduce new issues. Whenever changes are made, all relevant sections are re-tested to confirm stability.

- **Automation Support**: Use automated testing scripts where possible to check previously validated functionality.
- **Manual Verification**: For complex or interdependent features, manual regression testing is recommended.

2. Test Automation in Game Development

Automating repetitive test cases helps maintain consistent testing and accelerates the QA cycle. Automation is particularly useful for regression testing and load testing.

a. Automated Functional Testing

Automate interactions for simple gameplay features using tools like Unity Test Framework, Unreal's Functional Testing Framework, or custom scripts for C++ games.

- **Scripting Basic Interactions**: Automate common actions like movement, combat, and basic UI interactions.
- **Event-Based Tests**: Automate scenarios such as enemy spawn, NPC interaction, and inventory management.

b. Performance Testing Automation

Automated performance tests track game performance metrics and identify areas for optimization. Automated profiling tools capture frame rates, memory allocation, and CPU/GPU load over time.

- **Profiling Tools**: Tools like NVIDIA Nsight, Intel GPA, or Visual Studio Profiler help gather performance data across platforms.

- **Stress Test Scripts**: Set up automated tests to stress-test scenarios, like large battles or dense asset environments, for consistency.

c. Continuous Integration (CI) Testing

Set up a CI pipeline to automatically build and test the game whenever new code is added. CI integration platforms like Jenkins, GitHub Actions, or GitLab CI allow for automated builds and regression tests, accelerating the QA process.

- **Automated Builds and Testing**: Every code commit triggers builds across different configurations and runs test cases.
- **Bug Reporting Integration**: Automatically log bugs and issues in a tracking system if tests fail during CI.

3. Manual Testing: Where It's Essential

While automation is valuable, manual testing remains essential for aspects that require human insight, such as user experience and game feel.

a. Playtesting

Playtesting involves having testers or players try the game to provide feedback on gameplay experience, balance, and difficulty.

- **Internal Playtests**: Developers and team members test early versions for basic functionality and design feedback.
- **External Playtests**: Open testing to select players or conduct closed beta sessions to gather feedback on gameplay, pacing, and enjoyment.

b. User Interface (UI) Testing

UI testing ensures all interface elements are intuitive, responsive, and functional. Manual testing of UI often reveals usability issues that automated scripts miss.

- **UI Responsiveness**: Check buttons, menus, and interactive elements on different screen sizes and resolutions.

- **Accessibility**: Ensure accessibility features (like text-to-speech, color-blind modes) work smoothly and meet required standards.

4. Bug Tracking and Quality Assurance Workflow

A structured QA workflow and bug-tracking system streamline the process of identifying, prioritizing, and fixing issues.

a. Bug Tracking Software

Use bug-tracking tools like JIRA, Bugzilla, or Trello to log, categorize, and manage reported issues. Organize bugs by priority, status, and assignment for efficient tracking.

- **Issue Prioritization**: Label bugs based on severity, such as "Critical" for game-breaking issues and "Minor" for visual inconsistencies.
- **Collaborative Tracking**: Allow team members to collaborate on bugs, add screenshots, comments, and assign tasks.

b. QA Workflow and Best Practices

An effective QA workflow ensures smooth transitions between testing, bug reporting, and fixing phases.

1. **Test Planning**: Develop a test plan outlining which tests to perform at each development stage.
2. **Issue Reporting**: Log bugs immediately upon discovery, detailing reproduction steps and attaching relevant media.
3. **Fix and Validate**: Developers fix the bugs, and testers validate the fixes through re-testing.
4. **Post-Release Monitoring**: Even after release, monitoring player-reported issues and updating the game as needed is critical.

5. Post-Release Quality Assurance

After release, post-launch QA is essential to maintain game quality, address new bugs, and update content. Here are common approaches:

a. Hotfixes and Patches

Rapidly deploy hotfixes for critical bugs that impact the user experience. Develop a system to roll out quick patches without extensive downtime.

- **Prioritizing Critical Fixes**: Address issues impacting gameplay stability, user progress, or major visual bugs as soon as possible.
- **Scheduled Updates**: Release minor updates on a regular schedule for non-critical fixes and performance improvements.

b. Collecting Player Feedback and Bug Reports

After launch, player feedback is invaluable for identifying overlooked bugs or gameplay issues. Include an in-game reporting tool or provide an official platform for feedback.

- **In-Game Reporting**: Allow players to report bugs or provide feedback directly within the game for streamlined collection.
- **Community Monitoring**: Monitor community forums, social media, and reviews to track common issues or requests.

c. Telemetry for Long-Term Insights

Implement telemetry to track how players interact with the game, which provides valuable data for future updates and optimizations.

- **Event Tracking**: Log events such as quest completions, deaths, or frequent locations to analyze player behavior.
- **Performance Metrics**: Use telemetry to continuously monitor performance, identifying areas for optimization in future patches.

Effective QA is integral to a smooth, engaging, and bug-free gaming experience. From detailed testing strategies to automated and manual tests, a well-executed QA process ensures a high-quality product that players can enjoy across platforms.

Releasing on Digital Platforms: Steam, Itch.io, and Epic Games Store

383

Releasing a game on popular digital platforms is key to reaching a broad audience. Each platform has its unique requirements, community dynamics, and distribution tools, making it essential to understand how to leverage them effectively. This guide outlines how to prepare, publish, and market a game on Steam, Itch.io, and the Epic Games Store.

1. Steam

Steam is the most popular game distribution platform with a vast community of players and extensive tools for developers.

a. Setting Up a Steamworks Account

To publish on Steam, you need a Steamworks account. The setup involves an application fee, which allows access to Steam's publishing tools and API.

- **Fee**: $100 per application, refundable once the game reaches a certain revenue threshold.
- **Access to Tools**: The Steamworks SDK offers access to features like achievements, cloud saves, and multiplayer services.

b. Building a Store Page

The Steam store page is crucial for attracting attention, so it's essential to invest in high-quality visuals, trailers, and an engaging description.

- **Visual Assets**: Include high-resolution screenshots, trailers, and cover art. These are critical as they make a first impression.
- **Description and Tags**: Use descriptive tags and keywords that help Steam's recommendation engine match the game to potential players.
- **User Reviews and Community Hub**: Encourage early users to leave positive reviews and engage with the community to build rapport and trust.

c. Using Steam's Marketing and Promotional Tools

Steam provides various marketing and promotional opportunities to help increase game visibility.

- **Steam Sales Events**: Participate in seasonal sales like the Summer Sale or Winter Sale to boost visibility and reach.
- **Discount Strategies**: Offering discounts on launch or during special events can attract a wider audience.
- **Wishlists and Notifications**: Encourage wishlists from early marketing stages so followers receive notifications on updates, release dates, and discounts.

d. Implementing Steamworks Features

Steamworks provides tools to enhance user experience, including achievements, cloud saves, and Steam Workshop for user-generated content.

- **Achievements and Leaderboards**: Adding achievements and leaderboards fosters player engagement.
- **Cloud Saves**: Enable cloud saves to let users play across multiple devices.
- **Steam Workshop**: For moddable games, Steam Workshop lets players share custom content, extending a game's longevity.

2. Itch.io

Itch.io is a popular platform for indie games, offering a lower barrier to entry and a developer-friendly revenue model. It also supports a wide range of genres and experimental projects.

a. Creating an Itch.io Developer Account

Setting up an Itch.io account is simple and free, making it a great option for indie developers or small studios with limited budgets.

- **Flexible Revenue Sharing**: Developers choose their revenue share percentage, with the standard being 10%.
- **Game Jam Community**: Itch.io hosts game jams, providing a platform to showcase your game in events that encourage experimental designs.

b. Designing an Appealing Game Page

A well-designed Itch.io page is crucial, as it acts as the main point of contact between the game and potential players.

- **Page Customization**: Itch.io allows extensive customization, enabling a game's page to match its branding and style.
- **Visual Assets and Descriptions**: Use eye-catching visuals, trailers, and detailed descriptions to engage users.
- **Developer's Devlog**: Regular updates or a devlog keep players engaged and informed about development progress.

c. Building a Community on Itch.io

Itch.io has a supportive community that values transparency and developer-player interaction.

- **Devlog and Comments**: Regularly update the devlog with development insights, and interact with players in the comments section.
- **Community Involvement**: Join game jams, provide feedback on other games, and interact with other creators to grow visibility.

d. Monetization Options on Itch.io

Itch.io supports several monetization options, from traditional sales to donations, making it an adaptable platform.

- **Pay-What-You-Want**: Allow players to pay what they think the game is worth, potentially increasing accessibility and earnings.
- **Bundles and Sales**: Collaborate with other developers on bundles or organize sales to increase visibility.
- **Early Access**: Release the game in an early access format to gather feedback and build an audience before the full launch.

3. Epic Games Store

The Epic Games Store (EGS) is a curated platform known for its exclusivity, high revenue split, and support for both indie developers and larger studios.

a. Becoming an Epic Games Partner

Applying to publish on EGS requires approval, as the platform is more selective than others. This selectivity, however, results in less competition on the storefront.

- **Revenue Split**: EGS offers developers an 88/12 revenue split, more favorable than most other platforms.
- **Exclusive Deals**: Epic sometimes offers exclusive deals or funding to developers, providing financial support for development.

b. Creating a Compelling Storefront Page

The storefront page on EGS is essential for conveying the game's value and capturing user interest.

- **High-Quality Visuals**: Showcase professional-quality screenshots and a trailer, highlighting unique aspects of gameplay or visuals.
- **Game Description and Tags**: Describe the game effectively, focusing on features and gameplay style to attract the right audience.
- **Early Access and Pre-Orders**: EGS supports early access and pre-orders, allowing players to support the game's development.

c. Leveraging Epic's Marketing and Support

Epic offers promotional support for some games, including Epic-sponsored sales events and spotlights for certain titles.

- **Sponsored Sales Events**: Participate in EGS's seasonal or special sales events to boost visibility.
- **Epic Game Store Exclusives**: For games offered exclusively on EGS, Epic provides additional promotional support, including features on the homepage.
- **Engagement with Unreal Engine Integration**: If using Unreal Engine, Epic offers tools for seamless integration with EGS, allowing access to advanced engine features and support.

d. **Cross-Platform Play and Cloud Saves**

EGS is known for its emphasis on cross-platform compatibility, particularly for multiplayer games.

- **Cross-Platform Features**: Use Epic's cross-platform tools to allow gameplay across EGS, Steam, and consoles.
- **Cloud Saves and User Profiles**: Enabling cloud saves improves user experience, especially for players switching between devices.

4. Cross-Platform Publishing Strategies

Publishing on multiple platforms allows developers to maximize reach and appeal to diverse audiences. Here are some best practices:

- **Unified Build Pipeline**: Use a build system like CMake or Unity's build pipeline to streamline deployment for different platforms.
- **Platform-Specific Features**: Leverage each platform's unique features, like Steam achievements or EGS cross-platform play, without creating compatibility issues.
- **Testing Across Platforms**: Thoroughly test the game on each platform to ensure compatibility, and optimize performance for each operating system.

5. Marketing and Community Engagement Across Platforms

Marketing a game across multiple platforms requires consistent branding while adapting to the unique aspects of each platform's audience.

- **Early Promotion**: Start building interest before launch, utilizing wishlists on Steam, devlogs on Itch.io, and social media for EGS-exclusive titles.
- **Regular Updates and Player Engagement**: Engage with players on each platform's community hub, respond to feedback, and provide regular updates.
- **Cross-Platform Social Media Campaigns**: Use social media to drive

traffic to each store page, offering exclusive insights, videos, or behind-the-scenes content to maintain player interest.

Releasing on multiple platforms expands a game's potential audience and revenue streams. By understanding each platform's strengths, creating appealing storefront pages, and engaging with communities, developers can successfully launch and promote their games across Steam, Itch.io, and the Epic Games Store.

Marketing Strategies for Independent Game Developers

Marketing an indie game requires creativity, resourcefulness, and a strong understanding of your target audience. Unlike large studios, independent developers often have limited budgets, so choosing the right strategies and leveraging cost-effective tactics is key. Here's a comprehensive breakdown of essential marketing strategies for indie developers.

1. Build Hype Early with a Strong Pre-Launch Campaign

An effective marketing strategy starts long before the game's release. Pre-launch campaigns help build excitement and create an initial fanbase.

a. Social Media Presence

Maintaining a consistent and engaging social media presence is crucial for independent developers.

- **Choose the Right Platforms**: Focus on the platforms where your audience is most active, such as Twitter, Instagram, or TikTok.
- **Content Variety**: Post game development progress, behind-the-scenes insights, concept art, and early gameplay clips. Sharing relatable, humanizing content can increase engagement.
- **Consistent Posting**: Establish a posting schedule to keep your audience engaged without overwhelming them.

b. Devlogs and Blogging

Devlogs give potential players an in-depth view of the development process, which can create loyalty and anticipation.

- **Video Devlogs**: Platforms like YouTube or TikTok are effective for short, engaging devlog videos. Visuals are particularly appealing for audiences interested in the technical and creative process behind game development.
- **Written Blogs**: If video production isn't feasible, consider a written devlog on platforms like Medium, IndieDB, or a dedicated blog. Highlight milestones, discuss challenges, and share your creative vision.

c. Wishlist Campaigns

If releasing on Steam, encourage players to add your game to their wishlists early on.

- **Why It Matters**: Wishlists are a major factor in Steam's algorithm, which can lead to more visibility at launch.
- **Encouraging Wishlists**: Regularly remind followers on social media and in devlogs to wishlist your game. Offering sneak peeks or small rewards (like exclusive wallpapers or early screenshots) can incentivize wishlist additions.

2. Leverage Crowdfunding Platforms for Funding and Community-Building

Crowdfunding is both a financing and marketing tool, providing early visibility and building a community of invested supporters.

a. Kickstarter and Indiegogo

These platforms allow developers to raise funds and gain a loyal fanbase before release.

- **Define Clear Reward Tiers**: Offer rewards that appeal to backers, like exclusive in-game items, access to a private Discord server, or early demo versions.
- **Regular Updates**: Keep backers informed with updates on the game's

progress, milestones, and behind-the-scenes content to maintain excitement and trust.

- **Stretch Goals**: Use stretch goals to build further engagement, enabling backers to help shape the game's content and features.

b. Community Platforms like Patreon

Patreon is ideal for ongoing support, especially if you plan to develop games or content consistently over time.

- **Exclusive Content**: Offer patrons exclusive content, like early access builds, concept art, or Q&A sessions, in exchange for their support.
- **Building Relationships**: Engage patrons in development decisions by polling them on features or hosting monthly Q&A sessions. A strong community leads to dedicated, long-term fans.

3. Influencer Marketing and Content Creator Outreach

Partnering with influencers, streamers, and content creators is one of the most effective ways to reach a larger audience.

a. Identify Relevant Influencers

Focus on influencers who cover indie games or specialize in the genre of your game.

- **Micro-Influencers**: Smaller creators (with followers between 1,000 and 100,000) can be highly effective, often having dedicated, niche audiences.
- **Genre Alignment**: Partner with creators whose content aligns with your game. For instance, horror streamers are ideal for horror games, while strategy game YouTubers can boost a new strategy title.

b. Provide Early Access and Exclusive Content

Providing early access keys or exclusive gameplay footage can entice influencers to cover your game.

- **Playable Demos**: Offer a polished demo for influencers to showcase.

For smaller creators, even a simple build can generate interest.

- **Exclusive Content**: Consider offering exclusive content, like a sneak peek of an unreleased level or special in-game items, to encourage influencers to share unique gameplay footage with their audience.

c. Engage with Content Creators Directly

Form genuine relationships with influencers to create long-term partnerships.

- **Custom Emails**: Personalize your outreach emails to show that you're familiar with their work and explain why you think your game is a good fit for their audience.
- **Community Involvement**: Engage with influencers' content by leaving thoughtful comments or participating in their community discussions. This visibility can create organic interest in your game.

4. Utilize Indie Game Festivals and Showcases

Participating in indie game festivals and showcases is a valuable way to gain exposure, get feedback, and attract press coverage.

a. Popular Indie Game Festivals

Submit your game to festivals like the Independent Games Festival (IGF), PAX, and Ludicious to gain visibility and attract potential fans and press.

- **Networking**: Festivals are ideal for networking with other developers, publishers, and media outlets.
- **Awards and Recognition**: Winning or even being nominated can provide powerful promotional material to use on your game's store page and marketing materials.

b. Online Showcases and Digital Events

For developers unable to attend physical events, digital showcases provide an alternative platform.

- **Platforms**: Consider events like the Steam Game Festival, Guerrilla Collective, or Itch.io's digital festivals.
- **Live Demos**: During digital events, offering live-streamed demos or Q&A sessions can engage audiences in real-time.

5. Engage with the Community through Forums and Social Platforms

Building a loyal community is essential for long-term success. Engaging with fans keeps them invested and fosters word-of-mouth promotion.

a. Discord and Reddit Communities

Discord and Reddit offer vibrant communities where indie game fans gather to discuss and discover new titles.

- **Game-Specific Discord**: Create a Discord server dedicated to your game. Use it to share exclusive updates, organize events, and interact with fans directly.
- **Subreddits**: Engage with relevant subreddits, such as r/IndieDev or r/gaming. Share devlog updates or participate in discussions to organically attract interest.

b. Answering Community Questions and Providing Support

Regularly interacting with fans shows transparency and builds a positive reputation.

- **Q&A Sessions**: Host Q&A sessions on platforms like Twitter, Reddit, or Discord to answer questions and provide insights.
- **Feedback and Suggestions**: Actively solicit feedback on gameplay, art style, or features to show fans that you value their input.

6. Create a Memorable Launch Event

The game's launch is a critical point in the marketing timeline, and creating buzz around it can drive initial sales and reviews.

a. Launch Day Livestream

Host a livestream event on platforms like Twitch or YouTube, showcasing gameplay, and interacting with fans.

- **Special Guest Playthroughs**: Invite popular streamers or influencers to join the event and play the game live.
- **Giveaways**: Hold giveaways during the stream to increase viewer engagement and attract more followers.

b. Email Marketing and Social Media Blasts

Engage with followers on social media and send out email blasts to ensure that everyone in your network is aware of the launch.

- **Countdown Campaign**: Start a countdown campaign on social media a week before the launch to build excitement.
- **Press Release**: Prepare and distribute a press release to announce the game's release, targeting both indie and mainstream gaming news outlets.

c. Encourage Early Reviews and Word-of-Mouth

Positive reviews are crucial for gaining traction on platforms like Steam or Epic Games.

- **Incentivize Feedback**: Encourage early adopters to leave reviews. Consider providing minor in-game rewards to players who leave feedback.
- **Post-Launch Updates**: Keep players engaged with regular updates, new content, or bug fixes, which also signal your commitment to the game's quality and longevity.

An effective marketing strategy for an indie game combines early community engagement, creative promotional tactics, and strategic use of digital platforms. By following these steps, indie developers can maximize visibility, build a dedicated fanbase, and increase the chances of their game's success in a competitive market.